HAPPY HACKS

101 SCIENCE-BACKED WAYS TO BOOST HAPPINESS,
REDUCE STRESS, AND BUILD A MORE MEANINGFUL LIFE

David Schramm

ISBN's
Paperback: 979-8-9963400-0-2
Hardcover: 979-8-9912251-2-0
Ebook: 979-8-9912251-3-7

Published independently via Amazon KDP

For more resources, visit:
www.DrDaveSchramm.com

HAPPY HACKS

Known as "Dr. Dave" on campus and across the country, David Schramm is a professor and Family Life Extension Specialist in the Department of Human Development and Family Studies at Utah State University. He received his B.S. from Brigham Young University, his M.S. from Utah State University, and a Ph.D. in Human Development and Family Studies from Auburn University. He married his high school sweetheart Jamie, they have four children and are obsessed with being grandparents. He might have a slight addiction to peanut M&Ms, and the Schramm fam lives in North Logan, Utah.

Praise for Dr. Dave's *Happy Hacks*

"In *Happy Hacks*, Dr. Dave Schramm bridges the gap between research and real life in a way that is both refreshing and deeply useful. Each insight is clear, actionable, and rooted in what we know truly supports well-being. This is the kind of book that invites small changes that can lead to lasting impact."

—Emma Seppдlд, PhD, Author of
The Happiness Track & *Sovereign*, Lecturer at
the Yale School of Management

"A nice exploration of what true well-being actually requires — and a practical guide to building more of it, one small habit at a time."

—Laurie Santos, Professor of Psychology at Yale University and creator of *The Happiness Lab* podcast

"*Happy Hacks* brings the science of happiness where it belongs: into daily life. With clarity, warmth, and practical wisdom, David Schramm offers 101 evidence-based practices that can help readers reduce stress, strengthen relationships, deepen meaning, and build lasting wellbeing. I love this book. It makes the research accessible without oversimplifying it, and actionable without overwhelming the reader."

—Tal Ben-Shahar, author of *Happier*
and former Harvard University lecturer

"Dr. Dave Schramm has written the rare happiness book that takes hard things seriously. *Happy Hacks* pairs decades of positive psychology research with the warmth of someone who has clearly lived what he's writing about. It is exactly the kind of book we need right now."

—Michelle Gielan, bestselling author of
Broadcasting Happiness and *Resilient Optimism*

"Through extensive research and personal experience, Dr. Dave Schramm offers readers an approachable framework for connecting with the natural streams of happiness that surround us. His book of *Happy Hacks* reminds us that happiness is a process, not a destination."

—Sharon Salzberg, author of
Lovingkindness and *Real Life*

"David Schramm has given us a remarkable gift — a research-based, creatively crafted, engagingly written guide to living a thriving, meaning-filled, happy life. By blending wide-ranging scholarship with personal storytelling, *Happy Hacks* offers a buffet of practical wisdom that readers can draw from again and again."

—David G. Myers, Hope College, author of
The Pursuit of Happiness and *Exploring Psychology*

"As a psychiatrist dealing with the harsh reality of mental illness for so many, I needed a lift from *Happy Hacks*! Dr Dave's take shows that research and real living matter, that skepticism and enthusiasm can be balanced. It also reveals how gratitude, meaning, joy and even hard stuff can be hacked together to help reach for that elusive quality of happiness. I thoroughly recommend it for therapists, clients, students, everybody!"

—Dr. Christian Heim, Clinical Director of Mental Health, Author of *Resilient Relationships*, University of Queensland, Australia

"Wow! Dr. Dave Schramm has created a wonderful guide filled with 101 research-based ways to increase joy, reduce stress, and live more meaningfully. These are not just good ideas—they are practical habits that can strengthen our hearts, homes, and relationships. Don't wait! Start bringing these happiness hacks into your life today!"

—Dr. Wally Goddard, author of *Finding Joy in Family Life* and former Professor of Family Life

"In *Happy Hacks*, David Schramm accomplishes something rare: he democratizes well-being. True flourishing is often caught between the marginalized 'woo-woo' self-help movement and the overly academic, detached discussions of the ivory tower. This book sits neatly and powerfully right in the center. Schramm translates rigorous science into actionable, everyday behaviors, making a more meaningful life something that each and every one of us can immediately learn from and incorporate. I am deeply grateful for this book, and for the profound impact it will have not only on all who read it, but on everyone they touch."

—Craig Robinson, bestselling author of *The Happiness Reboot*

To my wife Jamie and the Schramm fam—
you've taught me more about happiness and meaning
than any study ever could.

TABLE OF CONTENTS

PREFACE

Why Happiness Isn't What You Think
(And Why That's Good News)

It was Christmas morning in 1987. I was ten years old. One of my older sisters, she was eighteen at the time, had drawn my name in our annual sibling gift exchange. When it was my turn, she disappeared into her bedroom and came back holding a large mason jar. It was her spare-change jar, half full of quarters, nickels, dimes, and pennies she'd collected over the years.

She smiled and said: "You can stick your hand in and take as many coins as you can grab, as long as you can still pull your hand out." I slowly reached in, scooped up the tightest fistful I could manage, and carefully eased my hand back through the opening. My five siblings cheered like I was pulling treasure from a pirate chest. Best present ever for a ten-year-old. It felt magical. I don't remember exactly how much money I ended up with. But I remember the excitement, and I remember exactly what that money meant to a ten-year-old boy: baseball cards.

If you had asked me in that moment whether I was happy, I would have told you I had never been happier in my life. Was that happiness? A jar of coins and a stack of baseball cards?

To my ten-year-old brain, absolutely. And here's the thing—it wasn't wrong. It just wasn't the whole story.

So, What Is Happiness?

If happiness were simple, most of us would have figured it out by now. We wouldn't keep asking questions like: *Why do I still feel empty even when things are going well? Why does something that made me happy last year barely register now? Why do some of the most meaningful moments of my life feel hard, not happy?*

I've spent much of my career as a family science professor and Extension specialist at Utah State University and the University of Missouri trying to answer those questions—reading the research, giving hundreds of presentations, designing workshops and courses on happiness and well-being. And after all of it, here's what I keep coming back to: There isn't just one kind of happiness. And there's more than one path to it.

The ancient Greeks understood this in a way our culture has largely forgotten. Their word for happiness, *eudaimonia*, didn't mean feeling good. It meant flourishing. Moving toward your potential. Living in accordance with who you actually are. It's not a feeling you have for an afternoon. It's a direction you move in over a lifetime. And that idea, that happiness is less a destination and more a way of traveling, turns out to be one of the most important distinctions in all of modern well-being research.

The founders of this country wrote about "the pursuit of happiness" as though it were something you could chase down and catch. And some forms of happiness do respond to pursuit. You can pursue goals, growth, health, connection, contribution. But the more I study this, the more I notice something that surprises people: not all happiness responds well to being chased. Some happiness shows up when we stop sprinting after it. Some settles quietly when we're fully absorbed in something that matters. Some appears when we turn outward—when we serve, notice, and love someone beyond ourselves.

I experience this in my own life all the time. Some happiness feels like a jolt—peanut M&Ms and a cold Diet Dr Pepper. Some feels like awe—watching humpback whales explode out of the ocean on a family cruise. Some feels tender—rocking my granddaughter as she dozes off to sleep. Some feels peaceful—sitting on the deck with my wife, watching a sunset that stops you mid-sentence. Some feels strong—jumping off cliffs into the water at Lake Powell. And some feels warm and quietly profound—taking our adult children to a care center at Christmas and listening to elderly residents share their stories. They're all happiness. But they're genuinely different, in texture, in duration, in what produces them and what sustains them. Understanding that difference is where this book begins.

The Four Directions of a Happier Life

Over two decades of research and teaching, I've noticed that the happiest, most resilient people tend to be doing four things well, even if they couldn't name them.

They search inward. They know their strengths, values, and what genuinely sustains them. They pay attention to the basics that make everything else possible: sleep, movement, nutrition, and the quiet work of understanding who they actually are.

They turn outward. They use what they have to serve others. They intentionally practice gratitude and kindness. They invest consistently in the relationships and communities where they live.

They look upward. They anchor themselves to something larger than their own comfort and convenience: meaning, purpose, awe, transcendence, faith, and the kind of spiritual grounding that gives difficulty a frame larger than the suffering itself.

And they press forward. They navigate hard things without being defined by them. They manage stress, process adversity, and keep moving through the inevitable losses and setbacks that visit every human life.

These four directions quietly organize everything in this book. You'll find them in every chapter, sometimes named, often simply present. They're not a formula or a program. They're a map. And like any good map, they're most useful not when you're comfortable but when you're lost.

A Word to the Skeptics and Those Seriously Struggling

Not everyone loves the happiness conversation. For some, "positive psychology" sounds like forced smiles, toxic optimism, or a message that boils down to: *just smile and think positive and everything will work out*. If that's what this book were about, I'd be skeptical too. It isn't.

This book isn't suggesting you should be happy all the time. Grief, anger, fear, and sadness are not signs of failure, they're part of a full human life. Some of the most meaningful seasons we walk through are not light or easy, and pretending otherwise helps no one. What I am suggesting is something both simpler and more hopeful: while we can't control everything that happens to us or around us, we have more influence than we realize over the conditions that shape our well-being. We can strengthen connection. We can appreciate what we have. We can train attention. We can build small habits that support safety, meaning, and growth. We can gently tilt the system.

One more thing worth saying clearly: this book is not a substitute for professional care. If you are living with clinical depression, anxiety, trauma, or any condition that has made daily life genuinely hard to navigate, these hacks may still be useful, but they are *not* the complete answer. Therapy works.

The right medication, for the right person, can be genuinely life-changing. A good therapist is not a luxury or a last resort, they are one of the most evidence-based investments you can make in your own well-being. If you are really struggling, please don't let a book be the only thing you reach for.

That said, the research is also clear that small, consistent actions, practiced alongside whatever else you're doing, can meaningfully support recovery, resilience, and daily functioning. This book is designed to be one useful tool, not the whole toolbox.

Happiness isn't about pretending life is perfect. It's about working with your brain and your humanity so that even in an imperfect life, more moments of peace, purpose, and connection become possible.

How To Use This Book

I've spent more than 25 years doing research, studying the research of others, and translating it into something real people can actually use—that's the heart of what Extension work is. This book is that same instinct applied to happiness. What you'll find here are 101 simple, science-backed practices—what I call "happy hacks." For each one, you'll learn what it is, why it works in plain language, and how to try it today. No academic jargon. No overwhelming theory. Just the good stuff, made practical.

The book is designed buffet-style. Read it front to back or flip to whatever calls to you. Try a few. Experiment. Notice what shifts. Some practices will resonate immediately. Others may not. That's okay. This isn't a prescription, it's an invitation.

On a deeper level, I believe one of the genuine purposes of life is to experience joy—not shallow pleasure alone, but rich, layered joy rooted in connection, meaning, growth, and love. These 101 practices are small movements in that direction.

1.

THE SCIENCE OF WHY YOU'VE BEEN WRONG ABOUT HAPPINESS

Let's start at the very beginning, with us as newborns, and what we ultimately need not just to survive, but to thrive. Drawing from the work of psychologist Rick Hanson and others, research suggests that across cultures and throughout history, human beings arrive in the world with at least three core psychological needs: Safety. Satisfaction. Connection. These needs don't disappear as we grow older. They simply become more complex.

Safety includes the obvious physical needs, food, clothing, shelter, but it goes much further than that. Emotional safety matters just as deeply. We need to feel respected, supported, seen, and heard. We need to feel like we can risk being ourselves without being burned, shamed, or humiliated. When safety is missing, the brain shifts into protection mode, vigilant, defensive, reactive. Energy that could be used for growth or connection gets redirected toward scanning for threats. When this need is genuinely met, the result is a quiet but powerful inner state: peace.

Satisfaction includes pleasure, comfort, and reward, but also growth, progress, mastery, and achievement. It's not just about indulgence. It's about engagement and forward movement. This need covers everything from enjoying your favorite bowl of ice cream to working toward a meaningful goal, building a skill, or finishing something difficult. When satisfaction is met in healthy ways, the result is contentment, the sense that life is good, that you're moving forward, growing, and being rewarded for your effort.

Connection is the third fundamental need. We're all born with a longing for belonging, a craving for connection to others and to something larger than ourselves. Even those who consider themselves introverts still benefit profoundly from healthy human connection. Ask most people what matters most in life, what they'd miss most if it were gone, and you'll hear the same words: family, relationships, friends, love. Connection includes both giving and receiving care. It involves kindness, understanding, and compassion, shared experiences, laughter, service, vulnerability, and attention. When this need is well met, the result is love, and with it, a deep sense of belonging.

When these three needs are reasonably met, well-being increases. When one is chronically neglected, imbalance follows. This framework quietly explains a lot. It's why someone can be financially successful and socially admired and still feel deeply lonely: pleasure is feeding satisfaction, but connection is starving. And it's why people living in humble and modest circumstances sometimes report extraordinary life satisfaction, because they feel safe, connected, and valued.

Understanding this changes the question we ask ourselves. Instead of *why am I not happier*, we can ask something far more useful: *which need might be undernourished right now?*

Three Pathways to Happiness

Now that we've looked at the underlying needs, we can explore how we actually move toward happiness day to day. Martin Seligman, one of the founders of positive psychology, described three foundational pathways: the Pleasant Life, the Engaged Life, and the Meaningful Life. These are not competing options. They are layers, and each one feeds something different inside us. Pleasure feels good. Engagement absorbs you. Meaning sustains you. When people lean too heavily on only one, things start to fall out of balance. A life built solely on pleasure lacks resilience. A life driven entirely by achievement may lack warmth. A life of constant service without rest can lead to burnout. Flourishing, the kind of deep, sustained well-being researchers write about, tends to come from weaving all three together.

Pleasure: The Fast, Flashy Feeling

Pleasure is about feeling good right now. Good food. Comfort. Entertainment. Novelty. Winning. Laughing. Celebrating. And let's be clear, pleasure gets a bad reputation it doesn't entirely deserve. My wife and I had a blast on our honeymoon at Disneyland, and we've returned many times with our kids. For us, there's something about the rush of a fast roller coaster, biting into a fresh Matterhorn macaroon at Jolly Holidays Bakery Cafe, or floating through Pirates of the Caribbean that just feels magical. For someone else it might be a bowl of chips and guac or carving through fresh powder on a snowboard. Those moments feel good, sometimes really good, and there's nothing wrong with that.

In the brain, pleasure activates reward systems that release dopamine. Dopamine is often called the happiness chemical, but it's more accurately the motivation chemical. It says: *that felt good, let's do that again.* Pleasure isn't selfish or shallow. It's essential. It motivates us to eat, connect, explore, and survive. The problem isn't pleasure itself. The problem is expecting pleasure to do a job it was never designed to do.

Harvard professor and happiness researcher Arthur Brooks identifies what he calls the "vicious four," the things the world tells us will make us happy: money, power, pleasure, and fame. They're not inherently evil. But they share a common flaw. They're all external, temporary, and deeply subject to comparison. The more you get, the more you want. And the admiration of others, what Brooks calls the applause of the world, is perhaps the most unstable foundation of all. It feels amazing when it arrives. It creates anxiety the moment it slows. Building your happiness on any of these, he argues, will reliably make you unhappier over time.

Sometimes we begin to believe that if a little pleasure feels good, more must feel better. That's when pleasure quietly turns into pursuit, the unending chase for the next thrill, the next purchase, the next distraction that dulls reality just enough to escape it. And here's the tricky part: it works at first. But when pleasure becomes our only strategy for happiness, something inside eventually begins to feel hollow.

A wise professor once told me something I've never forgotten: *you can never get enough of what you don't need, because what you don't need will never satisfy you.* Pleasure mostly feeds satisfaction, and if safety and connection are missing, satisfaction alone won't carry us very far. It's like eating cotton candy and expecting to feel full. It might taste wonderful in the moment. But try living on it.

There's another reason pleasure can't anchor a meaningful life: our brains adapt to it. What feels extraordinary at first soon becomes normal. This process, called hedonic adaptation, is why the first bite of dessert is incredible but the tenth bite barely registers. It's why promotions, purchases, and new possessions give us a lift, but not for long. This isn't a character flaw. It's biology. Pleasure fades by design so we'll keep striving and growing. But if we mistake temporary highs for lasting happiness, we can spend years chasing something that was never meant to stick.

Someone once compared happiness to a butterfly. If you spend all your time sprinting after it, it stays just out of reach. But if you lose yourself in helping others, it might just gently land on your shoulder without you realizing it. Pleasure is often the chase. The deeper kind of happiness usually comes when we stop sprinting and start building. Pleasure is wonderful. It just isn't enough.

Engagement: The Joy of Being Fully Alive

Joy is different from pleasure, and the difference is worth understanding. Pleasure feels good while it's happening. You know you're enjoying the dessert, the roller coaster, the massage. Joy, on the other hand, often shows up when you're not thinking about how you feel at all. You're simply in it. Psychologist Mihaly Csikszentmihalyi called this state flow, the experience of being fully absorbed in something that uses your strengths, where time bends, self-consciousness fades, and you're not evaluating whether you're happy because you're simply too engaged to notice. Seligman called this the Engaged Life (and the Good Life), and research consistently shows it produces a deeper and more durable sense of well-being than pleasure alone.

Think about an athlete locked in on the next play, barely aware of the crowd. A musician playing a difficult piece and losing awareness of the room. A parent so absorbed in building Legos with their child that an hour disappears. A writer whose ideas come faster than their fingers can keep up. Our son, who was a star football wide receiver in high school, used to describe being so "in the zone" that he stopped noticing the noise from the cheerleaders, the opposing team, even the crowd. He was "locked in" to the next route or the next play. For many of us, flow shows up in quieter places, working on a project, cooking a meal, tending a garden, getting lost in a meaningful conversation. For me, it happens on stage. There's a moment when I begin genuinely connecting with an audience and time both stands still and disappears. I'm not monitoring my performance. I'm simply present. That's flow.

Here's the key distinction: with pleasure, you feel it in real time. With flow, you often feel it afterward, when you look back and think, that felt alive. This is why someone can finish a hard workout or a difficult presentation feeling deeply satisfied, even if parts of it were uncomfortable. The joy isn't in the ease. It's in the engagement. Seligman emphasizes that engagement deepens when we use our signature strengths, the qualities that feel most natural and energizing. Kindness. Creativity. Curiosity. Humor. Gratitude. Love of learning. When you use your strengths, you don't just pass time. You flourish.

I genuinely love learning—books, podcasts, research, a good conversation with someone who knows more than I do. Give me something interesting to read and I lose track of time. For my wife, it's making sourdough bread or playing Mahjong. For my dad, it's woodcarving. He can disappear into a project for hours and emerge with sore hands and a deeply satisfied look on his face. That's a very different kind of happiness than a handful of chocolate-covered cinnamon bears. Engagement is less about intensity and more about alignment. It's not about adrenaline. It's about using your talents and strengths and being in sync with what you're built to do.

There's a quieter layer of joy worth naming: savoring. Savoring isn't chasing pleasure. It's slowing down enough to actually experience something good in the moment. It's sitting in your car for a minute after you arrive home, finishing listening to a song you love instead of immediately jumping out. It's standing in the kitchen while something bakes and breathing in the smell. For my wife it's noticing and soaking in the silence of the house before everyone wakes up.

Since becoming a grandfather recently, I've learned something about savoring I didn't expect. One of my new favorite things is holding our granddaughter in the quiet, wrapped in a blanket, singing softly while she dozes off. I just watch her little face in my arms. I slow down. Nothing else competes for my attention in that moment. It's seriously the best.

Moments like that have taught me something I believe deeply: the amount of good in your life often depends on your ability to slow down and notice it. There is good everywhere. When you search for it intentionally, you find it. And when you find it, don't rush past it. Stay there a little longer. That's what savoring is.

Meaning: The Deepest Layer

Then there is meaning, and it operates differently than either pleasure or engagement. Meaning isn't primarily about how good something feels. It's about why it matters. It grows out of purpose, values, belonging, contribution, faith, family, service, and love. And here's the important part: meaning is not always comfortable. Childbirth isn't comfortable. Parenting isn't always fun. Training for a marathon takes sustained effort. Caring for aging parents can be exhausting. Standing up for what's right can cost you something real. But meaningful? Absolutely.

Arthur Brooks offers a useful contrast here. Where the "vicious four," money, power, pleasure, and fame, pull us toward things that are external and temporary, the "virtuous four" point us toward what actually lasts: faith, family, friendship, and work that serves others. These aren't just nicer-sounding alternatives. They are the sources that research consistently connects to lasting well-being. Not because they are easy, but because they are real. They connect us to something larger than ourselves, and that connection is precisely what meaning is made of.

Meaning helps the brain put stress into context. It doesn't

erase pain, but it changes how pain is interpreted. Pleasure asks, *how do I feel right now?* Meaning asks, *why does this matter?* And lives built around meaning tend to be more resilient even when circumstances are genuinely hard.

Meaning often shows up in quiet, ordinary acts, giving your time to something larger than yourself, sitting with someone in grief, volunteering, coaching a youth team, showing up for a neighbor who's struggling. I find a deep sense of purpose when I visit people during difficult times. Sitting with someone in uncertainty has a way of rearranging your priorities. And I have never once regretted a single one of those visits.

My wife finds meaning in checking in and talking with others, dropping off her famous chocolate chip cookies, or taking dinner to a neighbor who needs a lift. It may seem small. It isn't. There's something about lifting others that lifts us in return. When we lose ourselves in service to something larger, something steadier grows inside us. Psychologist Jonathan Haidt calls this "elevation," a warm, open feeling in the chest when we witness moral beauty: acts of kindness, courage, quiet generosity. You've probably felt it when you heard about someone dropping off a meal for a family going through something hard, or watching a friend show up consistently for someone who had no one else showing up. Witnessing goodness feels good inside. It makes us want to be a little better and do a little better. Elevation isn't loud. But it lingers. And it changes us.

Meaning doesn't require grand gestures. When we talk about service, our minds often jump to the big moments, humanitarian trips, starting a nonprofit, fostering children. These are beautiful. But that same feeling shows up on ordinary Tuesdays when you might wake up and simply ask, *who needs me today?* Then you pause for a moment and notice the nudges, taking soup to a sick neighbor, listening patiently to a child tell a long story, or sending a quick message to check on a friend who's been on your mind.

A good friend once discovered that Crossing Guard Appreciation Day was coming up (yes, it's a real thing). The night before, he took his kids to the grocery store and they bought bottled water and snacks, bagged them up, and taped a small note to each one. The next morning, they drove around town looking for crossing guards, and his kids walked up to hand them the bags. Those kids learned something that morning that will outlast anything they missed in math, about service, about noticing people who are often invisible, about meaning. I guarantee they still remember the look on the crossing guards' faces. You don't need a passport to make a difference. You just need to first observe, then serve.

Where Happiness Comes From

So, if happiness has these layers, pleasure, engagement, and meaning, where does it actually originate? This is where the research gets both humbling and genuinely encouraging.

Psychologist Sonja Lyubomirsky and her colleagues have proposed that roughly 50% of the difference in happiness between one person and another is genetic, about 10% is circumstantial, things like income, marital status, and where you live, and the remaining 40% is influenced by intentional thoughts and behaviors. Researchers debate the exact percentages, and the picture is more nuanced than any simple chart can capture. But the takeaway isn't the math. The takeaway is this: happiness isn't entirely fixed, and it isn't entirely outside your control. What you do, how you think, move, connect, speak, rest, notice, and serve, matters more than most of us were ever taught. That 40% is where the 101 practices in this book live.

This also helps explain why circumstances disappoint us so reliably. Research by psychologist Daniel Gilbert on what he calls affective forecasting shows that human beings are surprisingly bad at predicting what will make them happy and how long that happiness will last. We overestimate how good the promotion will feel and how long the new car will lift our spirits. We overestimate how devastating the rejection will be and how long the heartbreak will linger. Gilbert calls this the impact bias, our tendency to overestimate the emotional impact of future events in both directions. The raise doesn't feel as good as we imagined, and the loss doesn't hurt as long as we feared. Why? Because we consistently underestimate our own resilience, what Gilbert calls the psychological immune system, the remarkable human capacity to adapt, reframe, and find meaning even in difficulty. Understanding this doesn't make happiness automatic. But it does prevent us from spending our lives chasing things that the research already knows won't deliver what we're hoping for.

Arthur Brooks adds an important reframe here. One of the biggest mistakes people make, he argues, is treating happiness as a feeling to be captured and held. Some people believe that if they just achieve enough, acquire enough, or arrange their circumstances correctly, they will finally arrive at happiness and stay there. But that's not how it works. Brooks calls this the arrival fallacy. You set a goal. You work toward it. You achieve it. And then life goes on. Olympic athletes who spend years pursuing a gold medal often report a surprising emptiness after they win it. Not because the achievement wasn't real, but because they believed it would deliver something it was never designed to deliver. Permanent happiness isn't a destination. It's a direction.

This is why celebrating the small wins matters so much. Not as a consolation prize for not having arrived, but because the journey itself, the daily progress, the growth and stretching, the gradual becoming, is where most of life's satisfaction actually lives. Brooks frames it simply: *happiness is things you have divided by things you want*. You can increase that ratio two ways. Get more. Or want less. The second turns out to be far more reliable. The goal, he points out, is not to get happy. It's to get *happier*. That's a self-managing project, one where you're making genuine progress every day. It requires the right understanding, the right expectations, and the right habits. Know yourself. Don't compare yourself to others. And then do something with what you learn: understand it, live it, and share it with others.

I've held onto a statement from Russell Nelson that captures something similar: *the joy we feel has little to do with the circumstances of our lives and everything to do with the focus of our lives.* I believe that, within reason. There are seasons when circumstances are genuinely horrendous, when grief or trauma or illness make joy feel completely inaccessible. In those moments, survival and stability are the goal, and this book isn't asking anything of you then. But over time, where we direct our attention begins to shape what we experience. And that's something we have more influence over than we often realize.

How the Brain Changes: The Science of Neuroplasticity

Here's something that genuinely changed how I think about all of this. For most of history, scientists believed the adult brain was essentially fixed. You got the brain you got, and that was largely that. We now know this is wrong. The brain is plastic, meaning it changes in response to experience throughout our entire lives. The pathways you use repeatedly grow stronger. The ones you neglect grow quieter. Neuroscientists describe this with a phrase worth memorizing: *neurons that fire together, wire together.* Every time you practice gratitude, it becomes slightly easier to feel grateful. Every time you ruminate, rumination becomes more automatic. Every time you reach toward someone in difficulty, compassion becomes more natural. You are, literally and measurably, shaping your brain through the habits you build and the thoughts you practice.

This matters enormously for happiness. It means that the

practices in this book aren't just producing momentary shifts in how you feel. Practiced consistently, they are gradually rewiring the neural architecture through which you experience your entire life. Neurochemistry is part of this too. Dopamine drives motivation and reward. Serotonin regulates mood and a sense of calm. Oxytocin, sometimes called the bonding hormone, surges during moments of genuine connection and trust. Endorphins reduce pain and produce euphoria during physical activity. These aren't abstract concepts. They are the actual biological substrate of your emotional life, and the practices throughout this book influence all of them in measurable ways. The brain you have today is not the brain you're stuck with. That's not a motivational sentiment. It's neuroscience.

The Science of Habit: How Small Actions Compound

Understanding how happiness works is one thing. Actually building it is another. And that requires understanding how habits form, because without habits, good intentions stay intentions. Here's what the research shows. Every habit follows a basic loop: a cue, a routine, and a reward. The cue triggers the behavior. The routine is the behavior itself. The reward reinforces it, making the brain more likely to run the loop again next time. This cycle, described in detail by researcher Charles Duhigg and others, explains why habits are so sticky in both directions. Bad habits are hard to break because the cue-routine-reward loop keeps running automatically. Good habits, once established, run just as automatically, which is exactly what we want.

Researcher BJ Fogg's work on tiny habits adds a crucial insight: the biggest mistake people make when trying to build new behaviors is starting too big. When we fail to maintain a large new habit, we blame our motivation or our willpower rather than our design. Fogg's research shows that when in doubt, start smaller. Much smaller than you think you need to. A habit that begins as a single push-up or two minutes of journaling is a habit that actually gets done. And once it gets done consistently, growth follows naturally. Neuroscientist Alex Korb, in his book The Upward Spiral (one of my "Dave Faves"), describes exactly this dynamic: small positive actions activate brain circuits that make the next positive action more likely, creating a self-reinforcing cycle that gradually pulls your mood, your energy, and your behavior upward.

This is why the practices in this book are called happy hacks rather than programs or overhauls. They are designed to be small enough to start today and sustainable enough to become part of who you are over time. You need a small win that makes the next small win easier to reach. As John Gottman puts it: *small things, often.* That's not a motivational platitude. It's how change actually works in the human brain.

Gainers, Drainers, and the Direction of Attention

The brain filters millions of pieces of information every second. Only a tiny fraction reaches conscious awareness, and what we repeatedly attend to shapes the neural pathways that define how we experience life. As my podcast co-host Dr. Liz Hale often says, *what we focus on grows.* As you read through this book, you'll begin to notice patterns. Some habits and thoughts are gainers. They feed safety, satisfaction, and connection. They expand your world, strengthen your relationships, and build the kind of energy that compounds over time. Others are drainers. They deplete the same resources, narrow your perspective, and leave you running on empty.

If we focus primarily on threat, scarcity, and comparison, those pathways strengthen. If we intentionally practice noticing connection, gratitude, progress, and contribution, those circuits strengthen instead. This isn't denial of pain. It's direction of attention. Over time, attention becomes interpretation. Interpretation becomes narrative. Narrative becomes identity. And identity shapes everything.

There is one practice worth naming here that feeds both connection and meaning at once: compassion. I've started thinking of it as seeing with *eyes of compassion*, slowing down enough to see people as human beings carrying invisible burdens, with their own needs, hopes, and fears, rather than as obstacles or inconvenient interruptions. When we see others differently, we treat them differently. Compassion softens judgment, widens perspective, and tempers the kind of chronic low-grade irritability that quietly drains well-being. Bitterness tightens the chest. Compassion opens it. And in that openness, real joy often follows.

The Bottom Line

Happiness is not a single feeling. It's a layered system. Pleasure stimulates. Engagement strengthens. Meaning anchors. Safety calms the nervous system. Satisfaction rewards effort. Connection sustains the soul. The brain that processes all of this is not fixed. It's shaped by what you practice, what you attend to, and the small habits you build and maintain over time. And the research is clear that roughly 40% of your happiness is influenced by what you intentionally think and do. That 40% is yours to work with.

The world will tell you to chase money, power, pleasure, and fame. But the research, and honestly, most people's lived experience, points elsewhere: toward faith, family, friendship, and work that serves. And here's perhaps the most liberating idea in this entire chapter: the goal is not to get happy. It's to get *happier*. That's a project you can actually work on every single day, in small ways, in the right direction. When you understand how the system works, you stop chasing what fades and start building what lasts.

That's where the 101 happy hacks begin.

2.

FIX THE FOUNDATION FIRST

I'm intentionally beginning this book with the body and brain. That might surprise you. When most people think about happiness, they think about mindset, gratitude, relationships, or purpose. And they're right. All of those matter enormously. But before we talk about meaning or mindset, we need to talk about physiology. Because no amount of positive thinking will reliably carry you through the day if your sleep routine is a wreck, your blood sugar is crashing, and your nervous system has been overstimulated since the moment you woke up.

I've seen this in my own life more times than I can count. There have been seasons when I was doing everything "right," practicing gratitude, staying connected, working toward things that mattered, and still felt like I was dragging. And almost every time I traced it back, the answer wasn't a mindset problem. It was a body problem. I wasn't sleeping consistently. I wasn't moving. I was running on Diet Dr. Pepper, Peanut M&Ms, and not much else. My foundation was cracked, and I was trying to build happiness on top of it anyway. I've heard enough people describe the same pattern—in my research, in my classes, and in conversations after presentations—to know it isn't just me. That's not a character flaw. It's biology.

Your brain is not floating independently above your body. It lives inside your body, and it responds, moment to moment, to the signals your body sends it. I sometimes refer to the most foundational elements as the "Big 3": sleep, movement, and nutrition. When one of these is off, you feel it. When two are off, you struggle. When all three are off, even ordinary stressors can feel completely overwhelming. You've probably experienced this. After a poor night of sleep, minor inconveniences feel personal. When you're dehydrated or hungry, patience disappears and small frustrations loom larger than they should. When you've been sitting too long and moving too little, your mood often dips before you even realize why. None of that is weakness. It's chemistry.

This section is about regulating the system before we ask it to do harder things. Before reframing thoughts or cultivating deeper meaning, we stabilize the foundation. We anchor your circadian rhythm, smooth out blood sugar volatility, and calm the nervous system. We support the neurotransmitters involved in mood, motivation, and resilience, and create enough physical predictability that emotional stability becomes more accessible. Not because life gets easier, but because your brain is better equipped to meet it.

The order of these hacks is intentional. Light and movement come first because they set your internal clock and establish the neurochemical tone of your day. Sleep comes next because it's when your brain repairs itself. Nutrition and hydration follow because your mood runs on chemistry and chemistry runs on fuel. From there we move into stress physiology, breath, temperature, touch, and environment, and finally to attention, specifically what enters your system first and last each day.

Think of this section as infrastructure. You wouldn't try to decorate a house before pouring the foundation. These twenty happy hacks pour the concrete. In fact, nearly one in five of all 101 practices in this book lives right here in this chapter, and that proportion is intentional. It reflects something the research makes hard to argue with: it is genuinely difficult to sustain gratitude, build meaningful relationships, manage stress, or pursue purpose when your body and brain are running on empty. Poor sleep, inadequate movement, and inconsistent nutrition don't just make you tired. They make every other happiness practice harder to execute and harder to maintain. Get the foundation right and everything that follows becomes more accessible. Once your system is steadier, the emotional skills, the relational repair, the meaning-making, the joy-building, all of it becomes more available to you. Not because the work gets easier. Because the brain doing the work is finally regulated enough to do it well.

Happiness is not built on exhaustion. It's built on a foundation. Start here.

1. Get Morning Sunlight Within an Hour of Waking

Start your day with the most powerful signal your brain understands: light.

What It Is

I'll admit this one took me awhile to actually do consistently. It sounds almost too simple to be worth talking about. Go outside? That's the hack? But once I made it a habit, the difference in how my mornings felt was hard to ignore.

Before checking email. Before scrolling your phone. Step outside. Within the first hour after waking, spend a few minutes in natural daylight. Not through a window. Not through a windshield. Outside. You don't need to stare at the sun. Just let the daylight reach your eyes while you do something simple. Walk the dog. Drink your protein smoothie on the porch. Check the mail. Stretch in the driveway. Take a quick loop around the block. On bright mornings, 5 to 10 minutes is enough. On cloudy days, aim for closer to 15 to 20. The goal isn't exercise, though that's a nice bonus. The goal is light.

Why It Works

Your brain runs on an internal 24-hour clock, and light is how that clock gets set each day. When natural light enters your eyes in the morning, it sends a signal to the brain that the day has started. That signal helps regulate when you feel alert, when your energy naturally dips, and when your body begins releasing melatonin at night so you can actually sleep. When this rhythm is working well, energy feels steadier, mood becomes more stable, and sleep gets deeper and easier.

Morning light also regulates cortisol in a healthy way, giving your body a natural signal to become alert rather than relying entirely on caffeine to do the job. It also supports dopamine activity in the brain, which plays a quiet but important role in motivation, focus, and overall mood. Your brain evolved outdoors. Modern life moved indoors. Morning sunlight simply returns your nervous system to the rhythm it was designed for.

Try This Today

- Step outside for 5 to 10 minutes before looking at your phone.
- Drink your coffee or morning smoothie outside instead of at the kitchen counter.
- Take a short walk around the block before the day gets busy.
- Park a little farther from work and walk in the daylight before heading inside.

Consistency matters more than duration. A few minutes every morning beats an hour once a week.

What If Your Mornings Are Complicated?

Life doesn't always cooperate. Winter mornings are dark. Schedules get tight. Weather is unpredictable. The good news is that even on cloudy days, outdoor light is far stronger than the lighting inside most homes and offices. If you wake before sunrise, step outside once the sun comes up. If the weather is rough, do what you can. Any morning light is better than none, and even an imperfect habit beats waiting for the perfect conditions that never quite arrive.

Bottom Line

Your brain needs light to function well, and morning is when that light matters most. Step outside for a few minutes, let the day begin with sunlight, and your energy, mood, and sleep will follow.

2. Move Your Body Early (Even Briefly)

Just a few minutes of movement can reset your mind.

What It Is

Have you ever noticed how stress seems to live in the body? Your shoulders tighten. Your jaw clenches. Your mind starts spinning through the same thoughts again and again. One of the fastest ways to interrupt that cycle is surprisingly simple: move your body. Not a full workout. Not an hour at the gym (although this is super helpful too). Just intentional movement early in the day. A brisk 10-minute walk. A few sets of squats or pushups. Stretching on the living room floor. Walking the dog with purpose instead of scrolling your phone. The key is simply to move. Experts and research findings suggest the same thing: moving your body moves your brain.

Why It Works

Your brain and body are deeply connected systems. When one changes, the other changes with it. I like to tell my students: *Move your body to move your brain.* Movement helps your body process the stress hormones that build up when life feels overwhelming.

Chemicals like adrenaline and cortisol begin to decrease, while mood-supporting chemicals like endorphins, dopamine, and serotonin start to increase.

Blood flow to the brain also improves with movement. That extra circulation supports clearer thinking, better focus, and more stable mood. Many people notice they feel mentally sharper after a short walk. Movement can also interrupt rumination, the mental loop where the same worries replay over and over. Walking, especially outdoors, gives the brain new sensory input and helps break that cycle.

There is also a simple evolutionary explanation. Stress was designed to be released through physical action. Our ancestors didn't sit still while feeling anxious. They moved. When you move your body, your brain receives a powerful signal: *we're handling this.*

Try This Today

- Take a 10-minute brisk walk within an hour or two of waking.
- Walk during lunch or between meetings if mornings are packed.
- Do a quick bodyweight circuit: squats, pushups, a plank.
- When stress spikes, take a short walk before responding to a difficult email or conversation.

Consistency matters more than intensity. Ten minutes most days is far more powerful than an occasional long workout.

What If You're Already Exhausted?

Many people think movement will drain what little energy they have left. In reality, gentle movement often creates energy rather than using it up. Start smaller than you think. Five minutes. A lap around the block. A few stretches in the living room. Even light activity like gardening, yard work, or playing with your kids or grandkids counts. You're not training for performance here. You're helping your nervous system reset.

Bottom Line

Stress builds up in a still body. Move, even briefly, and your mood, clarity, and energy often begin to shift. Your brain changes when your body moves. Give it the chance.

3. Protect Your Sleep Timing, Not Just Sleep Length

Your brain thrives on rhythm, and consistency matters more than most people realize.

What It Is

For most of my adult life I thought sleep was simple math. Get enough hours and you're fine. It turns out the timing matters just as much as the total, and that one realization changed how I think about the whole thing.

Your brain doesn't just want sleep. It wants sleep on a schedule. Going to bed and waking up at roughly the same time each day helps your body know when to be alert, when to wind down, and when to drop into the deep restorative sleep that actually leaves you feeling rested.

This isn't about rigid perfection. Life happens. Late nights are real. The goal is simply to keep your sleep within a general window most days of the week. When your timing becomes predictable, your body begins to cooperate in ways that feel surprisingly powerful.

Why It Works

Sleep isn't just rest. It's maintenance. During deep sleep, your brain activates a system that clears out metabolic waste that accumulates during the day. Scientists sometimes describe it as a nightly cleaning process. When sleep is shortened or inconsistent, that process becomes less efficient, and the effects show up in how you think, feel, and cope the next day.

Consistent sleep timing also improves emotional regulation. When the brain is well rested, the areas responsible for reasoning and self-control work more effectively, while the threat-detection system becomes less reactive. That's why even a single night of poor sleep can make everything feel harder. Stress feels bigger. Patience runs thinner. Small things feel personal. When your sleep schedule is steady, your internal clock stays anchored, and that stability quietly supports better mood, clearer thinking, and greater resilience throughout the day.

Try This Today

- Choose a consistent bedtime within a 30-minute range and aim for it most nights.
- Set an evening alarm to remind yourself to start winding down, not just a morning one.
- Dim your lights 60 to 90 minutes before bed to signal your brain that the day is ending.
- Commit to waking at the same time tomorrow even if last night wasn't great.

Your body recalibrates faster than you might expect when you give it consistency to work with.

What If Your Schedule Is Unpredictable?

Shift work, travel, young kids, late activities. I get it. Real life doesn't always cooperate and that's worth acknowledging honestly. If full consistency isn't possible, focus on one anchor point. Sleep researchers consistently point to wake time as the strongest lever for stabilizing your internal clock. Keep that one thing steady and the rest tends to follow more easily. Even partial rhythm helps more than none.

Bottom Line

Sleep is not a luxury. It's infrastructure. Protect your sleep rhythm and your mood, clarity, and emotional resilience become easier to access. Your brain does its best work while you sleep. Give it the time and consistency to do that work.

4. Stop Scrolling 60 Minutes Before Bed

Give your brain a chance to power down.

What It Is

Many nights end the same way. You climb into bed, pick up your phone, and start scrolling. One video turns into five. Five turns into twenty. Suddenly it's much later than you planned. This habit feels harmless, but it quietly works against the very thing you're trying to do: fall asleep.

This hack is simple. Try putting your phone away about an hour before bed. Not as punishment. Not as a rigid rule. Just as a small boundary that helps your brain shift out of daytime stimulation and into nighttime rest.

You don't need to sit in the dark doing nothing. Read a few pages of a book. Stretch. Talk with your partner. Write down tomorrow's tasks. The goal is simply to replace the endless stimulation of scrolling with something calmer.

Why It Works

Your brain follows signals from light and stimulation to decide when it should be awake and when it should prepare for sleep. Smartphones deliver both in large doses. The bright, blue-enriched light from screens can delay the release of melatonin, the hormone that helps your body fall asleep. Research in sleep science has shown that evening screen exposure can shift your internal clock later, making it harder to fall asleep when you intend to. The content itself matters too. Social media, news, and videos keep the brain mentally engaged. Instead of slowing down, your mind stays in problem-solving and stimulation mode.

Sleep researchers, including work from Matthew Walker (big fan of his TED talks), consistently show that the final hour before sleep strongly influences how easily we fall asleep and how restorative that sleep becomes. When you step away from screens, your nervous system gets the signal that the day is ending. Melatonin begins rising naturally. Your brain shifts from stimulation toward recovery. In other words, the quality of your sleep often begins with what you do before bedtime.

Try This Today

- Set a "screens off" alarm about 60 minutes before bed.
- Charge your phone outside the bedroom or across the room.
- Replace scrolling with something calming: reading, stretching, journaling, or quiet   conversation.
- If a full hour feels unrealistic, start with 20–30 minutes and build from there.

Consistency matters more than perfection.

What If Scrolling Helps You Relax?

For many people, scrolling feels like a way to unwind after a long day. And sometimes it does feel relaxing in the moment. The problem is that the brain interprets the light and stimulation differently than we do. What feels like relaxation to us can still signal "stay awake" to the nervous system.

If scrolling feels hard to replace, try swapping it for something that still feels enjoyable but less stimulating. A short podcast (my wife's go-to is true crime podcasts—how does she sleep after those!?), light reading, or quiet music can offer the same sense of unwinding without confusing your brain's sleep signals. The goal isn't discipline. It's giving your brain clearer cues.

Bottom Line

Sleep doesn't begin when your head hits the pillow. It begins with the signals you give your brain before bed. Put the phone down earlier, and falling asleep often becomes much easier.

5. Create a Consistent Wind-Down Routine

Teach your brain how the day ends.

What It Is

Most people try to fall asleep the moment their head hits the pillow, then wonder why it takes so long. The brain usually needs a little runway. A wind-down routine simply means doing roughly the same calming activities in the same order during the final hour before bed. Not a rigid checklist. Not a complicated nighttime ritual. Just a small pattern your brain begins to recognize.

It might look like dimming the lights, making a cup of herbal tea, stretching on the living room floor, reading a few pages of a book, or jotting thoughts in a journal before turning off the lamp. The exact activities matter less than the consistency. When your brain sees the same sequence each night, it begins to associate those cues with sleep, and over time that routine quietly becomes your nervous system's signal that the day is ending.

Why It Works

Sleep doesn't begin the moment you lie down. It begins earlier, as your nervous system gradually shifts from daytime alertness to nighttime recovery. The problem is that most of us move straight from stimulation to pillow and then expect our brain to power down on command. A consistent wind-down routine helps bridge that gap. When the brain repeatedly sees the same calming cues each night, it begins preparing for sleep before you've even turned off the light. Scientists call this a conditioned sleep response, and it's one of the more practical findings in sleep research.

There's also a stress-regulation layer worth understanding. Evening is when unprocessed thoughts from the day tend to surface, the conversation you're replaying, the task you didn't finish, the worry you've been too busy to sit with. Light journaling has solid research support for reducing the mental spinning that keeps people staring at the ceiling (check out all my unique helpful journals at www.DrDaveSchramm.com). Writing thoughts down externalizes them and signals to your brain that they've been acknowledged and don't need to be actively rehearsed in the dark. Light also plays a role. Bright screens and overhead lights delay your brain's release of melatonin, the hormone that helps initiate sleep. Dimming everything in the final hour sends your internal clock a clear signal that nighttime is approaching.

Try This Today

- Dim lights and reduce screentime about 45 to 60 minutes before bed.
- Do something calming like light stretching, a warm shower, quiet music, or reading.
- Write down unfinished tasks or lingering worries from the day to get them out of your head.
- End your routine the same way each night, even if it's just turning off the lamp at a consistent time.

Your brain learns through repetition. The more consistent the pattern, the stronger the signal.

What If Your Evenings Are Unpredictable?

Real life can make perfect routines difficult. Kids need attention. Work runs late. Evenings get complicated. If a full routine isn't possible every night, focus on one simple anchor. Maybe it's making the same cup of tea, washing your face, or dimming the lights at a certain time. Even a single repeated cue can start teaching your brain that sleep is approaching. The goal isn't perfection. It's a pattern your nervous system can recognize most nights.

Bottom Line

Your brain learns from the habits you repeat. A consistent wind-down routine tells your nervous system the day is finished and it's safe to rest. Give your mind a gentle landing and sleep becomes something you ease into rather than chase.

6. Eat Protein Early

Start your day with steady fuel.

What It Is

For a long time my morning routine looked like this: bowl of cereal, maybe a piece of toast if I was hungry, and then wondering why I felt scattered and irritable by mid-morning. It took me longer than I'd like to admit to connect those dots.

How you begin your metabolic day matters more than most people realize. Within the first hour or two after waking, try to eat something with meaningful protein. It doesn't have to be a big breakfast or a complicated meal. Just a small shift away from starting the day with pure sugar or refined carbs. Eggs. Bacon. Greek yogurt. Cottage cheese. A protein shake. Even leftovers from last night. The goal isn't dieting. The goal is stability. Giving your body steady fuel early in the day tends to produce steadier energy, clearer thinking, and fewer mood swings before lunch.

Why It Works

When you wake up, your body naturally produces a rise in cortisol. This isn't harmful. It's part of the system that transitions you from sleep to alertness. But what you eat next can either stabilize that process or amplify it. If the first thing you eat is mostly sugar or refined carbs, blood sugar rises quickly and then drops just as fast. That drop can show up as fatigue, irritability, brain fog, or intense cravings well before lunchtime. What feels like a mood problem is often a blood sugar problem. Protein slows digestion and creates a steadier release of glucose into the bloodstream, smoothing out that spike and crash cycle. It also provides amino acids, the raw materials your brain uses to produce neurotransmitters like dopamine and serotonin, which are directly involved in focus, motivation, and mood regulation. Starting the day with protein isn't about physique. It's about giving your brain a stable foundation to work from.

Try This Today

- Add a protein source to your morning meal: eggs, bacon, yogurt, cottage cheese, or a smoothie.
- Pair carbohydrates with protein instead of eating them alone.
- Prepare something simple the night before if mornings feel rushed.
- If you skip breakfast, make your first meal of the day protein-focused whenever it happens.

Small tweaks in your morning meal, done consistently, are far more powerful than dramatic overhauls.

What If You're Not Hungry in the Morning?

That's pretty common, and it often means late-night eating has shifted your hunger rhythms later in the day. You don't need to force a large meal. Start small. A boiled egg, a few spoonfuls of yogurt, or half a protein shake can still make a meaningful difference. Over time, eating earlier tends to gradually shift hunger earlier too. If mornings truly don't work for your schedule, simply make your first meal protein-rich whenever it happens. This isn't about rigid rules. It's about reducing the energy swings that make the day harder than it needs to be.

Bottom Line

Energy crashes often feel emotional but they're frequently physiological. Start the day with steady protein fuel and your mood, focus, and cravings tend to become steadier too. Stability early makes everything that follows a little easier.

7. Stay Hydrated Before Caffeine

Give your body what it actually needs before asking it to perform.

What It Is

I don't drink coffee or tea, so I had to think about this one differently. But the principle applies to everyone, whether your morning drink is coffee, an energy drink, a soda, or just the habit of diving straight into the day without touching a glass of water. After six to eight hours of sleep, your body wakes up mildly dehydrated. You've been breathing, regulating temperature, and going without fluids all night. Even a small fluid deficit can affect how you feel in those first foggy minutes of the morning. This hack is simple sequencing. Water first, then whatever else you reach for. It takes less than a minute and it can noticeably change how your morning feels.

Why It Works

Even mild dehydration affects how the brain functions. Research in nutrition and exercise science has found that losing as little as one to two percent of body weight in fluids can increase fatigue, reduce concentration, and make tasks feel harder than they actually are. Most people wake up already slightly behind that threshold without realizing it.

Drinking water first helps restore blood volume and circulation, which supports oxygen delivery to the brain. When those systems are running properly, mental clarity and energy tend to improve on their own. Caffeine works differently. It temporarily blocks a chemical called adenosine that builds sleep pressure in the brain, which is why it makes you feel more alert. But caffeine doesn't solve dehydration, and when it's layered on top of a dehydrated system it can sometimes amplify jitters, headaches, or that wired but tired feeling later in the morning. Hydrating first gives your body a stable foundation to build on. Then whatever you reach for next works more smoothly.

Try This Today

- Keep a glass of water on your nightstand so it's the first thing you reach for in the morning.
- Aim for 12 to 16 ounces within the first 10 minutes of waking before anything else.
- If you drink coffee or an energy drink in the morning, have your water while it's brewing or being prepared.
- Notice how your energy feels on days you hydrate first compared to days you don't.

A small shift in sequence can change the whole tone of the morning.

What If You're Just Not a Morning Water Person?

Fair enough. Try adding something to make it more appealing, a squeeze of lemon, a pinch of salt, or even just a cold glass straight from the fridge. I put a scoop of Re-Lyte electrolyte mix and a True Lemon Peach Lemonade packet in my Stanley jug every morning. The goal isn't to make it complicated. It's just to get some fluid into your system before the day starts pulling at you. Start with a smaller amount if a full glass feels like too much. Even half a glass is a meaningful improvement over nothing.

Bottom Line

Morning fatigue isn't always an energy problem. Often, it's a hydration problem wearing an energy-shaped disguise. Give your brain water first and your body has a steadier foundation to start from.

8. Master Your Breath (Lengthen Your Exhales)

Your breath is the fastest way to calm your nervous system, and it's available to you anywhere.

What It Is

Before I walked out for my TEDx Talk, I was nervous. Not a little nervous. The kind of nervous where your hands feel strange and your thoughts start racing. Then I gently reminded myself to slow my breathing and lengthen my exhales before stepping on stage. I did it for about two minutes backstage, and something genuinely shifted. Not perfect calm, but enough. Enough to think clearly, connect with the audience, and actually enjoy it. That experience made me a believer in this one.

When stress rises, most people try to calm their thoughts first. But the body has a shortcut. Slow your breathing and make your exhale slightly longer than your inhale. Inhale for four seconds and exhale for six. Or inhale for three and exhale for five. The exact numbers don't matter much. What matters is the ratio. Out longer than in. You don't need an app, a meditation cushion, or a quiet room. You just need a moment of attention and the breath that is already there.

Why It Works

Most calming strategies work from the outside in. You change your environment, call someone, go for a walk. Breathing works differently because it's always with you and it bypasses the thinking brain entirely.

Here's why it works so fast: your brain already knows that you only breathe slowly when you're safe. It has known this your whole life. When you slow your breath deliberately, you're borrowing a signal your nervous system already trusts. You're not trying to convince your brain that everything is fine. You're speaking to it in a language it already understands.

Research from Andrew Huberman and colleagues at Stanford confirms the effect is real and fast. A 2023 study found that just a few minutes of slow breathing with extended exhales improved mood and reduced anxiety, in some cases more effectively than traditional mindfulness practices. The mind follows the body. And the breath is the fastest way in.

Try This Today

- Inhale for 4 seconds and exhale for 6. Repeat for 2 to 3 minutes and notice what shifts.
- Take five slow breaths before responding to a stressful message or difficult conversation.
- Practice at a stoplight, in a waiting room, or anywhere you have a quiet moment.
- Add 3 to 5 minutes of slow breathing to your wind-down routine before bed.

You don't need a long session. Even two minutes can noticeably shift your state.

What If You Forget in the Moment?

That's completely normal. Stress has a way of making us forget the tools we have. Rather than waiting for crisis moments to practice, build the habit during ordinary ones. Try it while brushing your teeth, waiting for a page to load, or sitting at a stoplight. The more familiar the rhythm feels when you're calm, the more accessible it becomes when stress rises. Breathing is always available. It just works better when you've practiced using it on purpose.

Bottom Line

Your breath is a built-in regulator that most people never fully use. Lengthen your exhale and your nervous system listens. Calm the body first and the mind usually follows.

9. Get Regular Physical Touch

Your nervous system was not designed to regulate itself alone.

What It Is

I once heard a therapist say that many adults in modern life are living in a state of chronic touch deprivation without ever realizing it. That landed for me. We live busy, distracted, screen-filled lives, and somewhere along the way, simple physical connection quietly disappears from the daily routine.

It doesn't take much to change that. A hug that lasts a few seconds longer than usual. Holding hands on a walk. Sitting close on the couch instead of at opposite ends. A warm greeting instead of a quick wave across the room. For couples it might mean a longer hug before leaving the house. For parents, a little extra physical affection with the kids. For close friends, simply choosing connection over distance. These moments can feel small. To your nervous system, they are anything but.

Why It Works

Safe, affectionate touch triggers an immediate biological response. Oxytocin rises, cortisol drops, blood pressure softens, and stress reactivity decreases. These are not subtle effects. Even brief physical contact produces measurable changes in your physiology.

But the deeper mechanism is worth understanding. Your nervous system doesn't regulate itself in isolation. It co-regulates with the people around you. Research by social neuroscientist James Coan has shown that physical contact with a trusted person actually reduces the brain's threat response during stressful situations. When you're in safe physical contact with someone calm, your body begins to synchronize with theirs. Heart rate steadies. Breathing slows. Muscle tension releases.

This process starts in infancy and continues throughout adulthood. Decades of research in attachment and developmental psychology point to the same conclusion: physical connection is not a luxury or a personality preference. Touch isn't childish. It's biological. And it works.

Try This Today

- Give someone you trust a 15 to 20 second hug instead of a quick squeeze and notice how different it feels.
- Hold hands while walking or sitting together.
- Sit closer to your partner or a close friend rather than defaulting to distance.
- Greet people with a warm hug (if they're open to it) or a hand on the arm instead of a wave across the room.

Small, consistent moments of contact matter more than occasional grand gestures.

What If Touch Feels Uncomfortable or Isn't Available?

Comfort with touch varies widely and that's worth respecting. The key word throughout this entry is safe. Touch should always be consensual and appropriate. If affectionate touch feels unfamiliar, start small within relationships where trust already exists. And if physical connection with people isn't available right now, research shows that interacting with animals provides similar calming benefits. Petting a dog or cat has been shown to lower cortisol and improve mood. Your nervous system is simply looking for signals of safety.

Bottom Line

Safe physical touch lowers stress, strengthens connection, and calms the body in ways that words simply cannot replicate. Your nervous system was designed for contact. Give it what it needs, and everything tends to settle a little more easily.

10. Schedule Bodywork: Massage, Self-Massage, or Similar

Stress settles in the body. Help it leave.

What It Is

Have you ever had one of those days where your shoulders feel like rocks and your jaw has been clenched for hours without you even noticing? That's not just stress in your mind. It's stress in your body. This hack is about intentionally releasing that tension on a regular basis. That might mean a professional massage. It might mean foam rolling on the living room floor, using a massage gun, rolling your back on a tennis ball on the ground, stretching before bed, soaking in a hot bath, or spending five minutes working through the knots in your neck and shoulders with your own hands. It doesn't have to be fancy. It doesn't have to be expensive. It just needs to be intentional and reasonably consistent.

Your body keeps a running record of your days. In your jaw. Your neck. Your shoulders. Your lower back. Your hips. If that tension is never released, it tends to build. Bodywork is one of the simplest ways to interrupt that buildup before it becomes your new normal.

Why It Works

Stress changes the body in very physical ways. Muscles tighten. Breathing gets shallower. Heart rate rises. The nervous system shifts into a more guarded, activated state. Researchers who study stress physiology, including work influenced by people like Herbert Benson and Stephen Porges, have helped show that the body and nervous system respond strongly to cues of safety and release. When muscles soften, pressure decreases, and the body begins to feel supported rather than braced, the nervous system often starts to settle too.

Massage and similar forms of bodywork appear to help through several pathways. They can reduce muscle tension, improve circulation, and lower the physical arousal that often accompanies chronic stress. Some research also suggests massage can lower cortisol and support a calmer mood, especially when practiced regularly rather than occasionally.

In simple terms, bodywork helps send the body a message it rarely gets during a stressful week: you can let go now. Sometimes the mind calms the body. But often the body can calm the mind first.

Try This Today

- Spend 5–10 minutes massaging your neck, shoulders, jaw, or feet.
- Use a foam roller or massage gun in the evening, especially after long hours sitting.
- Take a warm bath or shower and consciously relax one muscle group at a time.
- Schedule a professional massage once a month or once a quarter if that fits your budget.

- Lie on the floor and slowly scan your body for tension, then release what you can.

Small, consistent release does more than occasional relief.

What If This Still Feels Like a Luxury?

That's a common reaction, especially when the word *massage* brings to mind robes, candles, and expensive spa menus. But the deeper idea here is not luxury. It's maintenance. Self-massage, stretching, foam rolling, heat, and simple muscle release practices can all help without costing much. The benefit does not depend on a professional setting. It depends on whether you make space to release tension before it becomes chronic. And if professional massage is available to you even once in a while, it may help to think of it the same way you think about dental cleanings, annual checkups, or fixing something on your car before it breaks down. Your nervous system deserves maintenance too.

Bottom Line

Stress doesn't just live in your thoughts. It lives in your body. Release tension regularly, and your muscles, mood, and nervous system all tend to benefit. Treat bodywork like upkeep, not indulgence.

11. Consider Magnesium for Relaxation and Sleep Support

Sometimes a restless nervous system needs a little nutritional support.

What It Is

My wife introduced me to this one, and I'll be transparent, I was skeptical at first. Another supplement someone swears by? But after trying it I noticed that my evenings felt a little easier to wind down, and the research behind it actually made sense. If you've ever felt exhausted but somehow still wired at night, magnesium might be worth paying attention to. It's a mineral your body uses in hundreds of processes, especially those related to muscle relaxation, nervous system regulation, and sleep. The catch is that many adults don't get enough of it, particularly during stressful seasons. And the frustrating part is that stress itself depletes magnesium further, meaning the people who need it most are often the ones losing it fastest. This isn't about turning supplements into a solution for everything. It's simply about recognizing that sometimes the body is missing a basic ingredient it needs to relax properly.

Why It Works

Your brain has a natural braking system. It's called GABA, a neurotransmitter responsible for slowing neural activity and promoting relaxation. Magnesium is what helps that system work effectively. When magnesium levels are low, the braking system becomes less efficient and the nervous system grows more excitable, showing up as muscle tension, irritability, restlessness, or that frustrating experience of lying in bed exhausted but unable to settle.

Magnesium also supports muscle relaxation directly. If you tend to clench your jaw, carry tension in your shoulders, or feel physically wound up at night, improving your magnesium intake may help soften that baseline tension. Clinical studies suggest magnesium supplementation can improve sleep quality and help people fall asleep faster, particularly for those who are deficient. It doesn't force sleep the way a sedative does. It simply makes the conditions for sleep easier to reach.

Try This Today

- Talk with your healthcare provider about whether magnesium makes sense for you, especially if you take other medications.

- If you try a supplement, take it in the evening as part of your wind-down routine rather than in the morning.
- Start with a modest dose. Too much magnesium can cause digestive upset for some people, so more is not always better.
- If you prefer a food-first approach, leafy greens, nuts, seeds, beans, and whole grains are all good natural sources.

What If You're Unsure About Supplements?

Not everyone needs supplements and magnesium can interact with certain medications, so a conversation with your healthcare provider is worth having first. A food-first approach is always sensible. But if stress is high, sleep has been inconsistent, or your diet isn't always ideal, magnesium is one of the more widely studied and generally well-tolerated nutrients to explore with a professional. The key point is that it should support your healthy habits, not replace them.

Bottom Line

Relaxation isn't always just psychological. Sometimes it's biochemical. If your system feels chronically tight or sleep feels just out of reach, magnesium may help create the conditions for calm and rest to emerge more naturally. Just start low, go slow, and check with your doctor first.

12. Optimize Vitamin D (Especially in Winter)

Sometimes the winter blues are partly biological.

What It Is

A few years ago I had my vitamin D levels tested almost as an afterthought during a routine checkup. They came back low, which surprised me because I spend a fair amount of time outdoors. My doctor explained that where I live, the angle of the sun in winter months means your skin produces almost no vitamin D even on a sunny day. That was news to me.

If your energy and mood tend to dip during the darker months, vitamin D is worth paying attention to. Your skin produces it in response to sunlight, but during fall and winter, especially in northern climates or for anyone spending most of the day indoors, that production drops significantly. The tricky part is that deficiency doesn't always announce itself clearly. It often shows up quietly as fatigue, lower mood, or feeling less resilient than usual without any obvious explanation.

Why It Works

Vitamin D receptors are found throughout the brain, including areas directly involved in mood regulation and cognitive function. Low levels have repeatedly been linked to higher rates of depressive symptoms, fatigue, and seasonal mood changes in large population studies. This isn't a fringe finding. It's one of the more consistent associations in nutritional research.

Winter compounds the problem in ways many people aren't aware of. In many northern regions, the sun's angle from roughly October through March makes meaningful vitamin D synthesis nearly impossible regardless of how much time you spend outside. Your shadow being longer than your height is actually a simple indicator that the sun is too low for effective production.

Vitamin D also works alongside other nutrients in the body. It plays a key role in calcium absorption, immune regulation, and muscle function. When it comes to supplements, the type matters. Vitamin D3 is the form your skin naturally produces and is generally better absorbed than D2. Taking it with a meal containing healthy fats, like eggs, avocado, or olive oil, significantly improves how well your body actually uses it. Some research also suggests that taking magnesium alongside vitamin

D helps with its activation in the body, which is one reason the two are often recommended together.

Try This Today

- Ask your healthcare provider to check your vitamin D levels during a routine blood test, especially heading into fall or winter.
- If supplementing, look for vitamin D3 rather than D2 and take it with a fat-containing meal for better absorption.
- Get outside during midday when possible. Even 10 to 15 minutes with arms and face exposed makes a meaningful difference in warmer months.
- If your doctor recommends a supplement, consistency matters more than the occasional high dose.

What If You Get Plenty of Sun?

You may not need supplementation at all, but it's worth verifying rather than assuming. Many people overestimate their effective sun exposure, particularly those who work indoors, use sunscreen consistently, or live north of roughly the latitude of Los Angeles or Atlanta, where winter sun angles are too low to trigger meaningful vitamin D production for several months of the year. Skin tone also affects production rates significantly, with darker skin requiring more sun exposure to produce the same amount of vitamin D. Testing removes the guesswork entirely and takes about thirty seconds at your next checkup.

Bottom Line

Mood is not just mental. It's biological. If winter consistently feels heavier than it should, vitamin D may be part of the picture. Test your levels, correct deficiencies if needed, and give your body the raw materials it needs to function at its best.

13. Take a Short Nap Instead of Powering Through

A brief reset can change the whole afternoon.

What It Is

I have to come clean here. When my afternoon energy crashes, my first instinct is usually a Diet Dr. Pepper or handful (or two) of peanut M&Ms. Or just ploughing through while digging for a little more willpower—just more task before taking a break. But I've learned that sometimes my brain isn't asking for effort. It's asking for recovery.

A short nap, somewhere between 10 and 20 minutes, can provide a surprisingly effective reset. Set a timer, lie down somewhere quiet, and close your eyes. Even if you don't fully fall asleep, the pause itself tends to restore energy in ways that pushing through simply doesn't. There's an important distinction worth naming here. Fatigue and laziness are not the same thing, and many people treat them as if they are. When your brain is genuinely depleted, more effort rarely helps. Recovery does.

Why It Works

Your brain naturally moves through cycles of higher and lower alertness throughout the day. For most people there's a predictable dip in the early to mid-afternoon, and this isn't poor discipline. It's biology. Part of the reason is the buildup of a chemical called adenosine, which accumulates the longer you stay awake and creates increasing pressure to sleep. A short nap helps clear some of that buildup and refreshes mental energy without requiring a full sleep cycle.

Sleep researchers including Matthew Walker (again, go watch his TED talks) have shown that brief naps improve attention, reaction time, memory, and mood. The key is keeping them short. Research consistently finds that 10 to 20 minutes provides meaningful cognitive benefits without causing sleep inertia, that groggy disoriented feeling that follows longer daytime sleep. There's also an emotional benefit worth noting. Fatigue lowers stress tolerance and makes ordinary problems feel larger than they are. A short nap can restore patience and perspective faster than caffeine, which tends to delay fatigue rather than actually resolve it.

Try This Today

- Set a 15-to-20-minute timer and lie down somewhere quiet in the early afternoon.
- If sleep doesn't come, simply close your eyes and breathe slowly. The rest alone is beneficial.
- Keep naps before 3pm to protect your nighttime sleep.
- If lying down isn't possible, try a five-minute eyes-closed reset at your desk or in your car (not while driving).

Short and intentional naps work better than long accidental ones.

What If Naps Ruin Your Nighttime Sleep?

For some people, particularly those dealing with insomnia, daytime naps can reduce the sleep pressure needed to fall asleep easily at night. If that's your experience, experiment cautiously. Keep naps brief and earlier in the day, and if nighttime sleep worsens, skip the nap and focus on protecting your sleep schedule instead. The goal is restoration, not trading one sleep problem for another.

Bottom Line

Fatigue makes everything feel heavier than it actually is. A short nap can restore clarity, patience, and focus in ways that willpower simply cannot. Sometimes the most productive thing you can do is pause.

14. Use Heat Intentionally—Shower, Bath, or Sauna

Warmth is one of the body's oldest signals of safety.

What It Is

There's a reason people have been soaking in hot springs, sweating in saunas, and relaxing in warm baths for thousands of years. Roman baths, Finnish saunas, Japanese onsens, sweat lodges across countless cultures—they all reflect the same instinct. When people need to recover, they reach for warmth. It turns out that instinct is well supported by science.

This doesn't require anything elaborate. A warm shower before bed. A bath after a hard day. Time in a sauna if one is available. Even a heating pad across tight shoulders while you decompress on the couch. The tool is simple. The effect on your nervous system is real.

Why It Works

When your body warms up, blood vessels expand, circulation increases, and muscles begin to loosen. Heat activates the parasympathetic nervous system, the branch responsible for rest and recovery. Heart rate slows. Breathing deepens. The body gradually shifts out of the high-alert state that stress keeps it stuck in.

Evening heat exposure has an added bonus for sleep. When you take a warm shower or bath, your core temperature rises slightly. When you step out, your body begins cooling down, and that cooling process mimics the natural temperature drop that signals your brain it's time to sleep. Studies show that warm bathing about 60 to 90 minutes before bed can help people fall asleep faster and sleep more deeply.

Sauna research is growing too, with longer-term studies linking regular use to improvements in cardiovascular health, stress reduction, and lower rates of depression symptoms.

Try This Today

- Take a warm shower 60 to 90 minutes before bed and let your shoulders actually relax while you're in it.
- Take a bath after a stressful day and focus on releasing tension rather than scrolling on your phone.
- If a sauna is available, try a short session and hydrate well before and after.
- Place a heating pad on your neck, shoulders, or lower back while you wind down for the evening.

A few minutes of intentional warmth is often enough to begin the shift.

What If You Don't Have Time?

You don't need an hour for this to work. Even five minutes in a warm shower can help your body downshift if you actually slow down while you're in it. Let the water hit your shoulders. Take a few slow breaths. It's worth it.

Bottom Line

Stress tightens the body. Heat helps it soften. Warm your body deliberately and your nervous system, your muscles, and your mood tend to follow. Sometimes restoration is as simple as stepping into warmth and letting your body remember how to release.

15. Try Cold Exposure for a Mood and Energy Reset

One of the fastest ways to reset your nervous system costs nothing and takes less than a minute.

What It Is

Let me be clear—I did not want to try this one. The idea of ending a perfectly nice warm shower with cold water sounded like something only elite athletes and people with something to prove actually do. But I tried it anyway, and the first thing I noticed was how awake I felt. Not jittery. Not caffeinated. Just genuinely alert and present in a way that was hard to explain. Yes, I did freak out at first, but then relaxed my muscles, told myself I was okay, and just took slow deep breaths.

You don't need an ice bath or a polar plunge. End your shower with 30 to 60 seconds of cold water. Splash cold water on your face when stress spikes. Step outside into crisp air with intention. The entry point is lower than most people expect, and the effect is faster than most people believe. Cold is uncomfortable, and that's not a flaw in the design. It's the mechanism. You're not trying to suffer. You're teaching your nervous system that discomfort and danger are not the same thing.

Why It Works

Cold exposure activates your stress response in a controlled, time-limited way. Heart rate rises. Breathing quickens. But unlike the emotional stress most of us carry all day, cold stress is predictable and finite. It starts and stops on your terms. When you stay with it and breathe through it rather than escape it, your brain learns something valuable through direct experience: discomfort and catastrophe are not the same thing. That lesson builds stress resilience in real time.

The chemistry is compelling too. Research shows cold exposure significantly boosts dopamine and norepinephrine, the chemicals behind alertness, motivation, and stable mood. Even short bursts can keep dopamine elevated for several hours afterward, producing calm focus rather than the spike and crash of caffeine. And cold demands presence in a way almost nothing else does. You cannot scroll or ruminate under cold water. You have to breathe. You have to be exactly where you are. Sometimes that's exactly what a stressed brain needs most.

Try This Today

- End your shower with just 20 seconds of cold water and focus on slow, controlled breathing while you do it.
- Splash cold water on your face the next time stress spikes and notice what shifts.
- Step outside into cool air for a few intentional minutes rather than staying in controlled comfort.
- Build gradually over days and weeks rather than trying to be impressive on day one (day one is awful, just sayin).

Short and deliberate beats long and chaotic. The goal is regulation, not endurance.

What If Cold Feels Intimidating?

That reaction is almost universal, and you are not alone. Start with lukewarm and move slightly cooler over time. Even small doses produce measurable effects. You don't need dramatic exposure to get meaningful benefit.

One note: cold exposure isn't appropriate for everyone, particularly those with certain cardiovascular conditions. Check with a healthcare provider if that applies to you.

Bottom Line

Discomfort, when chosen and controlled, is training. Brief cold exposure builds stress resilience, sharpens focus, and resets mood through neurochemistry rather than willpower. Lean in and teach your nervous system that it can handle more than it thinks it can.

16. Spend Time in Nature—Beyond Just Your Backyard

Nature calms the nervous system in ways that buildings simply can't

What It Is

Some of my clearest thinking happens while in the mountains near our home or hiking on a trail. Not because I'm trying to solve anything, but because something about being surrounded by trees and moving water quietly turns down the noise. I stop rehearsing conversations. I stop running through my to-do list. I just start noticing things. The light through the leaves. The sound of the creek. My own breathing. That's not an accident. Again, it's biology.

This hack is about intentionally spending time in natural environments, not just passing through them but genuinely entering them. A walk through a wooded trail. Sitting near moving water. Time in a park with mature trees. A hike where traffic noise fades and your senses can actually settle. Researchers have studied a Japanese practice called Shinrin-yoku, or forest bathing, which is simply the practice of being present in nature with your full attention. Not exercise. Not performance. Just presence.

Why It Works

Natural environments produce biological changes that indoor spaces simply don't replicate. Time in green space reduces cortisol, lowers blood pressure, and decreases activity in the part of the brain most associated with rumination, that repetitive mental loop that quietly fuels anxiety and low mood.

The reason goes deeper than scenery. Nature holds your attention gently without depleting it. Unlike screens and urban noise, which demand constant directed focus, natural environments let your brain rest while staying present. Researchers call this soft fascination, and it produces a genuinely different neurological state, one your brain slips into surprisingly quickly. Studies on forest bathing show improvements in mood, immune function, and feelings of vitality after even brief immersion, with effects that persist well beyond the time spent outdoors.

Your brain evolved in nature across hundreds of thousands of years. The sense of ease that settles over you near trees or water isn't nostalgia. It's recognition.

Try This Today

- Take a 20-to-30-minute walk in a park or wooded area without headphones and at a pace that lets your senses actually engage.
- Sit near water and leave your phone in your pocket. Just be there for a few minutes.
- Plan one longer nature outing this week, a trail, a canyon, a shoreline, and treat it as a genuine investment in your nervous system.
- On ordinary days, choose the route with trees over the route without them.

Presence matters more than pace. The benefit comes from attention, not distance covered.

What If You Live in a City?

You don't need wilderness to get meaningful benefit. Urban parks, tree-lined streets, community gardens, and time beneath mature trees all produce measurable effects in the research, smaller than a full forest immersion but real. Seek out the greenest space reasonably available to you and be intentional when you're there. Put the phone away. Look up.

If access to green space is genuinely limited, even tending houseplants or listening to natural soundscapes has shown modest but real effects on stress and mood. Start where you are and build toward more when you can.

Bottom Line

Step into green space regularly and let your mind soften, your stress drop, and your perspective quietly expand. Sometimes the clarity you've been trying to think your way toward is just waiting outside.

17. Laugh on Purpose

Your brain relaxes in laughter the way it never quite relaxes anywhere else.

What It Is

In our family we call ourselves the Schramm fam, and one of the things I'm most proud of is that we laugh a lot. Like, a lot a lot. We have fun together, we tease each other, we have inside jokes that have been running for years, and sometimes things go just a little too far, which somehow makes it even funnier. My wife and I have a genuinely witty dynamic that I treasure. Some of our best moments together have been laughing until it hurts over something completely ridiculous. I don't think that's a small thing. I think it's one of the reasons we're happy.

This hack is simple. Intentionally invite laughter into your day. Not forced positivity. Not fake enthusiasm. Just deliberate exposure to things that reliably crack you up. A short comedy clip. A funny podcast. A favorite ridiculous scene you've already watched a dozen times. A friend who makes you laugh without trying. A family inside joke that never gets old. We tend to wait for laughter to find us. But you can schedule it, and when you do, your nervous system responds just the same.

Why It Works

Laughter triggers immediate physiological changes. Cortisol drops, endorphins rise, and muscle tension releases. The physical relief is real, not just metaphorical. But the more interesting effect is cognitive. Humor reframes perspective in a way that deliberate positive thinking rarely can. When you laugh, your brain loosens its grip on threat-focused thinking. The problem doesn't disappear, but it loses its hold on your internal state. You get breathing room inside a difficult moment rather than being consumed by it.

Research shows that brief moments of levity during stress can prevent the kind of emotional constriction that, when sustained, contributes to anxiety and depression. Your brain cannot hold deep stress and genuine laughter at the same intensity simultaneously. One displaces the other, and even a temporary displacement breaks the cycle enough to matter.

Social laughter amplifies everything. Shared humor increases oxytocin, strengthens connection, and signals safety to a nervous system that is always quietly looking for it. But even solitary laughter, just you watching something hilarious alone on the couch, interrupts the stress cycle and resets your emotional tone.

Try This Today

- Watch a 5-to-10-minute comedy clip during a break instead of scrolling through news or social media.
- Text a friend who reliably makes you laugh, not to vent, just to connect.
- Keep a short mental list of go-to humor sources for your hardest days so you're not searching for funny when you're already depleted.
- Revisit a favorite scene or clip you already know cracks you up. Familiarity doesn't reduce the effect.

You don't need an hour. You need an interruption.

What If You Don't Feel Like Laughing?

That's actually the most important time to try. You're not overriding real emotion or pretending a hard season isn't hard. You're creating a small pocket of breathing room alongside it. Start with mild amusement if genuine laughter feels out of reach. Even a quiet smile begins shifting the physiology in the right direction. Laughter isn't denial. It isn't toxic positivity. It's regulation, and in genuinely difficult seasons, small consistent doses of levity can prevent emotional constriction from becoming your default state.

Bottom Line

Laughter lowers stress, shifts perspective, and creates breathing room in ways that willpower simply cannot replicate. Invite it on purpose. Schedule the ridiculous. A few minutes of genuine humor can soften the texture of an entire day.

18. Smooth Out Your Blood Sugar

What feels emotional is often metabolic.

What It Is

I'll be upfront: I'm not perfect at this one (but I'm getting better!). I have a weakness for sugary snacks, and there have been plenty of afternoons where I've crashed hard and wondered why everything suddenly felt challenging and more irritating than it should. Once I started connecting those crashes to what I'd eaten an hour or two earlier, things started making a lot more sense.

This hack isn't about eliminating carbs or obsessing over numbers. It's about reducing the large rapid swings in blood sugar that quietly wreak havoc on your mood, your patience, and your ability to think clearly. Most people don't realize that the irritability, brain fog, sudden fatigue, and vague sense of dread around 3pm aren't always emotional. They're often metabolic. And that means they're addressable.

Why It Works

When you eat refined carbohydrates or sugar without protein or fiber to slow things down, blood glucose rises quickly and then drops just as fast. That drop triggers a stress response. Cortisol and adrenaline rise to compensate, producing symptoms that can feel remarkably like anxiety: shakiness, irritability, difficulty concentrating, a sudden sense that everything is harder than it should be.

The mood connection is direct. Stable blood sugar supports stable neurotransmitter function. Repeated spikes and crashes create emotional volatility that people frequently attribute to stress or personality, when part of the instability is simply physiological and entirely fixable. Pairing carbs with protein and fiber slows digestion and smooths the glucose curve. Eating at regular intervals prevents the dramatic swings that come from arriving at a meal severely depleted. Neither requires dietary restriction, just a few simple habits applied consistently. The brain prefers consistency. So does your mood.

Try This Today

- Pair carbs with protein at every meal when possible: fruit with yogurt, toast with eggs, oatmeal with nuts or a scoop of protein powder.
- Avoid eating sugary snacks alone. Add something with protein or fat to slow the absorption curve.
- Eat at regular intervals rather than waiting until you're running on empty and grabbing whatever's closest.
- Pay attention to how you feel one to two hours after certain meals. The mood and food connection becomes obvious quickly once you start looking for it.

You don't need to eliminate foods you enjoy. You need to reduce volatility.

What If You Love Carbs?

Most people do, and carbs aren't the problem. The research doesn't support cutting them out, and rigid restriction tends to backfire in both mood and behavior over time. The goal is pairing and pacing, not removal. Add protein. Add fiber. Spread intake more evenly through the day. Keep the foods you love and simply change what surrounds them. Flexibility sustains. Restriction exhausts.

Bottom Line

Mood swings aren't always psychological. Sometimes they're biochemical, and blood sugar is one of the most overlooked drivers of daily emotional volatility. Smooth out the spikes and emotional steadiness becomes significantly more accessible. Feed your brain the right consistent combos and it tends to return the favor.

19. Spend Time Barefoot or Grounded Outdoors

Sometimes the simplest practices are the ones worth revisiting.

What It Is

Some of my favorite memories involve bare feet. Running through the grass playing spike ball with the family in the backyard. Walking along the shore at Bear Lake with the cold sand between my toes. There's something about direct contact with the ground that feels genuinely different from being in shoes, and it turns out there might be more to that feeling than nostalgia.

This hack is about occasionally spending time barefoot on natural ground, grass, soil, sand, rather than always maintaining a barrier between your feet and the earth. Not as a cure-all. Not as a mystical practice. Just intentional sensory contact. It's also worth noting this is different from the nature immersion entry earlier in this chapter. That one was about what your eyes, ears, and nervous system absorb from green environments. This one is more specific. It's about direct physical contact through your feet and what that connection might do for your stress physiology and present-moment awareness.

The research here is still emerging, and honesty requires saying that upfront. But the practice itself is free, low-risk, and worth trying.

Why It Works

Your feet contain some of the highest concentrations of nerve endings in the body. Walking barefoot on natural surfaces sends a continuous stream of sensory input to your brain that cushioned footwear significantly reduces. That stimulation increases present-moment awareness and pulls attention out of rumination in a way that is immediate and surprisingly hard to replicate indoors.

There is also a more debated mechanism called grounding or earthing, the theory that direct contact with the earth allows for small electrical exchanges that may reduce inflammation and influence stress physiology. Some studies show promising effects on cortisol and sleep. The evidence isn't definitive yet and healthy skepticism is warranted. But the proposed mechanism is plausible, the research is active, and the downside risk is essentially zero. What is well supported regardless of the electrical theory is the psychological shift. Being barefoot outdoors produces a different quality of attention, slower, more sensory, more present. That shift is real even if the full mechanism isn't yet mapped.

Try This Today

- Stand barefoot on grass for 5 to 10 minutes, ideally combined with your morning sunlight to stack two practices into one window.

- Walk slowly on sand or soil and pay deliberate attention to the sensations rather than letting the experience pass automatically.
- Remove your shoes while sitting outside even if walking barefoot feels impractical.
- Notice whether the quality of your attention shifts when your feet are in direct contact with the ground.

Simple exposure is enough. This isn't a performance.

What If You're Skeptical?

Good. You don't need to accept the electrical theory to experiment with sensory contact. The slowing-down effect and increased present-moment awareness are valuable on their own terms, regardless of what the grounding research ultimately concludes. Approach it as a low-stakes experiment. Try it a few times and simply notice what you notice. The science is still developing. The practice is simple. Those two things can coexist.

Bottom Line

Nature regulates, and direct contact may deepen that effect. Barefoot time is free, low-risk, and worth experimenting with even while the science continues to unfold. Some of the best things in life are also the simplest.

20. Move Your Body Before Checking Your Phone

How you start shapes how you feel, and what you hand your attention to first matters more than most people realize.

What It Is

My wife is genuinely better at this than I am. She wakes up and moves first, almost automatically. I still have to fight the pull of the phone some mornings. But on the days I win that small battle, the difference in how I feel is noticeable enough that I keep trying.

Before you reach for your phone in the morning, move your body first. Not for long. Not dramatically. Just enough to orient yourself before the external world rushes in. Stand up. Stretch. Step outside. Walk to the kitchen. Do a few squats. Let your body come online before your attention goes outward.

This isn't a repeat of the earlier entry on morning movement. That one was about what physical activity does for your brain chemistry and mood. This one is about something different: sequence and agency. What happens to your nervous system when the very first thing you do each day is hand your attention to a device. The movement here is almost incidental. It's a placeholder for something more important.

Why It Works

When you wake up and immediately check your phone, you invite external demands into your brain before your internal state has had any chance to settle. Notifications, headlines, emails, social media, each one triggers a small stress response before you've even fully registered where you are or how you feel. Research on attentional capture shows that these early inputs set a reactive tone that can persist for hours.

Moving first, even briefly, changes that. It gives your brain a moment to orient before the outside world rushes in, and it establishes the first action of the day as something you chose rather than something that happened to you. That distinction matters more than it sounds. Starting from agency feels different than starting from reaction, and that difference tends to carry forward into the rest of the day.

Try This Today

- Move for just 5 minutes before unlocking your phone: stretch, walk to the window, step outside, drink some water.
- Keep your phone across the room overnight so you have to stand before you can reach it, and once you're upright, stay upright for a few minutes first.
- Create one simple rule for yourself: body first, screen second. Put a sticky note on your nightstand if that helps.
- If you have to check your phone early for work, build in even two minutes of movement first. The principle still holds at smaller scales.

You don't need perfection. You need a new sequence.

What If You Use Your Phone as an Alarm?

Most people do, and it's a genuine obstacle because the phone is already in your hand the moment you wake up. Placing it across the room solves this directly. A cheap standalone alarm clock removes the obstacle entirely and costs less than a few cups of coffee. Either option gives you back the first moments of your day before your device reclaims them.

Bottom Line

Move before you scroll. Orient before you react. The phone will still be there in five minutes. Your morning mindset is harder to recover once it's gone.

3.

WHAT YOU FOCUS ON GROWS

Consider this: your brain receives an estimated 11 million bits of information every second from your senses. But you can only consciously process somewhere between 10 and 50 of them. Out of eleven million. That means attention, what you focus on and what you allow yourself to focus on, is one of the most consequential choices you make all day. And most of us are making it on autopilot, surrendering it to whoever or whatever is loudest, most urgent, or most algorithmically designed to capture it.

I remember hearing commercials years ago that said children spell love T-I-M-E. And while that was partly true, I've come to believe something has shifted. The golden gift is no longer just time. It's attention. You can be in the same room as someone for hours and never really give them your attention. But you can't give someone your genuine attention without it meaning something. Time is the container. Attention is what fills it. And when attention is absent, something quietly breaks down in our most important relationships. Lack of attention leads to loss of connection. Read that again.

I notice this in myself constantly. I can walk into the same room and depending on where my attention lands, feel grateful or frustrated, energized or depleted. Same room. Same life. Different focus. It's a little unsettling once you start paying attention to it, but it's also genuinely hopeful, because it means the lens is adjustable.

The brain's default setting leans toward negativity. Scanning for threats and problems requires less effort than noticing what's good. Left unchecked, that default pulls attention toward worry about the future and rumination about the past, leaving very little bandwidth for the present moment, where most of the good things in life are actually happening. And social media has turbocharged this tendency in a particularly insidious way. Psychologist Leon Festinger's research on social comparison, the deeply human tendency to evaluate ourselves by measuring against others, has been around since the 1950s. What's new is the scale. We now have access to a curated, algorithmically optimized feed of everyone's highlight reels, and our brains, already wired toward comparison, can spend hours scrolling through evidence that other people's lives are more exciting, more beautiful, more successful, and more together than ours. The research on upward social comparison is consistent and sobering: the more we measure ourselves against people who appear to have more, look better, or achieve more, the worse we feel about ourselves and our lives, regardless of how objectively good those lives actually are. Teddy Roosevelt called comparison the thief of joy. He didn't know about Instagram. The theft has only gotten more efficient.

This matters for attention because comparison is fundamentally an attention problem. It isn't happening to you. You are directing your attention toward it, often without realizing it, and your emotional state is following obediently. The good news is that what attention can move toward, attention can also move away from. That's what this chapter is about.

And here's something worth recognizing alongside all of this: the things we covered in Chapter 2, sleep, movement, nutrition, and physical health, all of them directly influence the emotional brain. A sleep-deprived, sedentary, under-nourished nervous system is a nervous system that is far more emotionally reactive and far less emotionally flexible. The body and the emotional life are not separate systems. They are deeply, constantly, bidirectionally connected.

Which brings us to the deeper truth underneath this entire chapter: we are emotional beings. Not occasionally, not inconveniently, but fundamentally. Child psychologist Haim Ginott once wrote that emotions are part of our genetic heritage. Fish swim, birds fly, and people feel. We don't get to choose which emotions arise in us. Anger, fear, sadness, joy, anxiety, excitement, they're all part of being fully human. But what we can develop over time is the ability to feel our emotions without feeding them. To recognize what we're experiencing clearly and choose how we respond to it. That gap between feeling and responding is small, but it's everything.

One simple framework I find useful: notice where your emotions are anchored in time. Emotions like anger, guilt, and regret are felt in the present but anchored in the past, centered on something that already happened. Emotions like worry, stress, and anxiety are also felt in the present but anchored in the future, responses to things that haven't happened yet and may never happen. Emotions like joy, peace, and love tend to live in the present moment itself. None of these are wrong. But it's worth asking how much time you're spending on each, and whether you're not just feeling those emotions but feeding them. As my wise sister JoLynn likes to say, *it's okay to glance in the rearview mirror of life but choose not to stare*. I've thought about that line more times than I can count.

The sixteen happy hacks in this chapter are about developing real, science-backed skills: naming what you feel, working with difficult thoughts rather than fighting them, managing worry and rumination, building self-compassion, reframing setbacks, and training your attention toward what's actually present rather than what your nervous system fears might be coming. These practices are drawn from cognitive behavioral therapy, acceptance and commitment therapy, mindfulness research, and positive psychology. They work not by eliminating difficult emotions, but by giving you more choice in how you respond to them.

You can't control every emotion that arises. But you have far more influence over where your attention lands and what you do next than most people realize. That influence is worth developing. And it starts right now, with what you choose to attend to.

21. Name the Emotion You're Feeling

Unlabeled emotion feels overwhelming. Named emotion becomes workable.

What It Is

I used to struggle with this. Someone would ask how I was feeling and I'd say "fine" or "stressed" and leave it there. It took me awhile to realize that wasn't actually naming an emotion. It was avoiding one. When you feel emotionally stirred, pause and name what's happening. Not analyze it. Not judge it. Not fix it immediately. Just label it. I'm frustrated. I'm anxious. I'm disappointed. I'm embarrassed. I'm overwhelmed. Be specific if you can. "Stressed" is a reasonable start, but "resentful," "discouraged," or "uneasy" is more useful. The more precisely you can name what you're feeling, the more effectively your brain can begin working with it. This isn't about dwelling on emotions longer than necessary. It's about identifying them, and that small act of naming changes what happens next in ways that are both measurable and immediate.

Why It Works

When emotions go unnamed they tend to feel bigger, more chaotic, and harder to manage. Research on what neuroscientists call "affect labeling," simply putting feelings into words, shows that naming an emotion reduces activity in the amygdala, the brain's threat detection center, while increasing activity in the prefrontal regions responsible for reasoning and regulation. In plain terms, naming an emotion shifts you from reaction toward reflection. It creates a small but meaningful pause between what you feel and what you do next, and in that pause, choice becomes possible.

Precision matters more than most people realize. The label you choose shapes the response that follows. "Angry" may lead to defensiveness. "Hurt" may open a conversation. "Overwhelmed" may point toward rest. When you misidentify an emotion or leave it unnamed entirely, you're essentially navigating without a map, responding to intensity rather than information.

Emotions are more than feelings. The word "emotion" comes from Latin, meaning "to move out" or "to move outward." Emotions are internal experiences that are meant to move us into action. Emotions exist for good reasons and carry real information about what you need. Naming them makes that information usable rather than consuming.

Try This Today

- Pause and complete the sentence quietly: right now I'm feeling ________.
- Write the emotion down in this book, a journal or notes app. Even one word helps.
- Reach beyond basic categories. If "bad" is all you have, ask whether it's closer to sad, angry, scared, ashamed, or disappointed.
- If you genuinely can't identify it, try "I'm noticing

something heavy" or "something feels tight." That's still naming, and it's still useful.

Clarity reduces chaos. Start there.

What If You're Not Sure What You're Feeling?

That's more common than most people admit, and it's worth treating with patience rather than frustration. Many people were never taught an emotional vocabulary beyond the basics. Start simple and refine over time. Emotional literacy is a genuine skill and like any skill it develops through deliberate practice. Some people find it helpful to keep a short feelings list nearby, not as a crutch, but as a reminder that the emotional landscape is richer and more specific than "fine" or "not fine."

Bottom Line

Put words to what you're feeling and your brain begins to do the rest. You don't need to get it exactly right. You just need to get closer. Naming emotions doesn't make them bigger. It makes them manageable.

22. Stop Arguing With Your Thoughts (Practice Defusion)

Notice your thoughts without believing everything they say.

What It Is

My mind can be a pretty loud place. On a bad day it runs a nearly constant commentary: you're behind, that went poorly, what if this doesn't work out, you should have handled that differently. For a long time I thought the solution was to argue back. Counter the negative thought with a positive one. Debate my own brain into submission. It's exhausting, and it mostly doesn't work.

The alternative is something called cognitive defusion, a core skill from Acceptance and Commitment Therapy, one of the most well-researched psychological frameworks of the past three decades. Instead of fighting difficult thoughts, you simply step back from them. When your mind says *I'm failing*, try shifting to: *I'm having the thought that I'm failing*. That small move creates real psychological distance. You're no longer inside the thought looking out. You're observing it from the outside. Your thoughts are real, but they aren't always true. And you aren't obligated to treat them as the same thing.

Why It Works

Your brain produces thoughts continuously—predictions, interpretations, warnings, judgments. Many are helpful. Some are distorted, exaggerated, or simply old patterns with no current relevance. The problem isn't having difficult thoughts. The problem is believing them automatically. When you think this is going to be a disaster, your body tightens as if disaster is already underway. Your stress response doesn't distinguish between a real threat and a convincing thought about one. It simply responds to what you've accepted as true.

Defusion interrupts that process. Adding the phrase "I'm having the thought that…" shifts you from the reactive part of your brain to the observational part. Research supports this. That small linguistic shift reduces emotional reactivity and recruits the prefrontal regions responsible for perspective and judgment.

The goal isn't to delete the thought or argue it into submission. It's simply to change your relationship to it. And that shift is often enough to loosen the thought's grip considerably. Here's the thing—fighting a difficult thought tends to strengthen it. Observing it with distance tends to shrink it. The thought may still be there. It just no longer runs the room.

Try This Today

When a sticky or distressing thought appears, try one of these:

- Add the phrase *I'm having the thought that...* before it and notice what shifts.
- Imagine placing the thought on a passing cloud and watching it drift by without chasing it.
- Write the thought down and label it "story" rather than "fact"—not to dismiss it, but to hold it more lightly.
- Say the thought out loud in a slightly silly voice. It sounds strange, but it works—humor is one of the fastest ways to reduce a thought's authority.

Distance creates choice. And choice is what defusion is ultimately about.

What If the Thought Feels Completely True?

It might be. Defusion isn't about pretending your thoughts are false—some of them are accurate, and dismissing real problems isn't the goal. The point is to create enough psychological space to evaluate the thought calmly rather than react to it automatically. From a position of distance, you can ask: *Is this thought helpful right now? Is it the complete picture? Is there another interpretation worth considering?* You're far better positioned to answer those questions as an observer than as someone fused with the thought itself.

You don't need to silence your mind. You just need to stop letting every thought it produces be treated as a directive.

Bottom Line

You are not your thoughts. You are the one observing them. Step back, even slightly, and you regain the space to choose how you respond. That space is where emotional freedom lives.

23. Practice Self-Compassion Instead of Self-Criticism

Harshness doesn't build resilience. Kindness does.

What It Is

I'll be straight with you: this one took me a long time to take seriously. Self-compassion sounded soft to me. Like an excuse. Like something you'd see on a motivational poster that doesn't actually help anyone do anything. It took reading the research and trying it myself to understand that I had it exactly backwards.

When you mess up, fall short, or feel inadequate, respond to yourself with kindness instead of attack. Not excuses. Not lowered standards. Not avoidance of accountability. Kindness. Think about how you'd respond if a close friend came to you after making a serious mistake. You almost certainly wouldn't say what's wrong with you or you should be ashamed of yourself. You'd acknowledge how hard it is, validate what they're feeling, and help them find a way forward. The invitation here is simple: offer yourself that same basic decency.

Research consistently shows that responding to failure with kindness rather than harsh judgment builds more resilience, more motivation, and faster recovery. It just requires unlearning the myth that beating yourself up is what drives growth. It doesn't. It just hurts.

Why It Works

When you attack yourself harshly after a mistake, your nervous system responds as though you're under genuine threat. Cortisol rises, thinking narrows, and defensiveness increases. You may force short-term compliance through self-punishment, but the psychological cost is high and the growth tends to be shallow.

Self-compassion works through a different pathway. Rather than activating the threat system, it activates the same neurological circuitry involved in caring for others. Emotional regulation improves, and from that calmer internal state you can actually see your mistakes clearly, understand what went wrong, and make meaningful adjustments without collapsing into shame first. Dr. Kristin Neff's research identifies three simple components: a gentle internal tone, the recognition that struggle is a universal human experience rather than evidence something is uniquely wrong with you, and an honest acknowledgment of difficulty without exaggerating or suppressing it. Self-compassion doesn't say *it doesn't matter*. It says *this is hard, I'm human, and I can respond wisely*.

Try This Today

- Ask yourself: "What would I say to someone I care about in this exact situation?" Then say that to yourself.
- Remind yourself that struggling doesn't make you broken. It makes you human.
- Replace "What's wrong with me?" with "What happened and what can I learn from it?"
- Notice your internal tone. You don't have to be harsh to be honest.

Gentleness isn't the opposite of accountability. It's what makes real accountability sustainable.

What If You're Afraid You'll Lose Your Edge?

The research doesn't support that fear. Self-compassion is consistently associated with greater persistence after failure, not less, precisely because it reduces the paralysis that shame produces. Shame makes you want to hide. Self-compassion makes it safe to look clearly at what went wrong and try again. High standards and a kind internal tone are not opposites. That combination tends to be more sustainable and more effective than the harsh alternative most people were taught to rely on.

Bottom Line

You don't have to be cruel to yourself to grow. You just have to be honest and human. Those two things are more than enough.

24. Talk to Yourself Like a Coach, Not a Judge

Judges define you by your worst moments. Coaches move you past them.

What It Is

The previous hack was about responding to struggle with kindness, the emotional support layer. This one is different. This one is about performance language, how you actually guide yourself through difficulty, pressure, and mistakes in real time.

A judge declares verdicts. A coach gives direction. A judge says: *you blew it, you always do this.* A coach says: reset, *here's the next move.* Self-compassion says *I'm human and this is hard.* The coach voice says *okay, what do I do now?* Both matter. They just do different jobs, and most people have plenty of the judge and not nearly enough of the coach.

I notice this most under pressure. When something goes sideways, my first instinct can be to run a quick verdict on myself before I've even figured out what actually happened. The coach reframe has been genuinely useful for me, not as a way to avoid accountability but as a way to stay functional when it counts.

Why It Works

The brain responds powerfully to the language you use internally, not just emotionally but functionally. When your inner voice issues harsh absolute verdicts, I'm terrible at this, I always mess things up, I can't handle pressure, it reinforces what psychologists call fixed identity statements. These are global judgments about who you are rather than specific observations about what just happened. They reduce cognitive flexibility, undermine motivation, and activate the same threat response as direct criticism.

Coaching language operates differently. It's specific, behavioral, and forward-focused. Instead of rendering a verdict about your character, it narrows attention to the next controllable action. That shift, from global judgment to specific next step, moves your brain from reactive emotional processing into the executive functioning systems responsible for planning and regulated action. Research on self-talk in performance psychology consistently shows that instructional and motivational self-talk improves focus, emotional regulation, and endurance under pressure. Elite athletes, surgeons, and high-stakes performers across disciplines use short directive phrases as precision tools, not motivational fluff, to redirect attention when pressure peaks.

A good coach sees the mistake clearly, names what needs to change, and redirects toward the next move. That's the model worth internalizing.

Try This Today

- Replace "I'm terrible at this" with "okay, what's the next right step?"
- Use short specific cue phrases: steady, reset, one thing at a time, stay in it.
- After a mistake, ask *what would a good coach say to me right now*, then say that.
- Instead of replaying the error, write one clear behavioral adjustment and focus there.

Direction builds momentum. Momentum rebuilds confidence.

What If You've Always Motivated Yourself Through Harshness?

Many people have, and for some it worked well enough long enough that it became the default. But there's an important distinction between short-term compliance and sustainable performance. Harsh self-talk can produce results under low-stakes conditions, but under sustained pressure it tends to produce shame, avoidance, and burnout rather than growth. Coaches who motivate exclusively through criticism lose their athletes over time. The same is true internally. Firm and kind can coexist. You can hold yourself to a genuinely high standard while speaking to yourself in a way that keeps you functional, focused, and in the game.

Bottom Line

Be firm. Be clear. Be specific. But speak to yourself in a language that points forward, because that's the only direction growth actually lives.

25. Schedule Worry Time

Worry expands to fill every available minute, unless you give it a container.

What It Is

Here's the truth: I worry less than I used to. Part of that is age, part of it is perspective, and part of it is genuinely learning to be more intentional about what deserves my mental energy. I once saw a presenter draw two large overlapping circles on a whiteboard. One was labeled "Things That Matter." The other was "Things I Can Control." The small overlapping space in the middle was where he said he tries to invest his worry. That image has stuck with me ever since, because most of what we spend mental energy on falls outside that overlap entirely.

This hack builds on that idea practically. Instead of worrying all day, choose a specific time to worry on purpose. Pick a 10-to-15-minute window in the afternoon or early evening and designate it as your worry time. During that window, think through your concerns, uncertainties, and unresolved problems.

Give them your full attention. Outside that window, when worries surface, gently redirect: not now, I'll think about this at 4:30 this afternoon. Then you actually do. This isn't denial. It's containment, and containment is one of the most underrated skills in emotional regulation.

Why It Works

Worry thrives on immediacy. The brain treats anxious thoughts as urgent even when they aren't actionable and even when thinking about them right now won't change anything. When you respond to every worry the moment it surfaces, you're training your nervous system to stay in a state of constant low-grade threat, always on, always scanning, always treating the next anxious thought as a summons that can't be ignored.

Research in cognitive behavioral therapy consistently shows that postponing worry, deliberately delaying engagement rather than immediately responding, reduces both the frequency and intensity of anxious thoughts over time. When you repeatedly demonstrate to your brain that anxious thoughts don't require immediate action, you gradually weaken the association between anxiety and urgency. The thought arrives. You acknowledge it. You redirect. Slowly, it loses its grip.

There's a second effect that surprises most people: when worry time finally arrives, many concerns that felt urgent hours earlier no longer feel as pressing. Some have dissolved entirely. What felt like an emergency at 10am often looks like a solvable problem at 4:30pm.

Try This Today

- Choose a consistent daily 10-to-15-minute worry window, the same time each day works best, and earlier evening rather than right before bed.
- When anxiety surfaces outside that window, write the

worry down briefly and tell yourself you'll give it full attention at the designated time. Then redirect.

- When worry time arrives, actually engage. Don't avoid it. This builds trust in the system.
- When the window closes, close the notebook and deliberately move on.

The writing step matters. Externalizing the worry onto paper or into your phone signals to your brain that the thought has been captured and doesn't need to be actively held onto.

What If Something Is Truly Urgent?

If a worry genuinely requires immediate action, respond to it. This practice isn't about ignoring real problems. But most worry is repetitive mental rehearsal, the same concerns cycling through in slightly different forms, rather than urgent problem-solving. Part of what this practice builds is the ability to distinguish between those two things. Real responsibility versus habitual rumination. That distinction alone is worth developing.

Bottom Line

Worry expands to fill every available minute unless you give it a container. Schedule it. Contain it. Reclaim the rest of your day.

26. Ask: "Is This a Problem to Solve or an Emotion to Feel?"

Applying the wrong response to either wastes energy you don't have.

What It Is

I catch myself doing this wrong more than I'd like to admit. Something hard happens and I immediately go into fix-it mode, trying to think my way through a feeling that isn't asking to be solved. Or I sit with a solvable problem and call it processing when what I really need to do is just make a decision and move on.

One question cuts through the confusion: is this a problem to solve, or an emotion to feel? Sometimes the honest answer is both. But more often than we realize, we confuse the two, and that confusion is where a surprising amount of wasted effort and unnecessary suffering comes from. We analyze grief like it's a logistics problem. We sit inside solvable situations and wonder why we still feel stuck.

Why It Works

Problems respond to action: generating options, making a plan, taking a next step. Emotions respond to something entirely different. Research on emotional processing shows that allowing feelings to move through naturally, without suppression or over-analysis, leads to faster recovery than trying to think your way through them. Emotions aren't problems to solve. They're experiences to move through, and the system already knows how if you get out of the way.

The reverse is equally true. Sitting with helplessness when a solvable problem is right in front of you creates unnecessary suffering of its own. Trying to fix sadness prolongs it. Treating loneliness like a scheduling problem misses what it's actually asking for. One simple question redirects all of that energy toward the right response.

Try This Today

- Pause and ask directly: *is this a problem to solve or an emotion to feel?*
- If it's a problem, write one specific next step and take it.
- If it's an emotion, pause, breathe, and observe the physical sensation with curiosity rather than alarm. Let the wave move through without feeding it with more thought.
- If it's both, separate them deliberately: *first I'll feel this, then I'll decide what to do.*

What If You're Not Sure Which It Is?

Default to emotion first. Most immediate distress is emotional before it's logistical, and clear thinking rarely happens inside the first wave of a difficult feeling. It happens after the feeling has been acknowledged and allowed to move through. Feel it first. Then assess. You'll almost always think more clearly on the other side.

Bottom Line

Some things need strategy. Some things need space. Ask the question and let the answer point you toward the right response.

27. Write It Down—The Case for Expressive Writing

Unwritten thoughts circle. Written thoughts settle.

What It Is

Another Dr. Dave confession: I'm not as consistent with this one as I'd like to be. I know the research. I've seen it work. And still there are weeks where something is weighing on me and I just keep carrying it around in my head instead of doing the one thing that would actually help. When something feels tangled, heavy, or unresolved, write about it. Not polished writing. Not for anyone else to read. Just honest, unfiltered words on paper or screen. Set aside 10-to-20 minutes to write freely about something emotionally significant. What happened. How you felt. What it meant. What still lingers. No grammar rules. No structure. No audience. Just clarity through language.

Why It Works

Psychologist James Pennebaker spent decades studying what happens when people write honestly about difficult experiences. His research consistently shows that expressive writing improves mood, reduces anxiety, strengthens immune functioning, and produces measurable improvements in long-term psychological and physical health across cultures and age groups.

The mechanism is organizational. Unprocessed experiences tend to live in the mind as fragments, looping thoughts and unfinished narratives the brain keeps returning to because they haven't been resolved into meaning. That fragmented state quietly consumes cognitive resources, like browser tabs running in the background draining processing power. Writing forces the brain to impose sequence and language on raw experience. That act of structuring recruits higher-order brain regions involved in regulation and integration, moving the experience from emotional loops to something more organized and metabolized. You're helping your brain finish what it's been carrying, and finishing is what it's been waiting for.

Try This Today

- Set a timer for 10-to-15 minutes and write continuously about something weighing on you. Don't stop, don't edit, don't judge what comes out.
- Write not just about what happened but how it affected you and what emotions it stirred. The emotional layer is where the benefit lives.
- If it feels overwhelming, start with five minutes. Even brief expressive writing produces measurable effects.
- When you finish, close the notebook deliberately as a small signal to your brain that the session is complete.

What If You're Not a Writer?

Completely irrelevant to this practice. Expressive writing has nothing to do with literary skill or sentence quality. Bullet points count. Fragments count. Pennebaker's research showed benefits across every skill level. What mattered was emotional honesty, not craft. If something feels too raw to approach directly, start at the edges. Write about what you learned, or what you'd tell a friend going through the same thing. Any structure is more useful than silent rumination.

Bottom Line

Unwritten thoughts circle. Written thoughts settle. Put it on paper and give your brain the chance to finish what it's been carrying.

28. Replace "Why Me?" With "What Now?"

You may not choose your circumstances, but you almost always get to choose your next move.

What It Is

In March of 2021 my mom was told she had liver cancer. I remember the Zoom call with my five siblings clearly. We all cried. It was one of those moments where the world just stops for a minute. And in the middle of that grief, what struck me most was my mom's reaction. She is one of the most positive people on the planet, and almost immediately she started asking not why this was happening, but what she was going to do next. That question, "what now?", has stayed with me ever since.

When something hard happens, notice the first question your mind reaches for. Most of the time it's some version of why me? Why did this happen? Why is this so unfair? These questions feel natural because they are. But there's a different question available, and it leads somewhere more useful. What now? Not as a way to bypass the pain. Not as forced positivity. Just as a deliberate redirect from explanation toward agency, from the past toward what's actually within reach.

Why It Works

"Why me?" is a natural response to pain. The mind searches for explanation because understanding causes can make us feel less helpless. The problem is that many difficult experiences, loss, illness, unfairness, don't have satisfying answers. And even when answers exist, they rarely change anything. Repeatedly asking why tends to activate rumination, keeping the brain locked on the problem rather than moving toward what's possible. It feels like processing but often just keeps you stuck.

"What now?" creates a fundamentally different shift. It moves attention toward planning, agency, and the next step forward. Research on resilience shows this pattern consistently. People who redirect attention toward small controllable next steps tend to recover from setbacks more effectively, not because they feel less pain, but because they direct their energy toward what they can still influence. You may not control what happened. But you almost always have some influence over what happens next.

Try This Today

- Notice the "why me?" narrative without judging yourself for having it. It's human and it makes sense.
- Pause and ask quietly: *okay, what now?*
- Identify one small next action, even if that action is rest, reaching out to someone, or simply deciding to revisit the situation tomorrow.
- If nothing can be done immediately, ask *what is within my control today, and start there.*

The action doesn't need to be significant. It just needs to point forward.

What If the Situation Truly Is Unfair?

It might be, and this practice doesn't ask you to pretend otherwise. Some circumstances are genuinely painful and outside your control. Grief deserves real space. Anger can be entirely appropriate. This entry isn't asking you to skip the emotional layer. It's about what becomes available after you've moved through it. Even within genuine unfairness, even within legitimate grief, the question eventually becomes: what now?

Not because the pain wasn't real, but because forward is the only direction life actually moves.

Bottom Line

"Why me?" keeps you anchored to what can't be changed. "What now?" returns you to what can. That question, asked repeatedly in hard moments, is what resilience is actually built from.

29. Reframe Setbacks as Data, Not Failure

Failure interpreted as identity shuts down growth. Failure interpreted as data fuels it.

What It Is

When our daughter told my wife and me she was getting an annulment, we were heartbroken for her. It was rough, not going to lie. We hurt because she was hurting. But over time, through all the hard stuff, she became a stronger, wiser person. She remarried, and she is on such a better path now. Looking back, what felt like a devastating setback turned out to be some of the most important data of her life.

When something doesn't go the way you hoped, a mistake, a missed goal, a hard conversation, a plan that falls apart, pause before you interpret it. Not as failure. As data. Data is information. Failure is identity. One opens a door. The other closes one. This doesn't mean pretending disappointment doesn't hurt or rushing past emotion that deserves space. It means separating what happened from who you are. Instead of "I failed", try "that approach didn't work this time." Subtle shift. Genuinely powerful difference.

Why It Works

The brain is highly sensitive to threats to identity. When a setback is interpreted as proof that something is wrong with you, it triggers a threat response similar to physical danger. Shame rises, avoidance increases, and thinking narrows. Instead of asking *what can I learn from this?* The mind starts asking *how do I escape this feeling?* That shift makes growth much harder.

When a setback is reframed as information, something different happens. It becomes feedback about strategy, timing, or circumstances. Curiosity replaces defensiveness. Problem solving replaces rumination. Carol Dweck's research on mindset shows this pattern clearly. People who view setbacks as part of the learning process persist longer, recover faster, and improve over time. They still feel disappointment, but they treat outcomes as information rather than verdicts on their worth. Athletes review game footage. Entrepreneurs study failed launches. Scientists analyze unexpected results. In each case the same principle applies: the outcome is data, not identity.

Try This Today

- Say quietly: *interesting, what does this teach me?*
- Ask: *what part of this is within my control to adjust next time?*
- Write down one specific behavioral adjustment rather than replaying the mistake. Forward focus, not forensic analysis.
- Replace "I'm bad at this" with "that particular approach didn't work" and notice how differently those two statements feel.

Information is useful. Identity attacks are not.

What If It Feels Personal?

Sometimes it genuinely is, and that deserves acknowledgment rather than bypass. Rejection hurts. Embarrassment stings. Loss is real. This entry isn't asking you to skip the emotional layer. Feel the disappointment first. Then, when the intensity has settled enough, extract the data. You can grieve a setback and learn from it at the same time. Those two responses aren't in competition. They work best when they happen in order.

Bottom Line

Treat setbacks as information and you stay curious and motivated. The outcome doesn't define you. What you do next does.

30. Practice One Minute of Mindfulness

Train your attention and your entire emotional life becomes steadier.

What It Is

I'm not someone who meditates for thirty minutes on a cushion. That's just not me. But I've learned to find small pockets of stillness that actually work for me. Sometimes I turn off the music on my drive to work and just drive. Other times I turn my chair away from my keyboard, close my eyes, and take a few slow breaths. That's it. And it genuinely helps.

Set a timer for one minute. Sit still. Pay attention to your breath. Not controlling it. Not optimizing it. Just noticing it. The air moving in. The air moving out. The subtle rise and fall of your chest. When your mind wanders, and it will, probably within the first ten seconds, gently bring it back without judgment. One minute. That's the whole practice. It sounds almost insultingly simple, but the research behind what happens in that single minute is anything but.

Why It Works

Attention is a skill, and like any skill it can be trained. Most people never intentionally train it. Research by Daniel Gilbert found that people spend nearly half their waking hours thinking about something other than what they're actually doing, and when the mind wanders, people consistently report lower happiness. That constant mental drift has a real cost in anxiety, emotional reactivity, and reduced satisfaction.

Mindfulness strengthens attention by giving the mind something steady to return to. Each time you notice your attention drifting and bring it back, you're practicing focus and self-regulation. Neuroscience shows this practice activates brain regions responsible for attention and emotional control while gradually calming the threat detection system. Even brief, consistent practice reduces stress and improves emotional regulation over time. Perhaps most importantly, it interrupts autopilot. Instead of thoughts and emotions automatically triggering reactions, you learn to notice them first. That small pause creates space for a more thoughtful response.

Try This Today

- Set a 60-second timer and focus only on your breathing. Nothing else has permission to exist for that minute.
- Count your exhales from one to ten, then start over. When you lose count, simply begin again without frustration.
- Practice between meetings, before a stressful conversation, or at any natural transition point in your day.
- Daily consistency at one minute outperforms occasional sessions at ten. Start small and stay consistent.

What If You Can't Clear Your Mind?

You're not supposed to. That's not the practice. Mindfulness isn't the absence of thoughts. It's awareness of thoughts without being automatically pulled by them. Every time your mind wanders and you return to your breath, you've completed one repetition of the actual exercise. Think of it like a bicep curl for your attention. The moment of return is the curl. Wandering is simply the weight going down before you lift it again.

Bottom Line

Your breath is always available, in every room, every moment, every difficult situation. One minute of deliberate attention can interrupt a mental spiral and reset your emotional state. Start there.

31. Reduce Rumination by Changing Your Environment

Sometimes the fastest way out of your head is through your feet.

What It Is

Someone once described rumination to me like rocking in a rocking chair. It takes real effort, it feels like you're moving, and you end up exactly where you started. That image stuck with me because it's all to accurate. We remember what we rehearse and what we review, which means the more we replay something, the more grooved in it becomes in our noggin. Rumination isn't processing. It's looping. And the loop rarely leads anywhere useful.

When your thoughts start cycling, replaying a conversation, rehearsing what you should have said, predicting worst-case outcomes that probably won't happen, change your physical environment. Stand up. Leave the room. Go outside. Not to escape responsibility or avoid what needs to be addressed. Just to interrupt the loop. Rumination thrives in stillness and sameness, and a change of setting can disrupt it faster and more reliably than mental effort alone. You don't have to outthink the spiral. You can step out of it physically.

Why It Works

The brain forms strong associations between places and mental states. If you often worry at your desk, that location gradually becomes linked with rumination. If you replay stressful conversations in bed, your bedroom slowly becomes associated with tension rather than rest. Research in behavioral psychology shows that environments actively cue patterns of thinking and feeling, which means the space you're in isn't neutral. It's either reinforcing the loop or helping break it.

Changing your environment introduces new sensory input, different light, sound, temperature, and movement, which draws attention outward and gives the brain something new to process. That shift alone can weaken the mental loop. Movement amplifies the effect. Research on behavioral activation consistently shows that simple physical movement is one of the most reliable ways to interrupt negative thought spirals. It may not solve the problem, but it changes the mental state that keeps the spiral going.

Try This Today

- Stand up immediately and move to a different room. Don't negotiate with yourself about whether it will help.
- Step outside for five minutes. Natural light and fresh air accelerate the shift more than staying indoors.
- Walk around the block before continuing whatever conversation you're rehearsing in your head.
- Change your posture significantly: sit on the floor, stretch out, or shift locations entirely.

What If You Can't Leave?

Even micro-changes produce real shifts. Open a window. Change chairs. Turn on different lighting. Move from sitting to standing. Put on a different background sound. These adjustments introduce new sensory input to a brain locked in repetition. Small physical changes create genuine psychological ones. You don't have to stay where the loop began.

Bottom Line

Rumination feeds on stillness and sameness. One of the biggest drainers of happiness is a mind that keeps rehearsing what it can't change. Change your setting, change the neurological conditions that keep the loop running, and give your brain a chance to reset.

32. Let Go of Perfectionism for Progress

Done and imperfect beats perfect and unfinished almost every time.

What It Is

I'll admit I've gotten better at this one with age. There's something about accumulating enough experience to realize that waiting for perfect usually just means waiting. This book probably has grammar errors in it somewhere. And honestly, that's okay. I'm not losing sleep over it. Getting it into your hands matters more than getting every comma right.

Perfectionism often sounds admirable from the outside: high standards, careful work, strong attention to detail. But underneath the surface it frequently operates as something more corrosive, an identity fused to outcome, where every imperfect result becomes evidence of inadequacy rather than information about process. Progress framing sounds different. This is moving forward. This is better than yesterday. This is a draft, not a verdict. The shift is subtle. The impact on what you're willing to attempt and finish is profound.

Why It Works

Perfectionism is usually less about high standards and more about fear. Fear of judgment, rejection, or being seen as inadequate. When identity becomes tied to performance, every task can feel like a test of your worth. Small mistakes feel disproportionately large, and criticism can feel deeply personal. This activates the brain's threat response, increasing avoidance and procrastination, narrowing creativity, and making starting feel genuinely risky. Research links perfectionist thinking with higher anxiety, burnout, and lower performance over time.

Ironically, perfectionism often delays the very work it's trying to protect.

Focusing on progress breaks that pattern. When the goal shifts from is this flawless to is this improving, mistakes become part of the learning process rather than evidence of inadequacy. Carol Dweck's research shows that people who focus on effort and improvement persist longer, recover faster from setbacks, and produce stronger work over time. They still care about excellence. They just don't let fear of imperfection stop them from starting.

Perfectionism asks: *am I good enough?* Progress asks: *what am I learning?* One creates pressure. The other creates growth.

Try This Today

- Replace "is this perfect?" with "is this better than my last attempt?"
- Set a timer and produce a deliberate "version one" without editing. Forward movement over polish, just for that session.
- When you notice yourself stalling, try the phrase: done and imperfect beats perfect and unfinished.
- After completing something, ask *what improved here?* before asking *what's still wrong?*

What If High Standards Genuinely Matter in Your Work?

They probably do, and this isn't asking you to abandon them. The key is sequencing. Progress first, refinement second. Perfectionism as a final polish before submitting is a legitimate standard. Perfectionism as a starting gate is what creates paralysis. The best work almost always passes through imperfect versions on its way to good ones. Giving yourself permission to produce those versions isn't lowering the bar. It's how you eventually clear it.

Bottom Line

Perfectionism ties your worth to outcomes. Progress ties your growth to effort. Let yourself move forward imperfectly and you'll often find that what becomes possible from motion is far more than what was ever possible from waiting.

33. Use Curiosity Instead of Judgment

Get curious, not furious.

What It Is

I've learned this one the hard way enough times to actually believe it now. People do things for reasons that make sense to them. That doesn't mean their behavior is always right or that anything goes. It just means that jumping straight to judgment usually skips over the most important part: understanding. And without understanding, our responses tend to be reactive rather than wise.

When something triggers you, someone's behavior, your own reaction, a moment that doesn't add up, try replacing your first judgment with a question. Judgment sounds like: what's wrong with them? What's wrong with me? I shouldn't feel this way. Curiosity sounds different: I wonder what's going on here. What might explain this? What am I not seeing yet?

One lesson I've learned in life: be slow to judge and quick to love. Curiosity is often the path that gets you there. It doesn't excuse behavior. It expands understanding. And expanded understanding almost always leads to wiser responses than reactive certainty does.

Why It Works

Judgment is fast by design. The brain moves quickly toward labeling, right, wrong, threat, safe, because rapid categorization was useful for survival. Once something is labeled as wrong or threatening, attention narrows, defensiveness rises, and the mind closes around its conclusion. You're in protective mode, and protective mode is not a particularly creative or flexible place to operate from.

Curiosity activates a genuinely different neurological mode. Research on what psychologists call "epistemic curiosity", the drive to understand and resolve uncertainty, shows that it engages the brain's reward and learning systems, broadening attention and increasing cognitive flexibility rather than narrowing it. You shift from mobilizing a defense to gathering information.

There's a relational dimension worth naming too. A significant portion of interpersonal conflict escalates not because of what actually happened but because of the stories we construct about intent. Judgment says *I know exactly what that meant*. Curiosity says *I might be missing something*. That second posture interrupts assumption-making before it hardens into narrative, which is where most conflicts do their real damage. Curiosity, it turns out, often creates compassion. And compassion tends to change everything about how a hard conversation goes.

Try This Today

- Replace "why would they do that?" with "I wonder what led to that?"
- Ask yourself: "what else could be true here that I haven't considered?"
- When reacting to your own behavior, try "interesting, what's happening here?" instead of "what's wrong with me?"
- In a conversation that's heating up, ask one genuine clarifying question before making your next statement. Just one.

What If the Behavior Really Is Wrong?

Sometimes it genuinely is, and curiosity doesn't change that. The point isn't to avoid accountability. It's to ensure that when accountability is needed, you're responding from clarity rather than reactive certainty. Boundaries enforced after genuine understanding tend to be firmer, clearer, and more sustainable than those enforced from pure reaction. Curiosity precedes judgment. It doesn't replace it.

Bottom Line

Judgment narrows. Curiosity opens. Get curious instead of furious and you'll almost always find something more useful waiting on the other side.

34. Practice Emotional Acceptance Before Action

Resisting difficult emotions amplifies them. Allowing them regulates them.

What It Is

My natural instinct when something uncomfortable shows up emotionally is to fix it, escape it, or argue myself out of it as fast as possible. I suspect I'm not alone in that. But I've learned, slowly and with some resistance, that the instinct to immediately eliminate an emotion often makes it worse rather than better.

When a strong emotion shows up, anxiety, sadness, anger, shame, grief, try something counterintuitive before doing anything else: pause and simply allow it to be present. Not indulging it. Not amplifying it. Just allowing it. Say quietly to yourself: *this is anxiety*, or *this is grief*. Then breathe and stay with it for a moment rather than immediately moving to make it stop. That pause between feeling and action is where some of the most important psychological work happens.

Why It Works

Much of human suffering comes not from difficult emotions themselves but from the war we wage against them. When you fight a feeling, telling yourself you shouldn't feel this or that, or something is wrong with you for having it, you add a second layer of distress on top of the first. Psychologists call this the second arrow. The first arrow is what happens to you. The second arrow is what you do to yourself in response.

Neuroscientist Dr. Jill Bolte Taylor proposed that the initial physiological surge of an emotion, the racing heart, muscle tension, flooding stress hormones, runs its natural course in roughly 90 seconds. The exact number is debated and emotions certainly vary by person and context, but the underlying principle is well supported: the physiological wave is brief. What extends it is the mental loop we attach to it. When we replay the event, assign blame, or catastrophize, we keep reactivating the emotional circuitry and the feeling persists far longer than it naturally would.

Acceptance and Commitment Therapy, one of the most well-researched frameworks in psychology, consistently shows that willingness to experience difficult emotions rather than suppressing them reduces long-term distress more effectively than almost any other approach. When you allow an emotion without immediately trying to correct it, the nervous system gradually recalibrates on its own. The wave passes, but only if you stop fighting it.

Try This Today

- Name the emotion simply and without judgment: this is anxiety, this is anger.
- Take three slow breaths without trying to make the feeling go away. Breathe alongside it.
- Notice where the emotion shows up physically, chest,

throat, stomach, and observe it with curiosity rather than alarm.

- Delay any significant decision until the intensity has lowered. Most things can wait five minutes.

What If the Emotion Feels Overwhelming?

Start small and build the skill gradually. Practice with mild irritation or low-level anxiety first—emotions manageable enough to observe without being swept away. As your capacity develops, stronger emotions become more navigable. And if emotions consistently feel overwhelming despite genuine effort, working with a professional can be genuinely transformative. Acceptance is a learnable skill, and sometimes the most effective way to learn it is with a skilled guide.

Bottom Line

Feel first. Choose second. That sequence, practiced consistently, changes the quality of your decisions, your relationships, and your relationship with your own inner life.

35. Make a Repair Attempt After Conflict

Conflict is inevitable in any relationship worth having. Disconnection doesn't have to be.

What It Is

This one can be hard, mostly because of pride. Something in us wants to wait for the other person to move first, or to hold our ground until the situation is fully resolved. I get it. I've been there. But I've learned that the longer you wait, the heavier it gets, and the heavier it gets, the harder it becomes to reach.

After tension, misunderstanding, or conflict, make a small move toward repair. Not a grand apology speech. Not a full resolution. Just a signal. Hey, can we reset? A hand on a shoulder.

A moment of unexpected humor. A simple acknowledgment: that escalated, and I care more about us than about winning. Psychologist John Gottman calls these repair attempts, small gestures that interrupt negativity and reestablish connection. After decades of research studying thousands of couples, his lab identified repair attempts as one of the strongest predictors of relationship stability and longevity. And relationship stability, research consistently confirms, is one of the most powerful predictors of lasting happiness.

Why It Works

Conflict itself is not what damages relationships most. It's the failure to repair afterward. When tension lingers unresolved, your nervous system stays activated, cortisol remains elevated, and you begin replaying the argument and rehearsing grievances. Defensive patterns harden. Gradually, often without either person fully noticing, the relationship begins to feel less like a source of safety and more like a source of threat.

Gottman's research shows that what distinguishes stable, happy couples from those who eventually disconnect isn't the absence of conflict. All relationships have conflict. It's the willingness to reach toward each other afterward, even imperfectly. A repair attempt communicates something the nervous system registers immediately: you matter more to me than being right does. That message begins restoring the sense of safety that conflict disrupts. Making a repair attempt also reduces your own rumination. Reaching out rather than retreating into silence interrupts the replay loop that unresolved conflict tends to sustain for hours or even days.

Try This Today

- Say simply: *I don't like how that felt between us. Can we try again?*
- Offer a brief acknowledgment of your part, even if it's small and imperfect.

- Use gentle humor to lower the temperature. Gottman's research shows humor is one of the most effective repair tools available (be wise though!).
- Reach toward physical connection: a hand squeeze, eye contact, a brief hug.

You don't need a perfect script. You need a bridge. And bridges don't have to be beautiful to hold weight.

What If the Other Person Doesn't Respond Well?

Repair attempts are invitations, not guarantees. Even when the other person doesn't reciprocate right away, your own nervous system benefits from moving toward connection rather than retreating into resentment. You've interrupted your own rumination loop. You've signaled your values. You can't control their response. You can control your reach.

Bottom Line

Make the repair. Protect the relationship. It's one of the most powerful things you can do for your own lasting happiness, and humility is usually all it takes to begin.

36. Practice Gratitude as Attention Training

What you repeatedly attend to shapes what your life feels like.

What It Is

Gratitude is one of my favorite topics in all of happiness research, and we're going to come back to it multiple times throughout this book because the evidence behind it is that compelling. But let's start with the reframe that changes everything: gratitude is not primarily an emotion. It's a direction of attention. You don't wait to feel grateful and then notice good things. You notice good things, deliberately and repeatedly, and feeling grateful becomes the natural result. That distinction matters more than it might seem. It means gratitude isn't something that happens to you when circumstances are good. It's something you practice regardless of circumstances. Not forced positivity. Not denial of difficulty. Just intentional noticing.

Why It Works

Your brain has a built-in negativity bias, a tendency to scan for threat and problems because historically, noticing danger improved survival. This isn't a design flaw. But left unchecked in modern life, where most of us face an endless supply of manageable problems and very few genuine threats, it skews perception in ways that quietly undermine happiness. What you repeatedly look for, you repeatedly find, and finding it reinforces the looking.

Gratitude practice interrupts and gradually retrains that scanning system. Research by Robert Emmons, one of the leading scientists in gratitude research, consistently shows that deliberately directing attention toward appreciation produces measurable increases in life satisfaction, reductions in depressive symptoms, improvements in sleep quality, and stronger relationship bonds. Emmons describes gratitude precisely as a cognitive and attentional practice rather than a passive emotional state. Something you do, not just something you feel when life happens to be good.

The mechanism is neurological as much as psychological. What you practice noticing becomes easier to notice. A brain trained to scan for good things alongside difficult ones develops a more balanced and accurate perception of life, not a rosier one, but a fuller one. Gratitude doesn't erase difficulty. It balances it. And that balance is closer to an accurate picture of most lives than either pure negativity or forced optimism.

Try This Today

- Write down three specific things that went well today. Specificity matters more than volume, and noting why they went well matters as much as what they were.
- Notice one ordinary detail, warm water, morning light, a text from someone you love, and pause with it for ten deliberate seconds rather than moving past it.
- When something good happens, say quietly to yourself: *I want to remember this.* Then let it actually land.
- At the end of the day, ask: *what is one thing today I don't want to take for granted?*

What If Life Feels Too Heavy for Gratitude Right Now?

Start smaller than you think you need to. Gratitude in difficult seasons doesn't require big moments or silver linings. It can be as quiet as: I got through today. The coffee was good. Someone was kind to me for thirty seconds. You are not minimizing real pain by noticing small things alongside it. You're simply widening the lens enough to see more of what's actually there.

Bottom Line

Train your attention toward what is good, steady, and present, and your experience of life shifts accordingly. Not because circumstances changed. Because your lens did.

4.

SMALL JOYS, BIG RETURNS

We tend to overestimate what grand gestures will do for our happiness, and underestimate what small ones will. We imagine that the vacation, the promotion, the milestone will finally deliver the sustained joy we've been waiting for. And those things matter. But the research tells a different story about where lasting happiness actually comes from. It comes from what John Gottman calls small things often—the quiet, repeated, easy-to-overlook moments that accumulate into something far more significant than any single big event.

I've come to think of this as a tension between two competing laws. I call the first one the Law of Least Effort. It's everywhere in nature. Your heart beats the minimum number of times needed to keep you alive. Your lungs take only the breaths required. You're probably blinking right now at the lowest frequency that keeps your eyes from drying out. There's a universal pull toward conservation, and our pursuit of happiness is no exception. We wait for something big enough to justify feeling good. We tell ourselves we'll slow down and enjoy life when things settle down. We walk past small moments of beauty, connection, and delight because they don't feel significant enough to stop for. The Law of Least Effort whispers that happiness should arrive on its own, and that if it requires intention it probably isn't real.

The second law pushes back. I call it the Law of Little Things, and it says that small, consistent actions repeated with intention produce outsized returns over time. Relationships thrive not because of grand romantic gestures but because of the daily small ones. Athletes improve not through occasional heroic efforts but through relentless attention to fundamentals. Happiness works the same way.

Barbara Fredrickson's research on positive emotions is one of the most important findings in all of positive psychology, and it deserves to be understood fully rather than just appreciated vaguely. Her broaden-and-build theory shows that positive emotions do something far more significant than simply feel good. Positive emotions like joy, curiosity, warmth, awe, and playfulness actually broaden your awareness in the moment, widening your field of attention, expanding your thinking, and making you more creative, more flexible, and more open to possibility. This is the opposite of what negative emotions do. Fear narrows focus to the threat. Anxiety tunnels vision toward the worst case. Positive emotions do the reverse: they open you up.

But here's the part that makes Fredrickson's research genuinely remarkable. Those broadened states don't just feel better in the moment. They build lasting psychological resources over time, things like resilience, emotional intelligence, social connection, and the capacity to navigate difficulty. Each small positive emotion is like a deposit. Individually modest. Collectively transformative. Fredrickson found that people who experience frequent positive emotions, even mild ones, develop measurably greater psychological resources over time than those who don't, regardless of their baseline personality or circumstances. The technical term is the broaden-and-build effect. The practical translation is simpler: small good things, noticed and savored regularly, compound into a life that feels meaningfully richer.

This is where savoring comes in (mentioned in Chapter 1).

Psychologist Fred Bryant, who has spent decades studying how people amplify positive experience, found that the key variable isn't how many good things happen to you. It's whether you slow down long enough to actually receive them. Most of us move through pleasant moments without ever fully inhabiting them. Bryant's research shows that deliberately savoring positive experiences, pausing, noticing, letting the moment land before moving on, produces significantly greater well-being than the same experiences rushed past. The good is already there. Savoring is simply the decision to stay in it long enough for it to matter.

I've seen this in my own life. The days that feel fullest aren't usually the ones with the biggest events. They're the ones where I actually stopped long enough to notice what was already there. Small joys. A good conversation. A song that hit at the right moment. Something beautiful I almost walked past. Something silly that made me laugh. Those moments were always available. I just had to be paying attention.

Martin Seligman, after more than three decades studying happiness, has noted that performing a kind act produces one of the fastest and most reliable boosts to well-being available. Not a grand act. Not a sacrifice. Just something kind, offered without needing it to be significant. Kindness turns out to be one of the clearest expressions of the Law of Little Things in action.

That's the spirit of this entire chapter. The twelve hacks that follow aren't about adding more to an already full life. They're about learning to receive what's already available, beauty, awe, music, play, creativity, connection, and letting it actually land. The small joys.

The Law of Least Effort says *keep scrolling*. The Law of Little Things says *stop, notice, and let it matter*. Small joys are not consolation prizes for a life without bigger ones. For most people, on most days, they are the happiness itself.

37. Let Music Move You

Press play. And actually listen.

What It Is

My wife and three daughters are devoted Swifties. Taylor Swift cranks through our house regularly, fills the car on family road trips, and has become the soundtrack to a lot of Schramm fam moments. And honestly, watching them light up when a favorite song comes on is its own kind of happiness research. There's something about music that bypasses all the noise and just reaches you.

Put on music that genuinely does something to you, and let it. Not as background noise. Not as a productivity tool. Not playing faintly while you answer emails. As the main event. Choose a song, an album, or a playlist that reliably reaches something inside you and give it your actual attention for a few minutes. Sit with it. Drive in silence except for it. Let the volume be slightly louder than usual.

You already know which music moves you. That response isn't accidental, and it isn't trivial.

Why It Works

Music is one of the most direct access points to the brain's emotional and reward systems available to us, and the research on why is genuinely fascinating. Listening to music you love triggers dopamine release, the same neurochemical involved in motivation, reward, and pleasure. Brain imaging studies show that peak emotional responses to music activate the nucleus accumbens, the same region involved in responses to food, love, and other primary rewards. Music isn't just pleasant. It's neurologically powerful.

Beyond dopamine, music measurably shifts cortisol levels, heart rate, and respiratory rhythm within minutes. Uplifting music reduces stress markers. Emotionally resonant music increases feelings of connection and meaning. Music also retrieves autobiographical memory with a vividness that almost nothing else produces, which is why a single melody can transport you to a precise moment years ago. That retrieval is emotionally regulating, connecting your present self to a broader sense of continuity and identity. Barbara Fredrickson's broaden-and-build research suggests the positive emotions music generates—joy, nostalgia, awe, tenderness—don't just feel good in the moment. They build psychological resources that compound over time.

You don't need a concert hall. You need a song and a few minutes of genuine attention.

Try This Today

- Put on one song that reliably moves you and listen without doing anything else simultaneously.
- Create a short playlist that consistently shifts your emotional state upward and use it intentionally on hard days.
- On your next drive alone, skip the podcast and play something that genuinely reaches you.
- Notice where you feel music in your body, chest, throat, the back of your neck, and stay with that sensation rather than moving past it.

What If You've Stopped Really Listening?

Start with a song from a period of your life when music mattered most. Let it carry some of that weight again. You don't need to discover new music. You just need to return attention to what's already there.

Bottom Line

Music is one of the most direct routes to emotional regulation, dopamine release, and genuine joy available to you, and it fits in your pocket. Press play. And actually listen.

38. Create a Moment of Sensory Awe

The world is more astonishing than the pace of daily life allows most of us to notice.

What It Is

It's become a running joke in our family. I'll step onto the back deck, see a stunning sunset, and say with complete sincerity, "Wow, we live in such a beautiful world." My kids have heard it so many times that now whenever something beautiful appears, someone will pause, gesture dramatically, and deliver the line before I can. We laugh every time. But I'm not even a little embarrassed about it, because I mean it every single time.

Sensory awe is the experience of encountering something vast, beautiful, or extraordinary through your senses. A sky that demands you look up. A view from high ground that shrinks your worries by expanding your perspective. A piece of music that makes time feel different. A natural landscape that makes the world feel larger than your daily life usually reveals. Unlike deeper transcendent awe, this version doesn't require a spiritual framework or a life-changing insight. It just requires your full attention and a willingness to let something beautiful actually reach you. Awe is available more often than most people realize. The obstacle isn't access. It's attention.

Why It Works

Psychologist Dacher Keltner has spent decades studying awe and what it does to the people who experience it. His research consistently shows that when you encounter something vast or extraordinary, the brain's default mode network, the part generating the constant internal monologue about your problems and to-do list, quiets. Keltner calls this the "small self" effect. Awe temporarily reduces self-focused thinking and places you in relation to something larger. Your ordinary concerns don't disappear, but they lose their grip. Perspective arrives not through effort but through experience.

Awe also measurably shifts time perception. People who experience awe consistently report feeling like they have more time available, not because the clock changes but because the quality of attention does. The physiological effects are equally real. Keltner's research shows awe reduces inflammatory markers, lowers stress hormones, and increases feelings of connection and meaning. And critically for this chapter, it's a small-effort, high-return practice. A two-minute pause to genuinely watch a sunset costs almost nothing and delivers far more than its size suggests.

Try This Today

- Step outside tonight and look at the sky with your full attention. Not a glance. A genuine pause.
- Find one piece of music, art, or natural scenery that has produced awe in you before and return to it deliberately, phone away, attention given fully.
- The next time you encounter something beautiful, stop. Stay thirty seconds longer than feels necessary. Let it actually register.
- Plan one small outing this week to a place that reliably produces the feeling: a view, a trail, a body of water.

What If You Can't Remember the Last Time You Felt Awe?

It's almost always an attention problem rather than an access problem. Awe tends to find people who are still enough to notice it.

Bottom Line

Seek beauty in small doses and let it stop you. We really do live in a beautiful world.

39. Go Outside for Joy, Not Just Recovery

Joy doesn't always need a reason. Sometimes outside is reason enough.

What It Is

Fall is my favorite time of year. The air turns cool and crisp here in northern Utah, the leaves change, and there's something about stepping outside on one of those mornings that just feels like a gift. We typically get a lot of snow from November through March, so I've genuinely learned to savor the nice days rather than take them for granted. When a beautiful day shows up, I try to actually be in it.

That's the whole idea behind this hack. Step outside not to decompress, not to exercise, not to recover from a hard day, but simply because being outside feels good. Most of us have learned to use the outdoors as a recovery tool. We go outside when we're stressed or burned out and need a reset. And it works beautifully for that. But this hack is about something different: going outside for the pleasure of it, the way you did as a kid without needing a reason. A walk with no destination. Sitting in the sun for ten minutes. Eating lunch outside instead of at your desk. Letting the light and air simply be enjoyable rather than medicinal.

Why It Works

The research on nature and well-being is extensive, but most of it focuses on stress reduction. This entry focuses on something equally supported but less discussed: nature as a direct generator of positive emotion. Psychologists Rachel and Stephen Kaplan's attention restoration theory explains why natural environments feel effortlessly pleasant in ways that built environments rarely do. Nature engages what they call soft fascination, a gentle low-demand form of attention that allows your mind to rest while staying pleasurably engaged. Unlike the directed effortful attention that work and screens require, soft fascination replenishes rather than depletes.

Studies examining positive affect specifically, not just stress reduction but genuine pleasure, vitality, and joy, consistently show that time in natural settings produces measurable increases in all three. Participants report feeling more alive, more curious, and more connected after time outdoors, even brief time, even in urban green spaces. There's also something researchers call a "being" rather than "doing" mode that matters here. Most of our time is spent in pursuit, working toward, accomplishing, moving forward. Nature invites something different: receptive, present, unhurried. That shift alone generates a quality of quiet pleasure that purpose-driven activity rarely produces.

Try This Today

- Eat one meal outside this week. Not at a restaurant, just outside wherever you are.
- Take a ten-minute walk with no destination and no podcast. Let your senses lead.
- Sit in natural light for a few minutes and do nothing except be in it.
- On the next genuinely nice day, treat it like the gift it is and actually go be in it.

What If You Don't Have Easy Access to Nature?

A patch of grass, a bench in the sun, a tree-lined street. Research shows that even modest natural elements produce meaningful positive emotions. What matters most is the quality of your attention while you're there.

Bottom Line

Your nervous system has recognized the outdoors as home far longer than any building has. Go outside not because you need to recover, but because it feels genuinely good to be there.

40. Grow Something—Plants, Herbs, or a Garden

Start small. Tend it. Let it grow. And notice what grows in you in the process.

What It Is

I grew up with a vegetable garden in the backyard. I learned to plant seeds, pull weeds, and watch things come up from the ground. There was something deeply satisfying about it. These days my kids tease me because I seem to be considerably better at growing weeds than anything intentional. But I still have raspberries, and tasting one you helped grow is a small joy that's hard to replicate any other way.

Plant something. Tend it. Watch it grow. Not as a hobby you have to be good at. Not as a productive side project. Just as a living thing in your care that requires small, regular attention and returns something quietly remarkable. A pot of herbs on the kitchen windowsill. A tomato plant on the back porch. A single succulent on your desk. The scale matters less than the act, the deliberate choice to nurture something living and show up for it in small ways over time.

Why It Works

Gardening and plant care produce well-being benefits through several distinct pathways, and the convergence of them is what makes this practice so reliably effective across such different kinds of people.

The most surprising finding involves the soil itself. Research has identified a common soil bacterium, Mycobacterium vaccae, that appears to stimulate serotonin production when humans come in contact with it through gardening or handling soil. This isn't metaphor. It's biochemistry. There may be a literal neurochemical reason that digging in the dirt feels good.

Beyond soil, gardening engages what psychologists call absorbed attention without pressure, a state similar to flow where your mind is fully present in a task that is clear, manageable, and intrinsically rewarding. Weeding, watering, planting, and pruning offer exactly this: simple, sensory, hands-on engagement that quiets mental chatter without demanding anything beyond the present moment. Research on caregiving behavior also shows that tending living things activates the same systems involved in bonding and connection, satisfying something in the human nervous system that is genuinely distinct from productivity or achievement.

Finally, growing things offers something increasingly rare in modern life: visible, tangible evidence of progress. In a world where so much of our work is abstract and invisible, watching something grow that you tended is deeply and measurably satisfying.

Try This Today

- Buy one herb, basil, mint, or rosemary, and put it somewhere you'll see it daily. Water it. Pay attention to it.
- If you have outdoor space, plant one thing this season and commit to tending it consistently.
- If space is limited, a single plant on a windowsill counts. The research doesn't require a garden. It requires a living thing in your care.
- Spend five intentional minutes with a plant today, not just watering on autopilot, but actually noticing what's changed.

What If You've Killed Every Plant You've Ever Owned?

Start with something genuinely hard to kill: pothos, snake plants, or succulents. Most plants die from overwatering, not neglect. You don't need a green thumb. You need a little attention and the willingness to start again.

Bottom Line

Growing something connects you to one of the most ancient sources of human satisfaction: nurturing life, watching progress, and caring for something beyond yourself. Even raspberries count.

41. Play for No Productive Reason

Play is not the opposite of serious work. It's what makes serious work sustainable.

What It Is

Not going to lie, I need to work on this one a bit more. I'm good at being productive. I'm good at staying busy. I'm less good at doing something purely because it's fun with zero justification required. But the research on this one is compelling enough that I've started paying attention to how rarely I actually play, and how much better I feel on the days I do.

Do something purely because it's enjoyable, with no goal, no output, no improvement arc, and no justification required. Not exercise disguised as play. Not a hobby you're trying to optimize. Just play. Toss a ball against a wall. Build something ridiculous with your kids' Legos. Mess around on an instrument you don't know how to play. Chase your dog around the yard. Do a puzzle with no interest in your finishing time. The defining feature of play isn't the activity. It's the absence of purpose beyond the activity itself. That distinction turns out to matter enormously, and most adults have quietly stopped doing it.

Why It Works

Psychiatrist Stuart Brown has spent decades studying play across the human lifespan, and his conclusion is both simple and striking: play is not a luxury. It's a biological necessity. Brown's research shows that play activates the brain's reward systems, promotes neuroplasticity, and enhances creative problem-solving in ways that goal-directed activity simply doesn't replicate. When you play, your brain enters a state of flexible exploratory processing, making unexpected connections and operating without the performance pressure that narrows thinking under serious conditions. Some of the most creative insights people report arrive not during focused work sessions but during or immediately after genuinely playful activity.

Play also naturally interrupts rumination. It's nearly impossible to replay a difficult conversation while you're genuinely absorbed in something fun. That interruption isn't avoidance. It's pattern-breaking from within the activity itself. Brown's research on play deprivation paints a concerning picture of what happens to adults who stop entirely: higher rates of depression, reduced creativity, diminished social connection, and a joyless rigidity in how they approach problems and relationships. Play isn't something we outgrow the need for. It's something modern adult life systematically removes, and the removal has real consequences.

Try This Today

- Give yourself 15 unscheduled minutes and fill them with something enjoyable and completely pointless.
- Play with a child on their terms, following their lead rather than directing the activity.
- Revisit a game, sport, or creative outlet you abandoned because you got too busy or too serious.
- Do something mildly silly today, something that serves no purpose except delight.

If you feel a reflexive need to justify the time, notice that impulse without obeying it. The need to justify it is exactly what makes it not play.

What If You've Forgotten How to Play?

Think back to what you did between ages eight and twelve purely for the joy of it. Not organized sports. Not lessons. The unstructured nobody's-watching stuff. Start there.

Bottom Line

Your brain needs play the way it needs sleep, not as a reward for productivity but as a biological requirement for creativity, resilience, and joy. Stop waiting until you've earned it.

42. Do Something Creative with Your Hands

Your hands are one of your brain's oldest and most reliable pathways to absorption, satisfaction, and joy.

What It Is

I used to love drawing as a kid. Bald eagles were my specialty. Something about trying to capture that detail with a pencil was genuinely absorbing. Then junior high hit, sports took over, and drawing quietly faded out of my life. I sometimes wish I had kept it up. This hack is a good reminder that it's never too late to pick something like that back up, or to find a new version of it.

Make something physical using your hands and whatever materials feel natural to you. Not to produce something impressive. Not to develop a marketable skill. Not to post the result anywhere. Just to make. Knit, draw, paint, bake bread, build something from wood, arrange flowers, fold origami, sculpt with your kids' Play-Doh. The material and the outcome matter far less than the act, hands engaged, mind absorbed, something taking shape that wasn't there before.

Why It Works

Psychologist Mihaly Csikszentmihalyi's research on flow, the state of deep absorption where time bends and self-consciousness fades, consistently identifies hands-on creative work as one of the most reliable pathways into that state. Making something with your hands provides exactly the conditions flow requires: a clear task, immediate feedback, and enough challenge to engage without overwhelming.

When your hands are occupied with something physical and creative, the brain's default mode network, the system responsible for worry and rumination, quiets naturally. You're not suppressing difficult thoughts through willpower. The absorption of making simply leaves no bandwidth for them. This is why knitting, woodworking, and baking have such consistent reputations for being meditative. The neuroscience supports what practitioners have always reported feeling.

Psychologist Kelly Lambert's research on what she calls effort-driven rewards adds another layer. Using your hands to produce a tangible result activates reward circuits in a way that passive or abstract activities simply don't. In an era when so much of our work is invisible, emails sent, documents revised, decisions made, the visibility of a made thing satisfies something deep and specific in the human nervous system. The brain doesn't reward the quality of the output. It rewards the act of making itself.

Try This Today

- Spend 20 minutes drawing, doodling, or sketching with no intention of the result being good.
- Bake something from scratch and pay attention to the process rather than just the result.
- Start one small physical project you've been putting off, building, fixing, assembling, or creating something tangible.
- If none of those feel accessible, try arranging flowers,

folding paper, or kneading dough. Let your hands do something deliberate and physical.

What If You Don't Consider Yourself Creative?

Creativity here has nothing to do with artistic talent. Baking bread is creative. Repotting a plant is creative. The research on effort-driven rewards doesn't discriminate between art and carpentry. It responds to the act of making regardless of the medium.

Bottom Line

Make something today, anything, and let the making itself be the point.

43. Savor Something Beautiful Today

Beauty is already present in your life. Slow down and let it land.

What It Is

Beauty is not scarce. It's present in ordinary life with remarkable frequency. What's scarce is the quality of attention we bring to it, the willingness to stop, notice, and let something genuinely register before moving on.

One of my favorite things in the world right now is holding my granddaughter while she sleeps. I could put her down. I don't. That's savoring. It's simply choosing to stay inside a good moment rather than moving past it.

Find one thing today that is genuinely beautiful and stay with it longer than feels necessary. Not scroll past it. Not photograph it for later. The morning light through a window. A piece of music that deserves real attention. A child's face when completely absorbed in something. Savoring is the willingness to be present with what's already there, made into a deliberate practice.

Why It Works

Psychologist Fred Bryant's decades of research on savoring consistently show it's one of the most powerful and underutilized tools for building lasting positive emotion. Most positive experiences pass through our lives without fully registering. We notice them peripherally, feel a flicker of pleasure, and move on before the experience has had time to consolidate into genuine well-being.

Savoring interrupts that pattern. Deliberate attention extends and deepens the emotional response your brain produces, and the experience encodes more richly into memory, continuing to generate positive emotion long after the moment has passed. The brain's reward system responds not just to the presence of something pleasurable but to the attention directed toward it. This is why the same sunset can feel transcendent one evening and barely noticeable another. The difference is rarely the sunset. Bryant's research also shows that people who practice savoring regularly become measurably better at finding pleasure in everyday life, not because their circumstances improve but because their attentional capacity does.

Try This Today

- Find one beautiful thing right now and give it thirty uninterrupted seconds of full attention.
- Eat one meal today without screens and actually taste it.
- Instead of photographing something beautiful, stay with it in the moment instead.
- Before bed, identify one beautiful thing from today and spend sixty seconds genuinely re-experiencing it.

What If You're Going Through a Hard Season?

Savoring doesn't require circumstances to be good. Even in hard seasons, beauty exists in small pockets. Widening the lens to see it doesn't diminish the difficulty. It just prevents difficulty from becoming the only thing visible.

Bottom Line

Slow down. Stay longer. Let something genuinely good actually land. Savoring costs nothing but attention, and the return is far greater than the investment.

44. Anticipate Something—Plan a Small Pleasure

Happiness doesn't only live in experience. It lives in anticipation.

What It Is

I love having something to look forward to. It doesn't have to be big. I've genuinely looked forward to Friday nights watching our son play football, to getaways with my wife, and honestly, some nights I just look forward to finally getting into bed and relaxing. All of it counts. And let's be real—sometimes the actual event doesn't quite live up to the anticipation. It's raining. It's hotter than expected. Someone's whining. But that almost doesn't matter, because the research shows the anticipation itself was generating real happiness the whole time.

Put something enjoyable on your calendar, something specific, something real, and something close enough to actually look forward to. Not a vague intention to do something fun someday. Not a grand vacation eight months away. A dinner at a restaurant you've been wanting to try. A hike on Saturday. A movie night this week. A morning where you sleep in without guilt. The size of the planned pleasure matters far less than the specificity and proximity of it.

Why It Works

One of the most counterintuitive findings in happiness research is that anticipation often produces more sustained positive emotion than the experience it precedes. Research by Leaf Van Boven and colleagues consistently shows that looking forward to something enjoyable begins generating positive emotions well before the event arrives, extending the total happiness value of that experience significantly. A dinner you've anticipated for a week produces more cumulative happiness than one you decided on that afternoon, even if both meals are identical.

The neurological mechanism involves dopamine, but not in the way most people assume. Neuroscientist Kent Berridge's research suggests dopamine is less of a reward chemical and more of an anticipation chemical. It surges in response to expected rewards, often more powerfully than it responds to the reward itself. Planning a small pleasure activates your brain's reward system right now, generating real positive emotion from an experience that hasn't happened yet.

The planning process itself adds another layer. Choosing and arranging a pleasurable experience produces its own positive emotion distinct from the anticipation that follows. You're generating happiness in multiple waves: during the planning, during the anticipation, and during the experience itself.

Try This Today

- Open your calendar right now and schedule one small pleasurable activity within the next seven days. Make it specific enough that you can picture it.
- If a larger experience feels out of reach, plan something tiny: a special breakfast, an evening walk, a phone call with someone who makes you laugh.
- Tell someone what you're looking forward to. Sharing anticipation amplifies it.
- Before bed tonight, spend a few minutes thinking about something upcoming that you're genuinely excited about.

What If You Feel Guilty Planning Pleasures?

That guilt is worth examining rather than obeying. Anticipated pleasure improves mood, reduces stress, and increases the patience available for everyone around you. You're allowed to have things to look forward to.

Bottom Line

Plan something small. Make it specific. Put it on the calendar. Talk about it. And let your brain start enjoying it today.

45. Keep Beauty in Your Environment

Your environment speaks to your nervous system constantly, whether or not you're listening.

What It Is

I spend eight or more hours a day in my office at Utah State University, so I've been intentional about what surrounds me there. Photos of my wife and kids where I can see them from my desk. Plants that add some life to the space. And yes, a jar of peanut M&Ms nearby, which may not be the most research-backed addition but does measurably improve my mood.

The point is that the spaces you inhabit are not neutral. They're sending your nervous system constant signals about order, beauty, and the quality of life happening inside them. This hack is about being intentional with those signals. Not an interior design overhaul. Not an expensive renovation. Just deliberate attention to what your eyes land on dozens of times each day. A plant on your desk. A photograph that means something to you. Fresh flowers on the kitchen table. A cleared surface instead of visual clutter. Natural light where artificial light was doing the job poorly.

Why It Works

Environmental psychology has produced a consistent and underappreciated body of research on how physical spaces shape emotional states, largely below the level of conscious awareness. Roger Ulrich's landmark research showed that hospital patients who had a window view of trees rather than a brick wall recovered faster, required less pain medication, and reported better emotional states, not because they went outside, but simply because natural beauty was visible from where they spent their days. What your eyes rest on, even passively, affects how you feel.

Research on restorative environments shows that spaces containing natural elements, aesthetic coherence, and visual order reliably reduce stress, improve mood, and restore cognitive capacity. Clutter works in the opposite direction. Visually cluttered environments increase cortisol, reduce focus, and create a persistent low-grade cognitive load as the brain continuously processes unresolved visual information in the background. Clearing a surface isn't just aesthetic preference. It's a stress reduction intervention.

Objects with personal meaning add another layer entirely. Photographs of people you love, mementos from meaningful experiences, gifts from important people, these function as memory cues that trigger brief but genuine moments of warmth and connection throughout the day. The key word is noticed. An object you've stopped seeing has lost most of its emotional value.

Try This Today

- Identify one surface that has become visually cluttered and clear it. Just one.
- Place one plant, one meaningful photograph, or one object of genuine beauty somewhere you'll see it regularly.

- Open the blinds and let natural light into a space that's been running on artificial light.
- Walk through your main living or workspace and ask honestly: *does this support how I want to feel, or does it quietly drain me?*

What If Your Environment Feels Beyond Your Control?

Even in constrained spaces, small changes are almost always available. A single plant, a cleared corner, a photograph on a desk. The research doesn't require beautiful surroundings. It responds to intentional ones.

Bottom Line

Choose, where you can, to surround yourself with what is beautiful, meaningful, and calm. Small deliberate changes to what you see every day compound into a life that feels measurably different.

46. Create Micro-Moments of Connection

Small connections, accumulated daily, are one of the quietest and most powerful sources of happiness available to you.

What It Is

My wife is genuinely gifted at this. She'll strike up a real conversation with a stranger waiting in line at a restaurant or sitting nearby at an airport, and by the end they're laughing like old friends. I've watched it happen dozens of times and I'm still a little in awe of it. What she understands intuitively is that brief human contact isn't trivial. It actually counts.

Make genuine human contact with the people you encounter in ordinary life and let those moments actually matter. Not networking. Not performed friendliness. Real, if brief, warmth. A genuine smile and eye contact with the person at the checkout. A real question to a neighbor that goes one sentence deeper than the weather. A moment of shared laughter with someone you'll never see again. Choosing to look up from your phone and actually acknowledge the person standing next to you. These are micro-moments of connection, and the research suggests they are far more significant to your happiness and health than their brevity implies.

Why It Works

Barbara Fredrickson's research on what she calls positivity resonance makes a claim that surprises most people: genuine connection doesn't require an ongoing relationship to produce real biological and psychological benefits. It requires only a moment of mutual care and shared positive emotion. The micro-moment of warmth you share with a stranger is not a pale imitation of real connection. It is real connection, brief, complete in itself, and producing measurable effects on both people involved.

These moments trigger oxytocin release, reduce cardiovascular stress reactivity, and increase vagal tone, a measure of the nervous system's capacity for flexible regulated response. People who experience more micro-moments of connection throughout their day show better physical health, stronger immune function, and greater psychological resilience than those who move through their days in social isolation even while surrounded by others.

Research by Nicholas Epley and Juliana Schroeder adds something worth knowing: people consistently underestimate how much they'll enjoy talking to strangers, and how much strangers will enjoy talking to them. The anticipated awkwardness is almost always worse than the actual experience. Once initiated, most micro-moments of genuine warmth feel natural and leave both people better than before.

Try This Today

- Make real eye contact and offer a genuine smile to the next person who serves you in any capacity.
- Ask one person today a question you're actually curious about and listen to the answer.
- The next time you're about to check your phone while waiting, look up instead and make brief friendly contact with whoever is nearby.
- Pay a specific, genuine compliment to someone you encounter today, not generic praise, but something you actually noticed.

What If You're Introverted or Socially Anxious?

Micro-moments were practically designed for introverts. They're brief by definition, low-stakes, and high-return. The research on social anxiety consistently shows that brief positive interactions with strangers are far more rewarding and far less depleting than introverts anticipate. Start with one genuine moment per day. That's enough to begin shifting what your social world feels like.

Bottom Line

Initiate. Make contact. Let the moment count. Connection doesn't have to be deep to be real.

47. Celebrate the Small Wins

Progress that goes unnoticed produces no benefit. Progress that lands builds everything that follows.

What It Is

Most people move through their days accomplishing far more than they register, checking things off, navigating difficulty, making small, good choices, and then arriving at the end of the day with a vague sense of not having done enough. This hack is the direct antidote to that pattern.

At the end of each day, identify one thing that went well, moved forward, or deserved acknowledgment. Not a major milestone. Not a completed project. Just a small win. A difficult email you finally sent. A healthy choice you made when an easier one was available. A conversation that went better than expected. A task you'd been avoiding that got done. A moment of patience when impatience would have been easier. Write it down. Say it out loud. Tell someone. Mark it in some small way that signals to your brain: that counted.

Why It Works

Teresa Amabile and Steven Kramer spent years studying what drives motivation and positive emotion in daily work life. Their findings, published as the Progress Principle, produced one of the most practically useful insights in modern psychology: of all the things that contribute to a positive inner work life, the single most powerful is making progress in meaningful work, even small progress, on a given day.

Small wins don't just feel good. They trigger a dopamine release that reinforces the behavior that generated the win and motivates continued effort. But the progress has to actually be noticed. Progress that goes unregistered produces no dopamine response and no motivational benefit. Modern life moves fast enough that accomplishments are immediately superseded by what hasn't been done yet. Over time this creates a chronic sense of inadequacy, not because you're not making progress, but because you're not pausing long enough to register it.

Psychologist Albert Bandura's research on self-efficacy adds another layer. Self-efficacy, your belief in your capacity to accomplish what you set out to do, is one of the strongest predictors of persistence and resilience. And it's built primarily through accumulated evidence that you are capable and effective.

Tracking small wins is the systematic practice of collecting that evidence rather than letting it evaporate unnoticed.

Try This Today

- At the end of today, write down one thing that moved forward, went well, or deserved recognition. Be specific rather than vague.
- When you complete something you've been avoiding, pause for 10 seconds before moving to the next task. Let the completion land.
- Tell someone about one thing that went well today, not to brag, but to let it register socially and verbally.
- If you use a planner or journal, add a single line at the bottom of each day's page for one small win.

What If Nothing Feels Like a Win?

Lower the bar until something clears it. Getting out of bed may be a win on some days. Choosing not to say the unkind thing was a win. On the hardest days, the win might simply be: I got through today. Write it down anyway.

Bottom Line

The wins are already there. You just have to stop long enough to see them.

48. Do Something Kind for a Stranger

It feels good to do good.

What It Is

This one is genuinely one of my favorites in the entire book. There is something about doing something kind for a stranger, with no expectation of anything in return, that produces an almost immediate lift. I don't think that's a coincidence. I think it's exactly how we were wired.

Do something genuinely kind for someone you don't know, without being asked, without expectation of return, and without needing it to be significant. Pay for the coffee of the person behind you in line. Help someone carry something heavy. Leave a generous tip with a handwritten note. Let someone merge in traffic without making them earn it. Compliment something specific and real about a stranger's effort or work. The act doesn't need to be grand. Research suggests the size of the kindness matters far less than the spontaneity and genuine intent behind it.

Why It Works

Martin Seligman, after more than three decades studying well-being, has described performing a kind act as one of the fastest and most reliable routes to happiness available, faster in controlled studies than almost any other positive intervention. The key word is performing. The happiness benefit flows to the giver, not just the receiver.

The neurochemical explanation involves what researchers call the helper's high, a measurable release of endorphins and oxytocin that follows prosocial behavior. Brain imaging studies show that giving to others activates the mesolimbic reward pathway, the same system involved in food, connection, and other primary rewards. Kindness isn't just morally good. It is neurologically rewarding in the most literal sense.

What surprises most people is the stranger dimension specifically. Research by Lara Aknin and colleagues has shown that spending money or effort on strangers produces happiness benefits comparable to spending on close friends, and in some cases slightly higher, possibly because the act feels more purely altruistic and less transactional. Your brain doesn't require a relationship to reward generosity. It rewards the act itself.

There's also a perspective-shifting effect worth naming. When you do something kind for a stranger, you briefly enter their world, imagining their day and what might matter to them. Psychologist Jonathan Haidt calls this elevation (mentioned previously), the warm uplifting feeling of moral beauty that transforms the person who experiences it. You're not just making someone's day slightly better. You're briefly becoming the kind of person who does that, and that identity shift has its own cumulative effect over time.

Try This Today

- Pay for the order of the person behind you in a drive-through or coffee line and leave before they can thank you.
- Write a genuine specific positive review for a small business whose work you've appreciated.
- Offer a sincere compliment to someone in a service role, not generic praise but something you actually noticed.
- Leave something small and unexpectedly kind somewhere a stranger will find it.

What If It Feels Awkward?

It often does at first. But research consistently shows that recipients of unexpected kindness almost universally feel touched and uplifted, rarely uncomfortable. The awkwardness lives in the anticipation, not the act. Do it anyway.

Bottom Line

Kindness is not just good for the world. It's good for the person offering it, neurologically, emotionally, and in ways that compound over time. Do something kind for a stranger today. You will feel it too.

5.

TURN OUTWARD: THE SCIENCE OF GRATITUDE

Some topics in happiness research get a footnote. Gratitude gets its own chapter, because the evidence for its effects is that strong and that broad. Marcus Tullius Cicero called gratitude not only the greatest of virtues but the parent of all others, the foundation from which kindness, empathy, humility, and generosity grow. That was two thousand years ago. Modern research has spent decades catching up to what Cicero felt, and the findings consistently confirm it: gratitude is not a pleasant add-on to a good life. It is one of its primary architects.

I'll be vulnerable about my own relationship with this one. Gratitude doesn't always come naturally to me in hard seasons. There are days when it feels like a discipline rather than a feeling, when I have to choose to look for what's good rather than waiting to feel it spontaneously. But that's actually the point. The research doesn't suggest that grateful people feel gratitude automatically. It suggests they practice it deliberately, and that the practice changes them over time.

Robert Emmons, the leading scientific researcher on gratitude, has found that people who practice gratitude regularly experience higher levels of positive emotion, sleep better, feel more connected to others, show greater resilience in adversity, and even report fewer physical health complaints. These aren't subtle effects. They're among the most robust findings in all of positive psychology, replicated across cultures, age groups, and life circumstances.

But here's what I think matters most about gratitude, and what the science often undersells: *gratitude is never really about you.* That's the key. Gratitude is fundamentally outward-facing. It turns your attention away from what you lack, what went wrong, or what you're worried about, and directs it toward the people, experiences, and ordinary gifts that already surround you. I think of gratitude and kindness as two sides of the same coin. When someone is kind, we feel grateful. When we feel grateful, we tend to act with kindness. Both are about turning outward, and turning outward, research confirms, is one of the most reliable paths to lasting happiness.

There's also something I've noticed personally: the more specific my gratitude is, the more real it feels. Vague thankfulness fades quickly. But pausing to genuinely appreciate a specific person, a specific moment, or a specific ordinary gift that I almost walked past, that tends to stay with me. It changes the tone of the day.

The ten practices in this chapter will help you develop gratitude as a genuine skill rather than an occasional feeling. Some are simple and daily. Some require more courage and reflection. All of them are about turning outward, and discovering again and again that when you do, there is far more to appreciate than you remembered.

49. Write Down Three Good Things Daily

What you repeatedly attend to shapes what your life feels like.

What It Is

One of our daughters has been a faithful journal writer for years. She keeps multiple journals, including one dedicated entirely to gratitude. I've watched that practice shape the way she moves through the world, and it's one of the clearest real-life examples I know of that this hack actually works.

At the end of each day, write down three things that went well. Not three extraordinary things. Not three things you're supposed to be grateful for. Just three things that were genuinely good, however small. The sun was out this morning. A conversation went better than expected. Someone held the door. You got enough sleep. Three things. Written down. Every day. It sounds almost too simple to matter. It isn't.

Why It Works

Martin Seligman and his colleagues tested this practice, sometimes called Three Good Things or What Went Well, in one of the most cited studies in positive psychology. Participants who wrote down three good things each day for just one week showed measurable increases in happiness and decreases in depressive symptoms, and those effects persisted for up to six months after the practice ended. Not six days. *Six months.*

The mechanism comes back to attention. Your brain's negativity bias means that without deliberate intervention, the day's difficulties claim a disproportionate share of your mental real estate. The good things happened. They simply didn't get registered with the same weight. Writing three good things each evening isn't manufacturing positivity. It's correcting an attentional imbalance that was always tilted against you.

The writing element matters specifically. Putting something

into words forces your brain to process it more deliberately than a passing thought allows, encoding it more richly into memory. Specificity strengthens the effect considerably. "Today was okay" produces almost no benefit. "The afternoon light through the kitchen window looked extraordinary and I actually stopped to notice it" produces a genuine neurological response. Over time this practice gradually retrains your brain to scan for what's good all day long, not just when you sit down to write.

Try This Today

- Keep a notebook beside your bed and write three things before you turn off the light tonight.
- Be specific about what went well and include, even briefly, why it went well or what it meant to you.
- If three feels like too many on a hard day, write one. One honest specific good thing is meaningfully better than nothing.
- If you miss a day, start again the next evening without self-judgment.

What If Nothing Good Happened Today?

Lower the bar until something clears it. The hot water in the shower felt great. You got through a difficult hour. Someone was kind for thirty seconds. This practice isn't asking you to pretend hard days aren't hard. It's asking you to insist that even hard days contain something worth noticing. Because they almost always do.

Bottom Line

Write down three good things tonight. Do it again tomorrow. The returns arrive quietly, and then one day you notice they've been accumulating all along.

50. Text 2 Before 10

Gratitude that stays inside is incomplete. Expressed gratitude is where its deepest benefits live.

What It Is

I came up with this one years ago and it's simple, yet powerful: Before 10am, send a genuine text to two people. Not a logistical message. Not a reply to something already in your inbox. A deliberate outward-reaching text that offers something real: appreciation, encouragement, warmth, a memory, a check-in, an invitation.

I've been thinking about you and wanted you to know I'm grateful for your friendship. That thing you did last week meant more than you know. I was just remembering the time we... You've been on my mind. How are you doing, really?

Two people. Before 10am. Every day. I've been sharing this practice in workshops for years and the response is consistently the same: people are surprised by how small it is and then surprised again by how much it changes things. Not just for the people who receive the texts. For the person sending them.

Why It Works

Gratitude at its most powerful doesn't stay inside. It moves outward, and the moment it does, something shifts for both people. Research by Martin Seligman on what he calls gratitude in action—gratitude expressed directly to another person rather than simply reflected on privately—consistently shows stronger and more lasting effects on well-being than private gratitude practices alone. When you tell someone what they mean to you, the emotional benefit is amplified for you as much as for them. The expression completes something the reflection alone leaves unfinished.

The morning timing matters more than it might seem. Most people begin their days in reactive mode, checking notifications, responding to demands, moving immediately into what the world needs from them. Sending two intentional texts before 10am reverses that sequence, making outward-directed warmth the first intentional act of your day rather than an afterthought saved for when time allows. For most people, that means it never happens at all.

There's also a relationship dimension that compounds powerfully over time. Two texts a day is 730 small relational investments per year. John Gottman's research on what he calls "turning toward," small consistent bids for connection honored rather than ignored, shows that relationships are built not through occasional grand gestures but through the steady accumulation of small ones. The effect on the quality and depth of your relationships over months and years is genuinely significant.

Try This Today

- Think of someone you appreciate but haven't told recently. Text them something specific before 10am tomorrow.
- Think of someone who has been on your mind and might need to hear from you. Reach out.
- Keep the message genuine and specific. A specific memory or quality lands far more powerfully than vague warmth.
- If two feels like a stretch, start with one. The principle holds at any scale.

What If You're Not a Texter?

The medium matters far less than the intention. A handwritten note, a voice message, a brief email. What matters is the deliberate morning practice of turning outward toward someone else before the day turns you entirely inward.

Bottom Line

Text two people something true and warm before 10am tomorrow. And notice what it does to the rest of your day.

51. Write a Gratitude Letter to a Former Teacher, Mentor, or Coach

You should never fail to thank those who have taught you well.

What It Is

Years ago I wrote gratitude letters to two people who had shaped me significantly, a former high school teacher and a religious leader who both made a real difference in my life. I can still remember how it felt to put into words what they meant to me. It was one of those experiences that stays with you, and I'm convinced it mattered as much to me as it did to them.

Think of someone from your past who shaped you in a meaningful way, a teacher who believed in you, a coach who pushed you further than you thought you could go, a mentor who saw something in you before you saw it yourself and write them a letter telling them so. Not a quick thank-you note. A real letter. Specific about what they did. Specific about how it affected you. Specific about who you became, at least in part, because of them. You don't have to send it, though the research suggests you should.

This is one of the most powerful exercises in all of positive psychology. Not one of the most complicated. One of the most powerful.

Why It Works

Martin Seligman and his colleagues developed what they call the gratitude visit, writing a detailed letter of appreciation to someone who significantly impacted your life and then delivering it in person. The results were striking. Participants who completed a gratitude visit showed the largest positive effect on happiness of any intervention tested, larger than any purely reflective gratitude practice, and the effects persisted for weeks afterward.

Writing the letter requires you to revisit specific memories, specific qualities, and specific moments of impact, generating positive emotion while consolidating meaningful parts of your own story with more clarity than you've likely brought to them before. When you deliver it, something even more significant happens. Teachers retire without knowing which students they changed. Coaches move on without knowing which athletes carried their belief forward for decades. This letter tells them. Seligman's research shows that both writer and recipient typically experience profound emotion, and people who receive such letters often describe it as one of the most meaningful moments of their lives.

Try This Today

- Think of one person who invested in you in a way that shaped who you became.
- Write specifically: what did they do, what did it mean at the time, and how has it stayed with you? Concrete and detailed is more powerful than general and vague.
- If the person is still alive and reachable, consider delivering it in person or sending it directly. Any form of delivery produces benefits that private writing alone does not.
- If the person has passed away, write the letter anyway. The research shows the benefits to the writer occur regardless of whether the letter is ever received.

What If It Feels Vulnerable?

It will. And that vulnerability is part of why it works. The discomfort is the doorway. Walk through it.

Bottom Line

Somewhere in your past is a person who helped make you who you are. They probably don't know the full extent of it. Tell them.

52. Express Appreciation in Relationships

The people you love most deserve to know not just that you love them, but that you love being theirs.

What It Is

There's a meaningful difference between telling someone you love them and telling someone you love being theirs. Most people have never fully felt it until they've either said it or heard it directed at them.

Tell the people closest to you, specifically and regularly, what they mean to you and what you love about being in their lives. Not just "I love you," though that matters too. Something more specific. Something that lands differently. *I absolutely love being your dad. Being your mom is one of the greatest gifts of my life. I'm so glad I get to be married to you.* A sticky note on the bathroom mirror. A text sent for no reason on a Tuesday. A quiet moment at the end of the day when you look at your child and say it out loud, unprompted, without the occasion of a birthday or a goodbye. What matters is the specificity, the naming not just of love, but of the particular joy of the particular relationship.

Why It Works

"I love you" is one of the most powerful phrases in human language and one of the most frequently repeated. For many people in long-term relationships, those three words have been said so many times in so many contexts that they've lost some of their original weight. This isn't a failure of love.

It's a predictable consequence of repetition, which the brain processes as familiarity rather than new information.

What hasn't been said as many times, and therefore lands with its original force, is the relationship-specific expression. *I love being your mom. I love being your husband.* These statements do something different neurologically and emotionally. They name the specific relational role as a source of joy, communicating something more particular, more chosen, and more meaningful than the general declaration alone.

Research by Sara Algoe on what she calls find, remind, and bind, the three functions of expressed gratitude in relationships, shows that specific appreciation reminds both people of what is good in the relationship and strengthens the bond in ways that general declarations don't fully achieve. John Gottman's research on the emotional bank account in relationships confirms that specific, consistent expressions of appreciation build the relational reserves that allow relationships to weather difficulty and the ordinary erosion of daily life. Specific appreciation says: *I see you. I notice you. I am glad, deliberately and particularly, that you are mine.*

Try This Today

- Write "I absolutely love being your mom/dad/partner" on a sticky note and leave it somewhere they'll find it today.
- Send a text right now that names the specific relationship as a source of joy.
- Say it out loud tonight, unprompted, slowly enough that it actually lands.
- Make it a weekly practice: tell one person close to you something specific about why you love being in their life.

What If It Feels Awkward?

For many people, especially in families or relationships where direct emotional expression isn't the norm, this kind of specificity can feel surprisingly vulnerable. That vulnerability is worth leaning into rather than around. The awkwardness usually lasts about as long as it takes to say the words. What follows—the look on your child's face, the pause before your partner responds, the quiet that settles after something true has been said—is almost always worth it.

Start with a sticky note if saying it out loud feels like too much. The written version lands just as powerfully, sometimes more so, because it can be held, reread, and kept.

Bottom Line

The people you love most deserve to know not just that you love them, but that you love being theirs. Say it specifically. Say it regularly. Say it in ways that land differently than routine. *I absolutely love being your dad* on a sticky note on a Friday morning. It costs nothing. It changes everything.

53. Practice Gratitude for Ordinary Things

It was never as ordinary as you thought.

What It Is

Turn your appreciation toward the unremarkable, the things so consistently present in your life that you've stopped noticing them entirely. Hot water when you turn on the shower. A bed that is comfortable and yours. The smell of coffee in the morning. A body that carried you through another day. A friend who picks up the phone. Electricity. A refrigerator full of food. These things are not small. They only feel small because they've been present so long that your brain has filed them under "expected" and stopped registering them as gifts. This practice is about reopening that file.

Why It Works

The brain's negativity bias has a partner called hedonic adaptation, the neurological process by which your brain adjusts to positive circumstances until they no longer register as positive at all. What was once remarkable becomes normal. What was once a source of genuine gratitude becomes invisible background. This is why a raise produces happiness for a few weeks before becoming the new baseline, and why the things that would devastate you to lose, your health, your relationships, your basic comforts, rarely produce active gratitude on the ordinary Tuesday when they are simply and quietly present.

Psychologist Sonja Lyubomirsky's research shows that one of the most reliable ways to counteract this process is deliberately directing attention toward everyday positive circumstances that have faded into the background. When you consciously notice something you've stopped seeing, you partially reverse the adaptation process. The thing doesn't change. Your perception of it does, and that perceptual shift produces genuine positive emotion from circumstances that were generating none.

Psychologist Timothy Wilson's subtraction technique takes this further: briefly imagine your life without something you currently take for granted, then return to the reality that it's still there. Research shows this mental subtraction produces a meaningful increase in appreciation, more effectively than simply trying to feel grateful for something's presence.

Try This Today

- Identify one completely ordinary thing today, something so routine it has become invisible, and spend sixty seconds genuinely appreciating it.
- Try the subtraction technique: imagine your life without one ordinary comfort or relationship, then return to the reality that it's still there and notice what shifts.
- As you move through your day, occasionally ask: *if I lost*

this tomorrow, would I miss it? Let the answer inform how you treat it today.

- At the end of today, write down one ordinary thing that went unnoticed until now and describe why it deserves more appreciation than it gets.

What If Your Life Genuinely Feels Hard Right Now?

This practice was partly designed for exactly that season. Gratitude for ordinary things doesn't ask you to be grateful for the difficulty or pretend circumstances are better than they are. It asks you to notice what is still present alongside the difficulty, the small steady ordinary things that hardship hasn't taken. Hot water. A quiet moment. Someone who checked in. The fact that you're still here.

In genuinely hard seasons, ordinary gratitude isn't a bypass around pain. It's a practice of widening the lens just enough to see what difficulty hasn't yet touched, and holding onto that, even briefly, as something real.

Bottom Line

The things you would grieve most if they disappeared are the things you're least likely to appreciate today. Look at what's ordinary in your life with new eyes. It was never as ordinary as you thought.

54. List Your Top Five People, Places, Experiences, and Things

There is more there than you think.

What It Is

Set aside 15 minutes, find a quiet space, and make four short lists. Your top five people. Your top five places. Your top five experiences. Your top five things. Not an exhaustive inventory.

Just an honest, unhurried answer to a simple question in four categories: what, and who, am I most grateful for?

Your top five people might be family members, close friends, a mentor, someone no longer living whose influence never left. Your top five places might be a childhood home, a stretch of trail, a city that changed you. Your top five experiences might be a birth, a journey, a conversation that rearranged something inside you. Your top five things might be simple, a book that shaped you, an object that carries meaning, something small that represents something large.

Write all four lists. Then read them back slowly. I've used this exercise in workshops for years and what happens in the room when people finish is always the same. A quiet settles. People look at what they've written with something between surprise and recognition. And almost everyone arrives at the same realization: there is more here than I remembered.

Why It Works

Robert Emmons describes gratitude as having two components: recognizing that good things exist in your life and recognizing that the sources of those good things are at least partly outside yourself. This exercise engages both simultaneously. The four-category structure matters because research on gratitude consistently shows its benefits are strongest when it is specific and varied, when attention is directed toward particular people, moments, and circumstances rather than vague general appreciation.

There's also a narrative identity dimension at work. Psychologist Dan McAdams' research on life stories shows that how we construct and interpret our personal narrative directly shapes our sense of meaning and well-being. When you identify what has mattered most, who has mattered most, where, and when, you are doing something more significant than making a gratitude list. You are clarifying what your life has actually been about. Reading the completed lists slowly then becomes what Fred Bryant calls savoring through reminiscing, deliberately revisiting what has been good, which generates genuine positive emotion in the present from experiences already past.

Try This Today

- Top 5 People: the individuals whose presence in your life you are most grateful for, living or not.
- Top 5 Places: the locations that have meant the most to you, for any reason.
- Top 5 Experiences: the moments or seasons you would least want to have missed.
- Top 5 Things: objects, books, or possessions that carry genuine meaning rather than just practical value.
- When you finish, read all four lists slowly. Then consider sharing them with someone close to you. What people include in their top fives reveals something true about them, and the conversation that follows is almost always worth having.

What If the Lists Feel Harder Than Expected?

Go gently. Gratitude for what was is as real and as nourishing as gratitude for what is. Let the lists be honest. Honest gratitude, even when it carries grief alongside it, is more sustaining than gratitude that stays safely on the surface.

Bottom Line

Make the lists. Read them slowly. There is more there than you think. Then keep adding to them.

55. Replace Entitlement With Appreciation

Subtract it briefly in your mind and what returns is closer to the truth of what you have.

What It Is

Let's be honest. If you're reading this book, you probably have a pretty good life compared to the majority of people on the planet. I include myself in that. Running water. A safe place to sleep. Food in the fridge. People who love you. And yet it's remarkably easy, even with all of that, to slip into entitlement without even noticing it happening.

Part of the problem is that we're swimming in messages that reinforce it. Marketing tells us we deserve it. Commercials say *have it your way*. The culture quietly suggests that comfort, convenience, and the good life aren't gifts to be appreciated but rights to be expected. And when expectations go unmet, we feel resentment rather than perspective.

Entitlement isn't usually malicious. It's what happens when good things are consistently present long enough that the brain stops registering them as good and starts registering them as expected. Expected things don't generate gratitude. They generate resentment when they're absent and indifference when they're present. Appreciation is the deliberate reversal of that process.

Why It Works

Psychologist Timothy Wilson and colleagues developed a practice called mental subtraction as a way of counteracting this drift and restoring genuine appreciation for what familiarity has made invisible. Rather than simply trying to feel grateful for something present in your life, you briefly and vividly imagine your life without it. Not as a dwelling exercise. Not as a source of anxiety. Just a genuine unhurried pause to inhabit the absence and then return to the reality that the thing is still there.

Research consistently shows that mental subtraction produces stronger and more genuine appreciation than directly trying to feel grateful for the same thing. The reason is neurological: the brain responds more powerfully to contrast than to steady-state presence. We feel the value of things most acutely at their edges, when they arrive or when they disappear. Mental subtraction artificially creates that edge, producing a felt sense of value that simple reflection rarely achieves.

Choose someone you love. A place that matters to you. Something ordinary you've stopped noticing. Ask honestly: *what would my life look like without this?* Sit with that absence for thirty seconds. Then return to the reality that it hasn't happened. That return is where appreciation lives.

Try This Today

- Choose one person, place, or ordinary comfort and briefly imagine your life without it. Then return to the reality that it's still there and notice what shifts.
- The next time you feel frustrated that something isn't meeting your expectations, ask: *would I miss this if it were gone?*
- Revisit your Top 5 lists from the previous entry and apply mental subtraction to one item from each category. Four minutes. Four genuine shifts in appreciation.
- When a commercial tells you that you deserve more, pause and ask whether what you already have is going unappreciated.

What If You Already Feel Grateful?

Then this practice will deepen what's already there. Mental subtraction doesn't manufacture gratitude artificially. It reveals what was always waiting for enough attention to become fully visible.

Bottom Line

Entitlement is what happens when good things stay long enough to become expected. Appreciation is what happens when you pause long enough to notice what you'd lose. Most of us have far more than we remember on an ordinary Thursday.

56. Keep a Gratitude Journal

A gratitude journal is where appreciation goes deep.

What It Is

This entry is different from the three good things practice earlier in this chapter. That one is about frequency, a brief daily habit that recalibrates your attentional default over time. This one is about depth, taking more time, less often, to write about gratitude with the kind of reflective detail that produces insight rather than just positive emotion. Think of them as different instruments playing the same note. The daily practice keeps your attention tuned. The journal goes deeper into what the tuning reveals.

Set aside a dedicated notebook specifically for gratitude, separate from a general diary or planner, and write in it with enough depth and regularity that it becomes a genuine practice rather than an occasional gesture. Not a checklist. Not three quick words before bed. A real engagement with what is good in your life, written with enough specificity that the writing itself deepens the appreciation rather than simply recording it.

Why It Works

Robert Emmons and Michael McCullough's foundational research on gratitude journaling found that people who wrote weekly about things they were grateful for reported higher positive affect, greater life satisfaction, more optimism, fewer physical complaints, better sleep, and more exercise. The effects were robust and appeared relatively quickly.

But subsequent research added a crucial nuance most people miss. Sonja Lyubomirsky and colleagues found that people who journaled about gratitude once per week showed greater well-being gains than those who did it three times per week. Depth and genuine engagement matter more than volume. Too frequent writing can make the practice mechanical and strip it of emotional potency.

When you write at length about why something or someone matters, tracing the specific ways a person has influenced you or articulating what you would lose if something were taken away, you engage the brain's meaning-making systems in a way that brief notation simply doesn't. There's also a compounding effect unique to journaling: the ability to read back. A gratitude journal kept over months becomes a document of what your life has actually contained. Reading it during hard seasons produces a quality of perspective that no single entry can generate alone.

Try This Today

- Choose a dedicated notebook kept specifically for this purpose.
- Write once or twice a week rather than daily. Regularity matters more than frequency.
- Write about fewer things with more depth. One person described specifically and at length is more powerful than ten items named and moved past.
- Include the why alongside the what. "I'm grateful for my sister because last Tuesday she called without a reason and said exactly what I needed to hear" produces far more benefit than "I'm grateful for my sister."

What If It Has Felt Hollow Before?

It's almost always a depth problem rather than a practice problem. Slow down, write less, and go deeper. Try writing about just one thing per session and don't stop until you've said everything true and specific about why it matters.

Bottom Line

A gratitude journal is not a record of pleasant things. It's a document of what your life has actually contained. Write slowly, write honestly, and let the pages remind you of what ordinary days bring that may be easy to forget.

57. Say "I Get To" Instead of "I Have To"

Change the words and watch the story change with them.

What It Is

This one is a simple little tweak, but don't let the simplicity fool you. When you catch yourself saying, out loud or internally, "I have to," pause and replace it with "I get to."

Not every time. Not as a forced performance of positivity. Just as a genuine experiment in perspective. *I have to take the kids to practice* becomes *I get to take the kids to practice. I have to go to work* becomes *I get to go to work. I have to make dinner again* becomes *I get to make dinner for people I love.* The words are small. The shift they produce is not.

"I have to" frames your life as a series of obligations imposed on you. "I get to" frames the same life as a series of privileges available to you, many of which would be desperately missed if they disappeared. The circumstances don't change. The orientation toward them does. And that orientation, practiced consistently, changes how your life actually feels to live.

Why It Works

Language doesn't just describe how we think. It shapes how we think. Research in cognitive linguistics and positive psychology consistently shows that the words we use to frame our experience influence our emotional response to it, often before we're consciously aware of any shift happening.

The "I have to" framing activates psychological reactance, the brain's resistance to perceived obligation and loss of autonomy. That framing costs you something emotionally before the activity even begins. "I get to" activates a different system entirely, framing the same activity as an opportunity, which in most cases is exactly what it is. Going to work is an opportunity if you consider the alternative. Taking your children somewhere is an opportunity if you consider how quickly that season passes.

Research by Sonja Lyubomirsky on positive reappraisal shows that this kind of linguistic shift produces genuine changes in emotional state, not just surface-level positivity. The brain responds to the reframe as real information. Over time repeated positive reappraisal rewires attentional habits, making the more appreciative orientation increasingly automatic rather than effortful. Many of the things we frame as obligations are things we get to do because we are alive, healthy, and present, because people we love are still here. "I have to" ignores that context entirely. "I get to" briefly restores it.

Try This Today

- For the next 24 hours, notice how often "I have to" appears in your internal monologue.
- Each time you catch it, try the substitution: "I get to."
- Pay particular attention to the "have tos" involving people, children, partners, aging parents, friends who need you. These are almost always "get tos" in disguise.
- At the end of the day, write down one "have to" that became something different when you reframed it.

What If the Reframe Feels Dishonest?

Sometimes it will, and that's worth respecting. Not everything is secretly a privilege. Start with the easy ones where the reframe is obviously true and let the practice build from there.

Bottom Line

"I have to" is a story about obligation. "I get to" is a story about privilege. Most days you're living far more of the second story than the first one your brain defaults to telling.

58. Practice Gratitude During Hard Moments

Hold the difficulty and the appreciation at the same time and discover you are capable of containing both.

What It Is

Before anything else, let me be clear about what this hack is not. It's not a trick. It's not a cure. It's not asking you to paste a smile over genuine grief or pretend that hard things aren't hard. If you are right in the thick of loss, trauma, or crisis, this is not the moment for this practice. Survival, support, and stability come first.

This is for the difficult-but-not-devastating moments, the ordinary hard days, the frustrating seasons, the circumstances that are painful but not catastrophic. In those moments, when the dust hasn't settled but the world hasn't ended either, there is a practice worth trying: look for something, anything, that is still worth appreciating. Not to replace the pain. Not to perform positivity. Just to refuse to let the difficulty become the only thing visible. Because when pain becomes the only thing visible, it doesn't just hurt. It consumes.

Why It Works

Robert Emmons, the leading scientific researcher on gratitude, puts it plainly: *"We know from studies that gratitude helps us recover from loss and trauma. It helps us to deal with the slow drip of everyday stress, as well as the massive personal upheavals in the face of suffering and pain and loss and trials and tribulations. Gratitude is absolutely essential. It's part of our psychological immune system."* That phrase has stayed with me. Psychological immune system. Not a feel-good add-on. A protective mechanism your mind uses to stay functional when life gets genuinely hard.

Barbara Fredrickson's research on what she calls the undoing effect of positive emotions shows that gratitude doesn't simply coexist with negative emotion. It actively accelerates physiological and neurological recovery from stress. People who experience genuine positive emotion during or following a stressful experience return to baseline measurably faster, not because the stress was less real, but because the positive emotion interrupts its persistence.

Research on post-traumatic growth consistently identifies gratitude as one of the central mechanisms through which people navigate hardship well. They don't avoid negative emotion or manufacture false positivity. They maintain what psychologists call a dual process, holding genuine pain alongside genuine appreciation, refusing to let either cancel the other. Viktor Frankl observed this from inside the most extreme circumstances imaginable. Meaning and gratitude, he wrote, were available even there, not as denial of suffering but as something that could coexist with it and ultimately transcend it.

Try This Today

- Ask quietly: *what is still present that I would miss if it were also gone?* Let the answer be small. Small is enough.
- Identify one person walking through the difficulty with you and let yourself feel genuine appreciation for their presence.

- Notice one thing the hard moment hasn't touched, a capacity still available, a relationship still intact, an ordinary comfort still present.
- If the moment is too acute for active reflection, simply name what you're feeling without resistance and return to gratitude when the intensity lowers. The practice doesn't require perfect timing. It requires the intention to return.

What If It Feels Impossible?

Sometimes it genuinely is, and that deserves honest acknowledgment. Come back to this practice when you have enough ground under your feet to stand on it. My mom navigating her liver cancer diagnosis has taught me something about this. There are days when the difficulty is simply the difficulty and nothing softens it. And there are other days, more than you'd expect, when something worth appreciating is genuinely present alongside the hard thing, waiting to be noticed. She has learned to notice it. Not to minimize what's hard. Just to refuse to let what's hard be the only true thing. That refusal, practiced consistently, is one of the most courageous forms of gratitude available to a human being.

Bottom Line

Gratitude during hard moments doesn't make the hard moments easier. It makes you harder to break. And according to the research, that's exactly what it was designed to do.

6.

HAPPINESS IS
A TEAM SPORT

I've asked more than 1,300 people across the United States two simple questions: To me, life is all about... and If I died tomorrow, what I would miss the very most would be... The answers were striking in their consistency. Across age groups, backgrounds, and life circumstances, people overwhelmingly said that life is about relationships and happiness, and what they would miss most, by a significant margin, was family, their children, and their spouse. Work and money appeared in less than 2% of responses.

Robert Waldinger directs the Harvard Study of Adult Development, the longest running study of adult life ever conducted, now spanning nearly 90 years and three generations of participants. When asked what the study's most important finding was, his answer was unambiguous: the people who were most satisfied in their relationships at age fifty were the healthiest at age eighty. Not the wealthiest. Not the most accomplished. Not the ones with the best diets or the most rigorous exercise routines. The ones with the warmest, most connected relationships. Waldinger puts it plainly: good relationships keep us happier and healthier. Period.

Researcher Julianne Holt-Lunstad at Brigham Young University has produced some of the most compelling and sobering evidence on what happens when those relationships are absent. Her landmark meta-analysis, examining data from more than 300,000 people across 148 studies, found that people with strong social relationships had a 50% greater likelihood of survival over a given period compared to those with weak or insufficient social connections. A follow-up analysis examining data from 3.4 million people found that loneliness, social isolation, and living alone were associated with a 26%, 29%, and 32% increased risk of premature death respectively, comparable to the health risks of smoking up to fifteen cigarettes a day and exceeding the risks of obesity and physical inactivity.

Let that land for a moment. Loneliness is as dangerous to your health as smoking. And connection is as essential to your long-term survival as food and water.

We live in a world that makes it remarkably easy to be physically surrounded by people while remaining genuinely disconnected from them. Technology competes for our attention during the moments connection could happen. Busyness crowds out the small, consistent relational investments that actually sustain bonds over time. Many of us save our best presence for screens and give the people we love what's left.

John Gottman's decades of relationship research offer a corrective. Happy, lasting relationships are not built on grand romantic gestures or dramatic moments of reconnection. They are built on what he calls "small things often," the daily bids for connection honored, the repair attempts made, the moments of genuine attention and affection offered rather than withheld. Relationships, like gardens, don't thrive on occasional heroic effort. They thrive on consistent, ordinary care.

That's what this chapter is about. The eighteen practices that follow aren't about overhauling your social life or becoming someone you're not. They're about making small, deliberate investments in the connections that research consistently identifies as the strongest predictor of how happy you'll be, how long you'll live, and how well you'll live while you're here.

The team you build and tend is everything. And building it starts with the very next person in front of you.

59. See the Person in Front of You—Practice Full Presence

One of the greatest gifts you can give another person is no longer your time. It's your all-in attention.

What It Is

No sugarcoating here. I need to be better at this one. When I'm waiting in line somewhere, my default is to pull out my phone and scroll. It's automatic. But every time I do it, I'm missing an opportunity to actually be present, whether that's with the person I'm with, a stranger nearby, or even just my own thoughts.

When you are with another person, give them the one thing no amount of money or good intention can substitute for: your full attention. Not partial attention with one eye on your phone. Not the performance of listening while composing your response. Full, unhurried, all-in attention that communicates without a single word that this person matters and that right now, nothing else competes with them.

Time and attention are not the same thing. You can spend time with someone and never really give them your attention. But you cannot give your attention without spending time. Attention is the more demanding gift, and in our distracted world, it has become the more meaningful one.

Why It Works

John Gottman's research on what distinguishes thriving relationships from deteriorating ones returns again and again to a single variable: responsiveness. Not grand gestures. Not conflict resolution skills. The degree to which people feel genuinely seen, heard, and responded to in everyday interactions. When someone feels truly seen, oxytocin releases, stress hormones lower, and the nervous system registers safety.

The absence of full presence does more damage than most people realize. Research by Sherry Turkle at MIT found that even the visible presence of a phone on a table, not in use, simply present, reduces the quality of conversation and the depth of connection felt. We don't have to be actively distracted to communicate distraction. The signal is ambient.

In my own research on technoference, the way technology interferes with face-to-face connection, 88% of participants agreed it is a significant problem in society and 62% acknowledged it as a problem in their own family. Relationships don't fail dramatically in most cases. They fade quietly, one half-present conversation at a time, one glance at a screen at a time.

Lack of attention leads to loss of connection.

Try This Today

- Put your phone in another room or face-down out of reach during your next meaningful conversation. Not silenced. Absent.
- The next time someone begins talking to you, stop what you're doing completely before responding.
- Make genuine eye contact during your next conversation, the kind that communicates: *I see you and I'm here.*
- The next time you're waiting in line, put the phone away and look up instead.

What If Your Mind Keeps Wandering?

It will. When you notice it has drifted, simply return without self-judgment, the same way you return attention to the breath during mindfulness practice. The return itself is the skill.

Bottom Line

Put the phone down. Turn toward them completely. See the person in front of you. That act alone, repeated in ordinary moments, can change everything between you.

60. Reach Out Before You Feel Motivated

The feeling follows the action. Don't wait for it to arrive first.

What It Is

I have a friend I met when I taught at the University of Missouri that I haven't talked to in way too long. I think about him occasionally, genuinely mean to reach out, and then the moment passes and another week goes by. Sound familiar? The gap grows, the bar gets higher, and a relationship that mattered quietly fades because neither person wanted to make the first move.

This hack is about reversing that sequence. Contact someone you care about before you feel like it, before the timing is perfect, before you have something significant to say. A text. A call. A voice message with no agenda. A note that says simply: *I've been thinking about you.* The motivation to reach out rarely arrives on its own. Waiting for it is one of the most reliable ways to let relationships that matter slowly disappear.

Reach out first. Let the connection follow.

Why It Works

Research by Peggy Liu and colleagues on what they call the undervalued connection effect found that people significantly underestimate the positive impact of a simple unexpected reach-out on the recipient. The anticipated awkwardness of contacting someone after a gap almost always exceeds the actual awkwardness experienced. We talk ourselves out of reaching out because we assume it won't matter as much as it does. It almost always matters more.

There's also a behavioral activation principle at work. Motivation in most areas of life follows action rather than preceding it. We don't feel like exercising and then exercise. We exercise and then feel better for having done it. The same pattern holds for social connection. The feeling follows the behavior. Waiting for it to arrive first inverts the sequence in a way that rarely works.

Try This Today

Try this right now, before you continue reading. Pause, quiet the noise for just a moment, and ask yourself: *who needs me today? Who might benefit from a text, a call, or a visit?* Notice what happens. A name appears. A face surfaces. That's the nudge. Follow it. Don't overthink it or wait for a better moment. The nudge itself is the information.

Send something genuine before the day ends. It doesn't need to be long or profound. I've been thinking about you is enough. I just wanted you to know I'm glad you're in my life is more than enough.

What If It's Been So Long It Feels Awkward?

That awkwardness is almost entirely self-generated. A message that acknowledges the gap directly, I know it's been too long and I've been thinking about you, is almost universally received with warmth rather than judgment. The awkwardness lasts about as long as it takes to press send.

Bottom Line

Somewhere in your life right now is a person who needs to hear from you. Part of you already knows who it is. Notice the nudges. Follow the feelings. The relationship is worth more than your hesitation.

61. Ask One Meaningful Question

Ask it. Then listen like the answer matters. Because it does.

What It Is

A while back I was sitting with some youth from our church eating pizza before an activity. Instead of asking how school was going or what was new, I asked them to tell me about their biggest fear. Then I asked about their plans for spring break. The conversation that followed was completely different from anything small talk would have produced. People lit up. They got real. They asked each other follow-up questions. All it took was one question that went a little deeper than the surface.

In your next conversation, ask one question that signals genuine curiosity. Something the other person might not have been asked recently. Something that opens rather than closes. What's something you've been thinking about lately that you haven't had a chance to talk about? What's been harder than you expected recently? What are you looking forward to most right now? What's one thing you wish more people understood about you?

One question, asked with genuine curiosity, followed by the silence that allows a real answer to arrive. That's it. And it can do more for a relationship than an hour of comfortable but shallow conversation.

Why It Works

Most people move through their days feeling more unknown than they appear. They interact with dozens of people, exchange hundreds of words, and arrive at the end of the day having been truly seen by almost none of them. Not because people don't care, but because ordinary conversation rarely creates space for anything beneath the surface to emerge.

Arthur Aron's research on interpersonal closeness, including his famous 36 questions study in which strangers asked each other increasingly personal questions and reported significantly increased feelings of closeness afterward, demonstrates that depth of conversation more than its duration or frequency is what generates genuine felt connection. Two people can talk for years at a surface level and feel less close than two people who have one honest, searching exchange. Depth is the active ingredient. Meaningful questions are how you create the conditions for it.

Research by Nicholas Epley shows that people consistently underestimate how much they and their conversation partners will enjoy going beyond small talk and consistently overestimate how awkward it will feel. Most people, when genuinely invited to go deeper, respond with more openness than either party expected.

Try This Today

- Prepare one question you're genuinely curious about before your next meaningful conversation.
- Ask it and then stop talking. Give the silence space to work.
- Listen to the full answer before responding, not to reply but to understand.
- Follow the thread of what they share rather than steering back to safer ground.

What If It Feels Intrusive?

Questions asked from obvious genuine curiosity are rarely experienced as intrusive. Start with questions about hopes and experiences rather than difficulties or vulnerabilities and build from there.

Bottom Line

Most people move through their days feeling more unknown than they look. One genuine question, asked with curiosity and received with full attention, can change that.

62. Practice Compassionate Listening

Listen not just with your ears but with your full attention and your heart.

What It Is

I got a text late one night from a friend who was going through a divorce and needed to talk. I threw on some clothes, he picked me up in his truck, and we drove around for more than an hour. He did most of the talking and crying. I mostly just listened, and if I'm being honest, shed a few tears myself. I didn't fix anything. I didn't have answers. But I think he felt heard, and sometimes that's everything.

Compassionate listening means when someone you care about is really talking, you lock in and listen with your whole self. Not to fix. Not to advise. Not to relate their experience back to something that happened to you. Not to rehearse your response while they're still speaking. Just to understand. To be genuinely present with what they're carrying. To communicate without a word: I hear you. What you're feeling matters to me.

This is meaningfully different from what most of us do when we think we're listening well.

Why It Works

Psychologist Carl Rogers, whose person-centered approach transformed modern therapy, identified empathic understanding as one of the most powerful forces in human healing and connection. Being truly heard at a deep level, he argued, is one of the rarest and most nourishing experiences available to a human being. Most people go through life never quite feeling fully understood by another person. Compassionate listening is the practice of offering that experience in the ordinary moments of ordinary relationships.

Research by James Pennebaker on emotional disclosure shows that expressing difficult emotions to someone who listens without judgment produces measurable improvements in psychological and physical health, reduced stress hormones, improved immune function, and lower rates of depression and anxiety. The benefits come not just from the expression itself but from the felt experience of being received without judgment. It's not enough that someone hears. It matters enormously how they hear.

When someone feels genuinely heard, their nervous system responds. Threat activation decreases. Cortisol lowers. The brain registers interpersonal safety, and from that place of safety, real conversation becomes possible in a way it simply isn't when someone feels dismissed or merely tolerated.

Try This Today

- Before responding, ask yourself: *do I understand what they're actually feeling right now?* If the honest answer is no, ask rather than assume.
- Resist the urge to fix or advise, at least until they feel fully heard. Try asking: do you need me to listen, or are you looking for input?
- Respond first to the emotion rather than the content. *That*

sounds really hard lands differently than immediately offering a solution.

- Let your body communicate presence: turned toward them, genuine eye contact, genuinely still.

What If You're Also Upset?

Name it honestly: I want to hear you and I'm not in a place to do that well right now. Can we come back to this in a few minutes? That's not avoidance. That's the self-awareness that makes genuine listening possible when you return.

Bottom Line

Most people don't need you to fix what they're feeling. They need to feel that what they're feeling matters to someone. That kind of compassionate listening doesn't just strengthen relationships. It heals them.

63. Respond to Bids for Connection

Every time someone reaches toward you, they're asking a quiet question: am I worth your attention?

What It Is

This is one of my favorite concepts to teach because once you see it, you can't unsee it, and it changes how you show up in every relationship you have. A "bid for connection," as researcher John Gottman defines it, is any attempt, however subtle, to attract your attention, interest, humor, affection, or support. Bids are rarely dramatic or explicit. Your partner mentions something they read and glances up from their phone. Your child tugs your sleeve and points at something outside the window. Your teenager makes an offhand comment about school. Your spouse sighs quietly while doing the dishes. A friend sends a funny meme with no caption. Every one of these is a bid. A small, tentative reach toward connection.

In each of these moments you have three options. You can turn toward the bid, acknowledging it and giving it your attention. You can turn away, missing it or staying in your own world. Or you can turn against it, responding with irritation or dismissal that makes the other person regret having reached out at all. The choice you make in these small moments, repeated hundreds of times over the course of a relationship, determines more about its quality than almost anything else.

Why It Works

Gottman's research in what he called the Love Lab produced one of the most practically important findings in all of relationship science. Couples who stayed together and reported high relationship satisfaction turned toward each other's bids approximately 86% of the time. Couples who eventually divorced turned toward bids only about 33% of the time. The difference wasn't in how passionately they felt about each other or how well they communicated during conflict. It was in how consistently they responded to the small, ordinary, daily bids that most people barely notice.

A bid is never really just about the thing being pointed at. It's a deeper question: are you there? Do I matter to you? Is this relationship a safe place to reach out? When bids are consistently met, the nervous system registers yes, and that yes, accumulated over time, builds the emotional safety that allows relationships to deepen and survive difficulty. When bids are consistently missed, people eventually stop reaching out. Gottman calls this flooding and withdrawal, the gradual disengagement that precedes the emotional distance most couples describe as what ended the relationship long before any formal ending occurred.

Try This Today

- Notice the small moments today when someone reaches toward you and consciously choose to turn toward them rather than past them.
- Watch for your children's bids specifically. They are often the most frequent and most easily missed, particularly as kids get older and the bids become less obvious.
- Put the phone down and say *tell me more.*
- At the end of today, ask honestly: *whose bid did I miss?* Not with self-criticism, but with the intention to do better tomorrow.

What If You've Been Missing Bids for a Long Time?

It's more common than most people want to admit. Simply increasing your awareness is the starting point. Most bid-missing isn't intentional. It's distraction. Naming the pattern honestly, even to the person whose bids you've been missing, is itself a "turning toward."

Bottom Line

Relationships are built in the small moments, not the big ones. Turn toward the people who are reaching toward you when possible. Answer yes.

64. Express Affection Daily

Love felt but not expressed is love only half given.

What It Is

I have a lot of favorites in this chapter, but this one is right up there. The power of a genuine hug, a slow I love you, a hand held for no reason, is backed by serious science and yet it's one of the first things that quietly fades in long-term relationships without either person quite noticing it happening. Express affection to the people closest to you every single day. Not just on birthdays or anniversaries. Not only when the relationship is feeling particularly warm. Every day, including the ordinary ones, including the hard ones, including the days when connection feels like one more thing on a list that's already too long.

A hug that lasts longer than three seconds. A text in the middle of the day that says nothing except thinking of you. Eye contact across a room that communicates warmth without words. A kiss hello and goodbye that doesn't get skipped because you're in a hurry. I love you said slowly enough that it lands rather than passing as routine. None of these are complicated. All of them, offered consistently, build something in a relationship that grand gestures alone never quite can.

Why It Works

Touch is one of the most fundamental human needs and one of the most underestimated tools for well-being in adult relationships. Research by Tiffany Field at the Touch Research Institute has consistently shown that physical affection triggers the release of oxytocin, reduces cortisol, lowers blood pressure, and strengthens immune function. These aren't subtle effects. Regular physical affection produces measurable improvements in both psychological and physical health, and the absence of it produces measurable deterioration over time.

Here's a specific finding worth knowing: research by Karen Grewen and colleagues shows that a warm embrace lasting twenty seconds or longer produces a significant oxytocin surge and a meaningful reduction in cardiovascular stress. Not a fake or forced three-second pat. A real hug, long enough to actually register in the nervous system as connection rather than greeting.

Gottman's research on the emotional bank account shows that daily expressions of affection make consistent deposits into the relational reserve that relationships draw on during conflict and difficulty. Couples who express affection regularly navigate hard conversations more effectively and maintain deeper friendship over time. Daily affection isn't separate from relationship resilience. It's one of its primary sources.

In long-term relationships, affection is among the first things to dwindle under the pressure of familiarity and busyness. It doesn't disappear dramatically. It fades gradually, one skipped kiss and one rushed goodbye at a time, until the relationship is running primarily on logistics rather than warmth. Daily affection is the direct antidote to that drift.

Try This Today

- Hug someone you love for at least twenty seconds. A real hug. Let it actually land.
- Say *I love you* slowly and deliberately, with eye contact, to someone who needs to hear it.
- Send an unprompted text to someone close to you expressing affection with no other agenda.
- Make physical contact at least once in each significant interaction today, a hand on a shoulder, a squeeze of the arm, a brief touch in passing.

What If Affection Doesn't Come Naturally?

Start with what feels most accessible. A text before a hug. A brief touch before a long embrace. The benefits begin accruing immediately, and the people on the receiving end will feel the difference long before the practice feels entirely natural to you.

Bottom Line

The people closest to you deserve to feel your affection not just on significant occasions but in the ordinary moments of ordinary days. Express it daily. Not because the relationship demands it. Because it deserves it.

65. Repair Quickly After Conflict

Move toward the person, not away from them—and do it soon.

What It Is

I remember relationships in high school where conflict was followed by the dreaded silent treatment. Both people waiting for the other to crack first, the tension hardening by the hour. It felt like a power move at the time. Turns out, in committed relationships, it's poison. When tension or conflict disrupts a relationship, move toward repair as soon as you're able. Not necessarily in the middle of the argument, and not before both people are calm enough to be genuinely present. But soon, before the silence hardens, before resentment takes root, before the distance that follows conflict becomes more familiar than the closeness that preceded it.

Repair doesn't require a formal apology or complete resolution. It requires a signal, a small genuine move that communicates: the relationship matters more to me than winning this. A quiet I don't like how that felt between us. A hand extended. An acknowledgment of your part, however small. A simple can we start over? John Gottman calls these repair attempts, and his research identifies them as one of the most powerful predictors of whether relationships thrive or gradually deteriorate over time.

Why It Works

Conflict itself is not what damages relationships. Every relationship experiences difficult differences. What determines whether conflict strengthens or erodes a relationship is what happens in its aftermath. When conflict goes unrepaired, the nervous system stays activated. Cortisol remains elevated. Both people carry the residue of the argument into subsequent interactions, a heightened sensitivity and slightly shorter fuse than before. Over time, unrepaired conflicts accumulate into what Gottman calls "negative sentiment override," a state in which partners begin interpreting even neutral behaviors through a lens of accumulated grievance. Relationships that feel unsafe produce less and less of the vulnerability and warmth that make them worth having.

Gottman's research found that the single most important factor in predicting relationship stability wasn't conflict frequency or communication style. It was the willingness to make and accept repair attempts, including imperfect, awkward, incomplete ones. Couples who repaired consistently, even clumsily, maintained significantly stronger bonds over time than those who waited for perfect resolution or let silence substitute for reconnection.

Timing matters more than most people realize. A repair attempt made within hours of a conflict is received very differently than one made days later, because early repair catches both people before resentment has consolidated into a hardened story about what happened.

Unresolved conflict is also one of the most reliable drivers of rumination, the mental loop that can occupy significant emotional bandwidth for hours or days. Repair doesn't just restore the relationship. It releases both people from the psychological weight of carrying it.

Try This Today

- Reach out with something simple: I've been thinking about what happened and I don't like the distance between us.
- Acknowledge your part in the conflict without waiting for the other person to go first.
- If words aren't ready yet, offer a physical signal, a hand on a shoulder, eye contact held a moment longer than usual.

What If the Other Person Isn't Ready?

Stay available. Even repair attempts that aren't immediately accepted shift the emotional tone. You cannot control the other person's readiness. You can control your willingness to keep reaching.

Bottom Line

Every relationship will experience conflict. Not every relationship will choose repair. The one you protect through consistent repair will still be there, deepened rather than diminished, on the other side of every hard season.

66. Spend Time With People Who Energize You

Spend more time with the people who leave you more alive than they found you.

What It Is

Pay attention to how you feel after spending time with the people in your life. Not every relationship produces the same effect. Some people leave you feeling lighter, more alive, more like yourself. One of my favorite people on this planet who energizes me is a great mentor, friend, and former colleague, Dr. Wally Goddard. Every few months we'll meet up for lunch (it usually includes lots of chips and salsa) and share what we've been up to. The time flies as we share ideas, insights, and inklings. We always leave with a warm hug but also feeling completely alive and energized. However, other people, through no fault of character on either side, consistently leave you feeling drained or vaguely worse than before you arrived.

This isn't a judgment about who is a good person and who isn't. It's an honest observation about relational chemistry and the fact that your social energy is a finite resource. The people who energize you are the ones who laugh with you, ask genuine questions and actually listen, challenge you in ways that expand rather than diminish, and leave you feeling more glad to be alive than before you sat down with them. Those people deserve more of your time than they probably get.

Why It Works

Not all social interaction produces equal well-being benefits, and the research is clear about why. Barbara Fredrickson's work on positivity resonance shows that the quality of social interaction matters as much as its quantity. Time spent in warm, mutually engaged, genuinely connecting interaction produces oxytocin release and reduced stress reactivity. Time spent in draining or merely obligatory interaction produces elevated cortisol and reduced well-being, even when the interaction is technically social. Not all time with people counts equally. Who you spend it with matters enormously.

Research on capitalization shows that good things feel better in the company of people who can genuinely celebrate with you. Sharing a success or an ordinary good moment with someone who is truly engaged amplifies the positive emotion for both people. The same experience shared with someone who responds flatly or redirects to themselves produces significantly less positive affect, sometimes less than experiencing it alone.

There's also an identity dimension worth naming. Research on what psychologist Brooke Feeney calls the Michelangelo phenomenon shows that the people we spend the most time with gradually shape who we become. Relationships that energize tend to affirm and draw out the best version of who we are. Relationships that drain tend to pull us toward versions of ourselves we're not particularly proud of. The people you choose to invest in aren't just sources of support. They are, over time, co-authors of who you're becoming.

Try This Today

- After your next several social interactions, notice how you feel afterward, more energized or more depleted? Let the pattern inform your priorities.
- Identify one person who consistently leaves you feeling better and reach out to schedule more time with them.
- When you're with someone who energizes you, be fully present. Don't take it for granted just because it feels easy.

What If Most Relationships Feel Draining Right Now?

It can point in two directions: specific people who deplete you, or a personal season of exhaustion that makes all interaction feel like effort. If it's the latter, withdrawal rarely helps. Start small. One person. One interaction. Notice what happens.

Bottom Line

Your social energy is finite. Where you invest it shapes not just how you feel but who you're becoming. Those relationships are not a luxury. They are some of the most important investments you will ever make.

67. Create Recurring Connection Rituals

The ritual doesn't have to be elaborate. It has to be protected.

What It Is

My wife and I have built up small rituals over the years that I genuinely treasure. Three hand squeezes that mean I love you. Regular getaways without the kids. Date nights that aren't always perfect but always happen. None of these are complicated. But their consistency is the point, and that consistency has compounded into something that feels like the backbone of our relationship.

Establish regular, protected times with the people who matter most and treat them with the same commitment you give to everything else on your calendar that counts. Not vague intentions to get together more. Not plans that form and dissolve with busy schedules. Recurring, reliable, anticipated rituals built into the structure of your life with enough regularity that the people in them can count on them. A weekly family dinner with phones in another room. A standing walk with a friend. A nightly check-in with your kids. An annual trip everyone protects regardless of what else is happening.

The specific ritual matters far less than its consistency. What recurring rituals provide isn't any single experience. It's the accumulated, compounding effect of showing up for the same people in the same way, again and again, until the ritual itself becomes part of the relationship's identity.

Why It Works

Research by sociologist Randall Collins on interaction ritual chains shows that repeated, emotionally significant interactions between the same people build what he calls emotional energy, a genuine psychological resource generated by shared, repeated ritual. The more consistent the ritual is, the more emotional energy it produces, not just in the moment but as a sustained background resource that strengthens the relationship between instances of connection.

Gottman's research consistently identifies shared rituals and traditions as one of the primary ways fondness and admiration are built and maintained in long-term relationships. Couples and families with rich ritual lives navigate difficulty more effectively and report higher relationship satisfaction than those whose time together is purely spontaneous.

Recurring rituals are also powerful sources of anticipatory positive emotion. As covered in Chapter 4, having something to look forward to generates genuine well-being in the present moment. You know the date night is happening Friday. That knowledge produces a low steady background hum of positive expectation that enhances the days leading up to it.

For parents, research consistently shows that family rituals, regular shared meals, consistent bedtime routines, predictable traditions, are among the strongest predictors of children's sense of security and emotional well-being. The ritual communicates something children need to hear without words: you belong here, and you are worth showing up for consistently.

Try This Today

- Identify one relationship that deserves a recurring ritual and propose one specific protected time, same day, same general time, recurring by default.
- If you have kids, establish one daily connection ritual that belongs entirely to them.
- Start smaller than feels necessary. A monthly ritual that reliably happens beats a weekly one that keeps getting cancelled.

What If Schedules Make Consistency Feel Impossible?

Find the interval that's actually sustainable and protect that. When life requires a cancellation, reschedule immediately. The rescheduling is itself a signal that the ritual matters.

Bottom Line

The relationships that matter most deserve more than good intentions. They deserve a place on the calendar, protected and anticipated. Create the ritual. Show up for it. Watch what grows in the space you've decided to protect.

68. Participate Instead of Just Attending

Attending puts you in the room. Participating puts you in the experience.

What It Is

When I first came across research showing that nearly half the time we're engaged in an activity we're thinking about something other than what we're actually doing, I was shocked. And then I felt a little guilty. Because I recognized myself in it. There's a meaningful difference between being present in a room and being genuinely engaged in what's happening there. Between sitting at the table and contributing to the conversation. Between attending an event and actually participating in it. Most of us have experienced both versions. The party where you stood near the food and counted the minutes. The meeting where you were physically there but mentally elsewhere. You attended. But you didn't participate.

Participation looks different. It's the person who introduces themselves first, asks the question that opens a real conversation, volunteers when something is needed, and leaves having contributed something, a laugh, an idea, a moment of genuine connection, rather than simply having been there.

Why It Works

Sonja Lyubomirsky's research on behavioral engagement consistently shows that active participation produces significantly higher positive affect than passive presence in the same setting. Two people at the same event can have measurably different emotional experiences based almost entirely on how actively they engage in what's happening.

The mechanism connects to self-determination theory, developed by Edward Deci and Richard Ryan, which identifies autonomy, competence, and relatedness as the three core psychological needs whose satisfaction drives well-being.

Active participation satisfies all three simultaneously. When you contribute to a conversation or initiate a connection, you exercise agency, demonstrate capability, and create genuine relatedness, all in a single act.

Research on sociometer theory adds another layer. Human beings have an evolved sensitivity to whether they are genuinely part of what's happening or merely adjacent to it. Active participation registers as belonging. Passive attendance often registers as isolation even in a crowded room, which is why it's entirely possible to feel profoundly lonely at a party.

The shift from attending to participating doesn't require a personality transplant. It requires a decision, made before you walk in the door or in the first moments after you arrive, to bring yourself rather than simply bring your body.

Try This Today

- Make one decision in advance: I will initiate at least one genuine conversation rather than waiting for someone to approach me.
- Introduce yourself to one person you don't know and ask something you're genuinely curious about.
- When you feel the pull toward your phone or toward the edges of the room, notice it and choose engagement instead.

What If You're Introverted or Socially Anxious?

Participation doesn't require being the loudest person in the room. For introverts, genuine participation often looks quieter, one meaningful conversation in the corner rather than working the room. One real conversation is worth more than an hour of surface-level mingling. Participate in the way that's authentic to who you are. Just make sure you actually participate.

Bottom Line

Show up. And then actually show up. The happiness difference between those two things is not small, and the choice between them is almost always yours to make.

69. Contribute to a Group Weekly

What you give to the group comes back to you multiplied.

What It Is

Sadly, group membership and community participation have declined significantly over the last few decades, and the research on what that's costing us isn't pretty. Loneliness is up. Meaning is down. And a lot of people are trying to meet a fundamentally social need through fundamentally individual solutions.

My wife gets up early five mornings a week to go to the gym. Yes, the exercise matters, but what she talks about when she comes home isn't just the workout. It's the women. The conversations before and after class. The friendships built through the shared ritual of showing up together, consistently, over months and years. Some mornings she joins a group of neighbors who rotate through exercise stations in a friend's indoor gym, and the connection that happens between those women is something no solo workout could ever replicate. That's the point. The group offers something the individual version simply can't.

Find a group, any group, and show up for it regularly, contributing rather than just consuming what it offers. A fitness class, a faith community, a book club, a volunteer organization, a recovery meeting, a sports league. Notice that this entry says contribute, not belong. Belonging is a feeling. Contributing is a behavior. And the research is clear that the behavior is what produces the deepest sense of belonging over time.

Why It Works

Julianne Holt-Lunstad's research on social integration shows that people embedded in multiple social groups have significantly better health outcomes and greater longevity than those whose social lives are limited to one or two close relationships. Close relationships are irreplaceable but not sufficient on their own. Group membership adds something distinct, a sense of collective identity and shared purpose that close relationships alone don't fully provide.

Research by Nick Haslam and colleagues on the social cure shows that actively participating in groups produces benefits well beyond social contact alone. Group members show lower rates of depression and anxiety, faster recovery from illness, greater resilience under stress, and higher levels of meaning than comparable individuals without strong group ties. The group doesn't just feel good. It functions as a genuine health resource.

The contribution element is what makes this practice distinct from simply showing up. Research on prosocial behavior consistently shows that giving to a group, your effort, encouragement, time, and presence, produces greater positive affect and meaning than receiving from it. When you contribute, you become a co-creator. The group becomes partly yours in a way it never does for someone who merely attends.

Try This Today

- Show up this week even when you don't feel like it. Consistency is the foundation everything else is built on.
- Contribute something specific, help set up, encourage someone, stay afterward to connect rather than leaving immediately.
- If you don't belong to any regular group, identify one that aligns with something you value and commit to six consecutive weeks before deciding if it's a fit.

What If You Haven't Found the Right Group Yet?

The sense of belonging almost never precedes consistent participation. It follows it. Show up before you feel fully at home. The belonging grows from the contribution, not the other way around.

Bottom Line

We were not designed to do this alone. Find your group. Show up consistently. Give something of yourself. What you give comes back multiplied.

70. Spend Time With Pets

Give them your time and attention. What comes back is worth far more than what you give.

What It Is

I miss our little Yorky, Max. We were lucky to have him for nine amazing years. I remember rubbing his belly and watching him get so happy and realizing that it made me genuinely happy too. At the time I didn't fully understand why. Turns out there's a lot of research behind that moment on the floor with a small dog who just wanted to be loved.

If you have a pet, give them your genuine attention and receive what they offer in return. Not the distracted, one-hand-on-the-phone kind of presence. Real time. A long walk where your phone stays in your pocket. Twenty minutes on the floor just playing and being together. A quiet evening with a cat in your lap, your attention nowhere else.

Pets love without agenda. They're glad to see you on your worst days as reliably as your best. They don't require you to explain yourself or perform wellness. They simply show up, and in doing so, they invite you to do the same.

Why It Works

The research on human-animal interaction has grown substantially over the past two decades and the findings are broader and deeper than most people expect. The most well-documented mechanism involves oxytocin. Research by Miho Nagasawa and colleagues published in Science found that mutual gazing between dogs and their owners triggers a significant oxytocin release in both human and dog, activating the same neurobiological bonding system involved in parent-infant attachment. This isn't metaphor. The bond between a person and their pet engages genuine attachment biology, the same chemistry that underlies our deepest human connections.

Beyond the neurochemistry, research consistently shows that time with pets reduces cortisol, lowers blood pressure, and decreases cardiovascular stress reactivity. A study by Karen Allen and colleagues found that pet owners showed significantly lower stress responses during challenging tasks than non-pet owners, and that the presence of a pet produced greater stress reduction than the presence of a close friend or spouse. The non-judgmental, unconditional quality of animal companionship creates a uniquely safe emotional environment that even beloved human relationships don't always replicate.

There's also a mindfulness dimension worth naming. Animals live entirely in the present moment, and spending genuine time with them pulls us there too. A dog on a walk doesn't ruminate about yesterday or worry about tomorrow. Time with animals is one of the most effortless invitations to present-moment attention available, and present-moment attention, as Chapter 3 established, is one of the most reliable contributors to happiness we know of.

Try This Today

- Take your dog on a walk where your phone stays in your pocket and your attention stays on the walk.

- Spend 15-20 minutes on the floor with your pet, playing or simply being together without another agenda.
- The next time your pet seeks you out, stop what you're doing and give them a genuine few minutes rather than a distracted acknowledgment.

What If You Don't Have a Pet?

Consider whether your life has room for one. If not, look for opportunities through friends, family, or local shelter volunteer programs. Even brief positive interactions with animals have been shown to reduce stress and increase positive affect.

Bottom Line

Pets offer something rare: unconditional presence, uncomplicated affection, and a daily invitation to be loved exactly as you are. The research confirms what pet owners have always known. Give them your time. What comes back is worth far more than what you give.

71. Reduce Technoference — Kick Technology Off Tables and Out of Beds

Two simple commitments. Profound and lasting returns.

What It Is

A few years ago I was deep in my own research on technology and relationships, and two simple ideas kept emerging from the data as the most practical and impactful things people could do immediately. I started sharing them in workshops and they stuck. K-TOOT and K-TOOB.

K-TOOT: Kick Technology Off Of Tables. When you sit down to eat with another person, the phone goes away. Not face-down beside the plate. Away. The table becomes a technology-free zone where the only things competing for your attention are the food and the person across from you.

K-TOOB: Kick Technology Out Of Beds. When you go to bed with a partner, the phone stays out of the bed. Not on the nightstand. Out of the space that should belong to the two of you, to conversation, to intimacy, to the kind of unhurried closeness that screens reliably crowd out.

Technoference, a term my colleague and friend Dr. Brandon McDaniel developed to describe the way technology interferes with face-to-face interaction, is one of the most quietly destructive forces in modern relationships. Not because technology is inherently bad, but because it competes for the exact moments when connection could happen and wins those competitions far more often than most people realize.

Why It Works

In my own research on more than 600 parents across the United States, 88% agreed that technoference is a significant problem in society and 62% acknowledged it as a problem in their own family. Nearly half considered it a significant problem in their marriage. More than one-third reported using technology in bed every night or almost every night, and nearly 25% said their partner's phone use in bed interfered with their sexual relationship.

Sherry Turkle's research at MIT found that even the visible presence of a phone on a table, not in use, simply there, reduces the quality of conversation, the depth of topics discussed, the empathy generated, and the sense of genuine connection felt by both participants. The device doesn't have to be active to divide attention. Its mere presence signals that something else might matter more than the person across from you.

Family meals eaten together without technology are associated with stronger family cohesion, better mental health outcomes in children, and higher relationship satisfaction in couples. The dinner table isn't just where food gets eaten. It's one of the primary places where families build and maintain the emotional connection that sustains them through difficulty.

Research on couple intimacy consistently identifies undistracted time together before sleep as one of the strongest predictors of relationship satisfaction. Technology in the bedroom doesn't just reduce sleep quality. It crowds out the specific closeness that the end of the day uniquely offers.

Try This Today

- Tonight, eat one meal with someone you care about with all phones put away before anyone sits down.
- Tonight, charge your phone outside the bedroom rather than on the nightstand. Notice what happens to the time before sleep.
- If you have children, make K-TOOT a consistent family practice.

What If Your Partner or Family Resists?

Start with yourself. Put your own phone away at the table. Charge your own phone outside the bedroom. Most partners and family members, given enough time to feel the difference in connection quality, will follow without being asked.

Bottom Line

The table and the bed are two of the most important relational spaces in your daily life. Technology doesn't belong at either one. K-TOOT. K-TOOB. Two simple commitments. Profound and lasting returns.

72. Schedule Face-to-Face Connection

Texts sustain relationships. In-person connection nourishes them.

What It Is

We tend to assume connection will happen naturally, but modern life rarely makes space for it. Without intention, even our best relationships drift into distance. We have to be intentional and jot it down in our calendars. Not "we should get together soon." Not the standing intention that never quite becomes a plan. Not the relationship that survives entirely on texts because actually being in the same room keeps getting pushed to when things slow down, which they never quite do.

A specific date. A specific time. A specific person. On the calendar. Protected. Lunch with a friend on the third Thursday of every month. A quarterly overnight trip with people you love. A coffee with a colleague you've been meaning to reconnect with, scheduled right now rather than someday. A visit to someone who lives alone and would be changed by an hour of your physical presence.

The research on what in-person connection does that digital communication cannot replicate makes a compelling case for treating face-to-face time not as a luxury to be enjoyed when schedules align, but as a non-negotiable investment in the relationships everything else in your life depends on.

Why It Works

Not all forms of connection are created equal, and the gap between in-person interaction and digital communication is larger than most people want to believe. Research by John Cacioppo, one of the foremost scholars on loneliness and social connection, found that the quality of social interaction, specifically its in-person embodied dimension, matters as much as its frequency in predicting well-being outcomes. Face-to-face connection engages the full range of social neuroscience that human beings evolved to need: reading facial expressions, regulating nervous systems through proximity, and the subtle attunement that happens between bodies in the same room in ways no screen can replicate.

Susan Pinker's research on what she calls the village effect documents the specific, irreplaceable health and longevity benefits of in-person social contact. Her analysis of the longest-lived communities in the world found that face-to-face contact was one of the strongest predictors of longevity, more predictive than diet, exercise, or many medical interventions. The villages that kept people alive longest weren't the ones with the best healthcare. They were the ones where people showed up in each other's physical lives consistently.

The scheduling element is essential, not incidental. Research on implementation intentions by psychologist Peter Gollwitzer shows that intentions paired with specific plans, who, when, where, are significantly more likely to be acted on than general intentions without those specifics. "I'll see them soon" fails the test. "Tuesday at 12:30 at the cafй" passes it. Specificity converts intention into behavior.

Try This Today

- Right now, text or call one person you've been meaning to see and propose a specific time within the next two weeks. Not "we should get together," a specific day, time, and place.
- Look at your calendar for the next month. If in-person connection is sparse, treat that as a problem worth solving today.
- Identify one person who is likely lonely or isolated and put a visit on your calendar this week. Not a text. A visit.

What If Distance Makes It Difficult?

Be honest about the difference between relationships where geography genuinely prevents regular in-person time and relationships where proximity exists but scheduling never quite happens. For the latter, the calendar is the solution.

Bottom Line

Schedule the time. Protect it when it's there. The people worth being with are worth showing up for, in person, on purpose, and with enough regularity that they know they can count on it.

73. Help Someone in Your Immediate Community

Making time to make a difference can make all the difference. You just need to look up.

What It Is

I've helped several families in our neighborhood move in or move out over the years. And I've never regretted a minute of it. There's something about showing up with your back and your time for someone who needs it that does something good for both of you. Shovel a neighbor's driveway before they wake up. Bring a meal to a family navigating something hard. Show up for a friend's moving day. Notice who on your street is struggling and do one concrete thing about it. Community at its most functional is not just a place you live. It is a web of mutual care built strand by strand through acts of contribution that accumulate into something neither person could create alone. Most of us just need to look up long enough to notice where we're needed.

Why It Works

Robert Putnam's landmark research on social capital shows that the strength of community bonds is one of the most powerful predictors of individual well-being. People embedded in strong, reciprocally supportive communities show better physical health, greater psychological resilience, and higher life satisfaction than those who live near others without genuine community connection.

Elizabeth Dunn and Michael Norton's research consistently shows that prosocial behavior produces greater happiness returns than comparable investment in personal pleasure. The helper's high is real, neurologically documented, and reliably produced by genuine acts of contribution regardless of their scale.

What distinguishes community helping from other forms of kindness is the relational continuity it builds. Research by Nicholas Christakis and James Fowler shows that one act of genuine help tends to generate reciprocal and pay-it-forward behavior that ripples well beyond the original exchange. Your decision to help a neighbor doesn't just benefit them. It gradually changes the social texture of the community both of you live in.

Research on place identity shows that actively contributing to a community strengthens felt belonging in ways that simply living there never does. When you help someone on your street, that street becomes more yours.

Try This Today

- Think of one neighbor going through something difficult and do one concrete thing for them before the week ends.
- Introduce yourself to a neighbor you've never spoken to and ask one genuine question about how they're doing.
- Pay attention this week to small needs that surface in your immediate circle and say yes to one you would normally let pass.

What If You Don't Feel Connected to Your Community?

Then this is exactly where to start. Connection follows contribution, not the other way around. Help first. The belonging grows from the helping.

Bottom Line

Community is not something that happens to you. It's something you build, one act of genuine contribution at a time. Look around. Notice who needs something. Show up for them. The web of mutual care you help weave becomes the safety net that holds you too.

74. Practice Forgiveness

Forgiveness is not a gift you give to the person who hurt you. It is the freedom you give to yourself.

What It Is

Earlier in this chapter we talked about repairing quickly after conflict, the small, timely repair attempts that keep relationships healthy and close. This entry is different. This is about the deeper, harder work of forgiving wounds that didn't get repaired, hurts that were never acknowledged, and grievances that have been carried long past the moment they were created.

Forgiveness is one of the most misunderstood practices in human experience. It's not condoning what happened. It's not pretending the harm wasn't real. It's not reconciliation. You can forgive someone completely without ever resuming a relationship with them. And it's not something you do because the other person deserves it. Forgiveness is something you do because you deserve it.

There is a saying that captures this with unusual precision: holding onto bitterness and resentment is like drinking poison and expecting the other person to die. The person who hurt you may be entirely unbothered while you carry the weight of what happened, replaying it, rehearsing responses, investing emotional energy in grievances that cost you daily while costing them nothing. Forgiveness ends that arrangement. It is, perhaps more than any other practice in this book, an act of self-liberation.

Why It Works

The research on forgiveness and well-being is among the most robust in all of positive psychology. Psychologist Everett Worthington defines forgiveness as replacing unforgiving emotions, resentment, bitterness, hostility, with positive other-oriented emotions such as compassion and goodwill. His research consistently shows this replacement produces significant reductions in anxiety, depression, and anger alongside meaningful improvements in life satisfaction and well-being.

The physiological effects are equally compelling. Research by Charlotte van Oyen Witvliet found that mentally rehearsing unforgiving responses elevated cardiovascular stress and cortisol significantly. When the same people practiced forgiving responses, their physiological stress markers dropped measurably. Forgiveness is not just emotionally liberating. It is physically regulating.

Fred Luskin's research at Stanford found that forgiveness training produced significant reductions in hurt, anger, and stress regardless of whether the person who caused harm ever apologized or acknowledged their actions. Forgiveness operates entirely within the person who practices it. It requires nothing from the person who caused the harm. Read that again.

Try This Today

- Identify one relationship where resentment is still costing you peace or energy and ask honestly: *who is this hurting more?*
- Try Worthington's REACH process: Recall the hurt

honestly. Empathize with the other person's humanity without excusing their behavior. Offer the Altruistic gift of forgiveness. Commit to it. Hold onto it when doubt returns.

- Write a letter you don't send, expressing fully what the hurt cost you, and then deliberately choosing to release it.
- If the hurt is deep, consider working with a therapist. Significant wounds sometimes require skilled guidance rather than solo effort.

What If What Happened Was Genuinely Wrong?

It was, and forgiveness doesn't change that. Forgiveness is not a verdict on what happened. It is a decision about how long you will allow what happened to continue shaping how you feel and function. You can acknowledge injustice fully and still choose to set the weight down.

Bottom Line

Holding onto resentment is drinking poison and expecting the other person to die. Set it down. Not because they deserve it. Because you do.

75. Spend Money on Others, Not Just Yourself

The purchase that produces the most happiness is rarely the one you bought for yourself.

What It Is

Just the other day I stopped at a gas station to grab a Diet Dr. Pepper. While I was waiting to pay, I noticed an older gentleman nearby putting a lid on his drink, and I caught him quietly counting out change from his pocket. Something in me just said: I've got this. I paid for his drink. He looked up, a little surprised, smiled, and said thank you. The whole thing took about fifteen seconds and cost less than two dollars. But that small jolt of joy stayed with me for the rest of the day in a way that my Diet Dr. Pepper, delicious as it was, absolutely did not.

The research, it turns out, has been tracking exactly this. When you have discretionary money to spend, consider directing some of it outward. Not because you should feel guilty about spending on yourself, but because the research consistently shows that spending on others produces significantly more happiness than the same amount spent on yourself, and most people find this genuinely surprising when they first encounter it.

This doesn't require large amounts. The effect holds across income levels and cultures, and the size of the gift matters far less than the fact of giving it. A coffee for a friend. Picking up the tab unexpectedly. A small contribution to something a colleague or friend cares about. A surprise treat for a child.

Why It Works

Lara Aknin and Elizabeth Dunn's research on prosocial spending is among the most replicated and cross-culturally robust findings in happiness science. In studies conducted across more than 130 countries, including some of the world's poorest nations, people who spent money on others reported significantly greater happiness than those who spent the same amount on themselves. The effect held regardless of income, culture, or the size of the expenditure. Giving, even very small giving, reliably produces more happiness than receiving.

The mechanism involves both social connection and meaning. Spending on others activates the brain's reward circuitry in ways that personal spending doesn't fully replicate, and it strengthens relational bonds in ways that produce lasting well-being returns well beyond the moment of the gift itself. Dunn's research also found that the happiness boost from prosocial spending is greatest when the giver can see the impact of their giving directly, which is one more reason to keep it local and personal rather than distant and abstract.

Van Boven and Gilovich's research on experiential versus material spending adds another layer: money spent on shared experiences with others produces more lasting happiness than money spent on things. And research by Ashley Whillans and Hal Hershfield extends this further in a direction most people find genuinely surprising: people who prioritize time over money, who are willing to spend money to buy back time or who make choices that protect their time and energy, report meaningfully greater day-to-day happiness than those who prioritize money over time. The implication is worth sitting with. Sometimes the wisest financial decision for your happiness isn't what to buy at all. It's what to trade money for: time with people you love, experiences that create shared memories, and the freedom to be present rather than perpetually productive.

All of these findings point in the same direction. The purchases most likely to make you genuinely happier are the ones that connect you to other people, either by being given to them, shared with them, or used to protect the time you spend with them.

Try This Today

- The next time you're buying yourself a small treat, buy one for someone nearby too and notice the difference in how it feels.
- Identify one person in your life who could use an unexpected, no-occasion gesture and spend a small amount on something specifically for them this week.
- The next time you're planning something enjoyable, invite someone to share the experience rather than doing it alone. Shared experiences compound the happiness of both the spending and the living.
- When you have a discretionary purchase to make, ask: *is there a version of this that involves someone else, or that buys back time with someone I care about?* Often there is, and often it's more enjoyable than the solo version.

What If Money Is Genuinely Tight Right Now?

The research is encouraging here: the size of the expenditure matters far less than the direction of it. Studies consistently show that even very small prosocial expenditures, a dollar, a coffee, a small gesture, produce the same happiness boost as larger ones. This isn't about how much you spend. It's about who you spend it on.

Bottom Line

The purchase most likely to make you happier isn't the one in your cart. It's the one you hand to someone else, share with someone you love, or trade for more time with the people who matter most. Spend a little outward this week and notice what comes back.

76. Build Friendships Through Shared Activities

The deepest friendships are rarely built face-to-face. They are built side-by-side.

What It Is

Stop waiting for deep friendship to arrive through conversation alone and start building it through doing things together. Not a dinner where the explicit purpose is to catch up. Those things have their place, but they are rarely where the deepest, most durable friendships are actually built. Friendships form most naturally side-by-side, in the shared pursuit of something beyond the relationship itself. The teammates who become lifelong friends through competing together. The neighbors who grow close through a shared project or a recurring walk. Think about the friendships in your life that have felt most genuine and sustaining. Most of them probably formed not through deliberate relationship-building but through something you were both doing, a class, a team, a project, a shared season of life that kept putting you in the same place at the same time.

That pattern is not accidental. It's the way human beings have always formed bonds.

Why It Works

Psychologist Robin Dunbar identifies what he calls pull-together activities as the most efficient and durable pathway to friendship formation. These involve coordinated effort, shared physical experience, or shared rhythm, and they produce bonding effects that conversation alone doesn't fully replicate. Physical synchrony, moving together, working together, creating together, triggers endorphin release through what Dunbar calls the grooming at a distance effect. This is why sports teammates develop unusual closeness and why people who exercise together report stronger feelings of connection than those who exercise alone.

Shared challenge adds another layer. Research on adversarial bonding shows that navigating difficulty alongside another person produces a quality of trust that comfortable shared experiences don't generate as quickly. A difficult hike, a challenging class, a competitive game, any shared experience requiring genuine effort from both people activates this bonding response.

Research by developmental psychologist Jeffrey Hall on adult friendship formation shows that developing a close friendship in adulthood requires an average of roughly 200 hours of shared time, and that the most efficient pathway to those hours is shared activity rather than explicit socializing. Activities provide the recurring, low-pressure, naturally occurring time that adult friendship requires without demanding the deliberate social investment that busy lives rarely accommodate.

Try This Today

- Invite someone to join something you already do regularly, a workout, a walk, a class, a hobby, rather than scheduling another coffee that may or may not happen.
- Join one activity-based group where you'll encounter the

same people repeatedly. The recurring overlap matters more than any single interaction.

- Think about the friendships you most want to deepen and ask: *what could we do together rather than just talk about doing together?*

What If You're Too Busy?

You may not need new time. You may just need different company during the time already there. The walk you already take alone, could someone join you? The class you already attend, is there someone worth showing up alongside more intentionally?

Bottom Line

Find the activity. Invite someone in. Let the friendship form the way it always has, not through trying, but through showing up together, again and again, for something beyond the friendship itself.

77. Respond to the Need, Not the Behavior

Behavior is the surface. Need is the story.

What It Is

When someone in your life is acting in a way that frustrates or hurts you, pause before reacting to the behavior and ask a more useful question: *what need might be underneath this?* A child who acts out at bedtime may need more connection before the day ends. A partner who snaps about something small may need to feel heard about something large. A teenager who withdraws may need reassurance that they're still loved without conditions. The behavior is the signal. The need is the message. And the relationships that last are almost always the ones where at least one person learned to read past the signal to the message underneath.

Why It Works

Every behavior in a relationship makes more sense when you understand the need it is trying, however imperfectly, to meet. This is the foundational insight of Cole Ratcliffe's Relationship Needs Circle, a framework I have used extensively in my own research and teaching. The sequence works like this. When a core emotional need goes unmet, the need for safety, connection, respect, understanding, or belonging, it first produces what I call "bummer emotions," the quieter, more vulnerable primary emotions like hurt, fear, shame, and loneliness. These are the real emotional story. But because they're uncomfortable, they rarely stay on the surface. They quickly trigger more reactive secondary emotions, the "boomer emotions," most commonly anger and anxiety. And it is these secondary emotions that drive the surface behaviors people react to: the snapping, the withdrawing, the shutting down, the picking fights.

The tragedy is that reacting to the behavior almost always makes the underlying need less likely to be met. She nags, so he withdraws. He withdraws, so she nags harder. These cycles can run for years while both people remain genuinely confused about why the relationship feels stuck, because neither person is addressing what's actually driving the dynamic.

Research in emotion-focused therapy developed by Sue Johnson provides the scientific grounding here. Johnson's attachment-based approach, which consistently produces among the strongest outcomes in relationship research, is built on exactly this insight: that the arguments couples have about surface behaviors are almost always about attachment needs, the deep human need to feel safe, seen, and securely connected. Gottman's research on conflict supports the same principle. The fight about the dishes is rarely about the dishes. Something deeper is asking to be seen.

Try This Today

- Pause and ask internally: *what need might be underneath this?* Even a few seconds of that question before responding changes what follows.
- Try addressing the possible need directly: it seems like you might be feeling overwhelmed right now, is there something I can do?
- With children especially, ask: *what is this behavior telling me about what my child needs right now?*

What If the Behavior Is Genuinely Harmful?

Responding to the need doesn't mean excusing the behavior. Both things can be true: the behavior is not acceptable, and there is a need underneath worth understanding. Understand the need. Address it where you can. Hold the boundary where you must.

Bottom Line

React to the behavior and the cycle continues. Respond to the need and something genuinely changes. Ask the question most people never think to ask: *what does this person actually need right now?* That practice, repeated over time, builds the kind of relationships that last.

7.

A LIFE THAT
MEANS SOMETHING

There is a kind of happiness that is pleasant but fragile, the happiness that depends on circumstances going well, on comfort being available, on life cooperating with your preferences. When things are good, it feels good. When things get hard, it evaporates. And then there is a different kind. Deeper, steadier, less dependent on whether today went the way you hoped. This is the happiness Viktor Frankl described from inside a Nazi concentration camp, the discovered truth that meaning can be found even in suffering, that a life oriented toward something beyond comfort and pleasure is a life with a foundation that difficulty cannot easily reach. Frankl called it the last of human freedoms: the ability to choose your response to any circumstance, and to find or make meaning within it.

I've thought about that a lot. Not because my circumstances have approached anything like what Frankl survived. But because I've watched enough people navigate genuine hardship to know that the ones who come through it with their spirit intact almost always share something in common. Not resilience as a personality trait. Not optimism as a default setting. Something more like orientation, a sense that their life is pointed toward something, anchored to something, part of something larger than the daily accumulation of comfort and inconvenience. I've seen it in people facing illness, loss, and circumstances that would flatten most of us. The ones with meaning don't just survive hard things. They come out the other side with something to show for it. That orientation is what this chapter is about.

Our three adult daughters all chose to go on a three-week humanitarian trip the summer after their junior year of high school, so we talked to our son Hayden about it. He wanted to go to Samoa to help build a school, but it conflicted with football camps he'd been planning on, and football was everything to this kid. He decided to go anyway. What happened in those 18 days changed his life. He traded video games and his phone for cold showers and bugs in his bed. For five days straight, he dug a massive hole for a septic tank under the Pacific sun. He mixed cement, shoveled rocks, and laid cinder blocks until he was wiped out. But somewhere in that physical exhaustion and discomfort, he felt something he hadn't felt before. He wrote us a letter that said, in part: "This has been the best experience I've ever had in my life and I wouldn't trade it for anything. My whole mind has changed. I've never been happier than I have here. Being here has just made me grateful for everything." Losing yourself in something larger than yourself can change everything. You don't need to travel to Samoa. You just need to pause and look around.

Martin Seligman's PERMA model identifies meaning as one of five essential elements of well-being, distinct from positive emotion, engagement, relationships, and accomplishment. You can have all four of the others and still feel, at some level, like something essential is missing. Meaning is what gives the other four their weight. It's what makes the pleasant things worth savoring, the achievements worth pursuing, and the relationships worth investing in. Without it, even a comfortable life can feel oddly hollow.

The research on meaning and longevity adds an urgency worth naming. Studies by Patricia Boyle and colleagues found that people with a strong sense of purpose lived significantly longer and showed dramatically lower rates of cognitive decline, even after controlling for health behaviors and baseline cognitive function. Purpose is not just psychologically enriching. It's biologically protective.

But here's what I find most important about meaning, and what the research consistently confirms: meaning is not found, it's made. And it's made most reliably when we stop letting life happen by default and start designing it with intention. Most of us spend more time planning a vacation than we spend thinking about what we actually want our lives to be for. We drift into careers, relationships, and daily rhythms through a series of reasonable decisions never organized around a coherent vision of what a meaningful life looks like for us specifically. Researchers Bill Burnett and Dave Evans, who developed the life design framework at Stanford, found that the people who report the greatest life satisfaction aren't necessarily those with the most impressive achievements. They're the ones who have taken the time to ask what they actually value, what kind of person they want to become, and whether the life they're living is pointed in that direction.

The 12 hacks in this chapter are organized around the specific ways meaning gets made in real life. Some are inward, clarifying your values, identifying your strengths, finding where challenge and purpose converge in your work. Some are outward, serving someone intentionally, anchoring yourself to something that will outlast you, thinking about legacy rather than just success. Some reach upward, practicing faith or spirituality in whatever form is genuinely yours, seeking the awe that briefly dissolves the small self and reminds you of what you're embedded in. And some look backward and forward at once, finding the glory in your life story, reframing the hard chapters through a growth lens, working toward something worthy of your sustained effort. Together, they close the gap between what we say we value and how we actually live. Because that gap, quiet and persistent, is where so much dissatisfaction hides.

In the introduction I mentioned that the happiest people I've observed tend to do four things well. They search inward. They turn outward. They press forward. And they look upward, toward something larger than themselves, something that gives the other three their deepest weight and their most lasting staying power. Of the four, this one is the hardest to manufacture and the most impossible to fake. You either have a sense that your life is pointed toward something that matters, or you don't. This chapter is about building that sense deliberately, one practice at a time.

Before you read any further, it's worth sitting with the question underneath all 12 of these hacks: What is your life actually for? Not what it has been—what do you want it to become? What do you hope to see when you look back from the end and ask whether it mattered? You already know part of the answer. This chapter will help you live it.

78. Clarify Your Values—Discover Your Core Four

The clearest map to the person you're becoming.

What It Is

In many of the happiness presentations I give, one of the things I invite people to do is clarify their values. Not because it's a warm-up exercise or an icebreaker, but because I genuinely believe that everything else, every decision, every relationship, every pursuit of happiness, works better when you know what you actually stand for and are trying to live true to it. It's surprisingly rare that people have done this work deliberately. And it's even rarer that the values they've clarified are actually showing up in how they live.

Take unhurried, honest time to identify what you actually

stand for. Not what you think you should value. Not the values that sound impressive when spoken aloud. The ones that, when you're living in alignment with them, make you feel most fully yourself, and when you're violating them, leave you with a quiet but persistent sense that something is off.

I call this discovering your Core Four. Your core values are not the things you value, your house, your career, your possessions. They are character strengths. Deep convictions about who you are and who you're becoming. The qualities that, at your best, define how you move through the world.

Here's how I invite audiences to find them. Imagine your own funeral. I know. Stay with me. Picture the people who loved you gathered together. Someone stands at the pulpit and describes not what you accomplished or owned, but the kind of person you were. Your character. And they can only use four words. What would those words be? Kind. Loving. Humble. Grateful. Courageous. Generous. Faithful. Present. Those four words are your Core Four. Not aspirations borrowed from someone else's life. Yours.

My mentor Dr. Wally Goddard has spent a career studying what separates people who truly flourish from those who simply get by. His central insight is worth sitting with: the happiest, most flourishing people he has known and studied are not those who accumulated the most or achieved the most, but those who became the most, who grew into increasingly generous, compassionate, and purposeful human beings oriented toward something beyond themselves. Your Core Four is the map for that becoming.

Why It Works

Research by Brian Little shows that people who pursue goals congruent with their core values report significantly higher life satisfaction than those pursuing goals driven by external pressure or social expectation. The alignment between what you value and what you pursue is one of the strongest predictors of whether achievement produces genuine happiness or leaves you strangely empty after reaching the destination.

Acceptance and Commitment Therapy, one of the most well-validated approaches in contemporary psychology I've mentioned previously, places values clarification at the very center of psychological well-being. Its foundational insight is that meaning and vitality come not from eliminating difficulty but from moving toward what genuinely matters, with clarity about what that is. Values don't make the hard things disappear. They make the hard things worth it.

Try This Today

- Do the funeral exercise. What four words would you want the people who know you best use to describe your character? Write them down. Those are your Core Four.
- For each value, write one sentence describing what living it looks like as a concrete daily behavior, not aspiration, but action.
- Share your Core Four with someone who knows you well and ask honestly: *do you see these in how I live?*

What If You're Not Sure What Your Values Are?

Start with what makes you angry or what makes you cry. The things that genuinely disturb you are often the most reliable map to what you actually value. Your Core Four is usually already there.

Bottom Line

A life without clarified values isn't necessarily a bad life. But it is a life navigated without a compass, shaped more by circumstance than by genuine conviction. Discover your Core Four and let it guide everything else.

79. Make Decisions Aligned With Your Core Four Values

Every decision you make is a vote for the kind of person you're becoming.

What It Is

When you face a decision, large or small, bring your Core Four into the room. Not as a performance. As a genuine first question: does this choice move me toward or away from the person those four words describe?

Most of us make decisions primarily on convenience, social pressure, or the path of least resistance. We say yes to things that crowd out what matters because we haven't made what matters explicit enough to defend it. We drift, not because we're uncommitted to our values, but because we haven't built the habit of consulting them before we act.

And sometimes we violate them outright. We lose patience with a co-worker. We snap at a partner over something small. We say something unkind to a child in a tired moment. That sting you feel afterward is not a sign that something is deeply wrong with you. It's a sign that something is deeply right. Your behavior bumped against your values and your values won the argument, even after the fact. You violated one of your Core Four. You feel it. You recommit.

That's not failure. That's the process. Aligning your behavior with your values takes a lifetime of mastery. Be patient with yourself and keep going. Because the closer your daily behavior moves toward those four words, the happier and more at peace you will be.

Why It Works

Sonja Lyubomirsky's research on sustainable happiness consistently identifies values-congruent living as one of the most reliable contributors to lasting well-being. When your choices align with your values, they simultaneously satisfy fundamental psychological needs for autonomy, meaning, and authentic self-expression. When they don't, a subtle but persistent psychological friction accumulates, the low-grade unease of living out of alignment.

Research on self-discrepancy theory by E. Tory Higgins shows that the gap between your actual self and your ideal self is one of the most reliable predictors of depression, anxiety, and dissatisfaction. Narrowing that gap through values-aligned decisions is psychologically and emotionally regulating in ways the research consistently confirms.

Try This Today

- Before your next significant decision, ask simply: *is this consistent with my Core Four?*
- When you feel the pull toward a choice that doesn't feel right, name the tension: this is convenient, but is this who I am?
- The next time you violate a value, practice the full cycle: feel the ping, name which value was bumped, recommit without excessive self-criticism, and move forward.
- Build a brief evening reflection into your day: did my choices today reflect my Core Four?

What If Your Values Conflict With Each Other?

They will, and that's not a flaw in the framework. Family and career. Generosity and self-care. Loyalty and honesty. When values conflict, identify which takes precedence in this specific situation for this specific reason. That's not compromise. It's the development of moral wisdom that values clarification is pointing toward all along.

Bottom Line

You won't always live the way you intend. Neither will anyone else. Feel the ping. Recommit. Keep going. The closer your daily behavior moves toward your Core Four, the more your life begins to feel like yours.

80. Serve Someone Intentionally—As a Meaning Practice

The self most fully realized is the one most freely given away.

What It Is

For years my mom had a sticky note on the bathroom mirror where all of us kids could see it. She had written the words: "And what did you do for someone today?" That wasn't just a note. It was a way of life. My parents modeled intentional service throughout their lives and taught all six of us kids what it looked like in practice. From sharing vegetables from their garden with neighbors, to taking soup and homemade bread to those who were sick, to simply going to visit someone who was lonely. They are the best examples I know of this.

Choose someone to serve, deliberately, specifically, and with your full attention, not as an item on a to-do list but as an act of meaning-making. Not the accidental kindness that happens when circumstances make it easy. Intentional service, the kind where you pause, identify someone who needs something you have, and give it as a conscious practice of turning outward.

The act itself can be small. What distinguishes this entry from the kindness and community entries earlier in the book is the intentionality. You're not just doing something nice. You're orienting your life, even briefly, toward something beyond your own comfort and convenience. That orientation, practiced consistently, is one of the most reliable pathways to a life that feels genuinely significant.

Why It Works

Martin Seligman's research on what produces the most lasting happiness consistently identifies meaningful engagement and contribution to others as the most durable sources of well-being available. Pleasant experiences fade through hedonic adaptation. Meaning does not. The satisfaction of having genuinely served someone, of having been useful in a way that mattered, accumulates rather than erodes.

Research by Michael Steger on meaning in life shows that people who engage in intentional, other-directed service report higher levels of both meaning presence and meaning search, the two dimensions of meaning that most reliably predict well-being and life satisfaction. Service doesn't just feel meaningful in the moment. It builds the felt sense that your life is pointed toward something that matters, a resource that sustains well-being through difficulty in ways that pleasure alone cannot.

My mentor Dr. Wally Goddard captures the deeper paradox well: those who spend their lives finding and aggrandizing themselves end up lost, while those who lose themselves in service find rich meaning, purpose, and identity in return. The self most fully realized is the one most freely given away.

Try This Today

- Ask the question my mom kept on her mirror: *what did you do for someone today?* Then ask: *what specifically do they need, and do I have it to give?*
- Choose one person carrying something heavy right now and do one concrete specific thing, not "I'll be there if you need me" but something delivered rather than offered.
- Make it a weekly practice: one person, one intentional act, one conscious choice to orient your life outward.

What If Service Feels Like One More Obligation?

The difference is almost entirely in the framing. Obligation asks: *what do I have to do?* Meaning asks: *who could I serve today?* Same act. Entirely different interior experience. Start with someone you already love and a service that feels genuinely chosen. Let the practice grow from there.

Bottom Line

Choose someone. Do something specific. Give it genuinely. Not because it's required, but because it's the kind of person you most want to become. And notice what it does to your sense of what your life is for.

81. Work Toward Something That Matters

A life with something meaningful to work toward feels more alive, more pointed, more like it's going somewhere worth going.

What It Is

I'll be honest, working on this book has been one of my own best examples of this hack. It has stretched me, kept me learning, and given me something to work toward that feels genuinely worthwhile. Having a meaningful project changes the quality of your daily life in ways that having nothing to work toward quietly and persistently diminishes.

Have something you're working toward that requires sustained effort, points beyond daily routine, and connects to what you genuinely care about. Not a vague wish. A real goal with direction and momentum. It doesn't need to be grand or publicly impressive. It needs to be genuinely yours, connected to your Core Four, worthy of the sustained effort it will require.

Why It Works

Viktor Frankl observed that human beings can endure almost any suffering if they have a sufficient why, a sense that their life is oriented toward something meaningful enough to justify the cost of getting there. Decades of subsequent research have confirmed the core insight: purposeful striving is one of the most powerful predictors of psychological resilience, well-being, and longevity.

Psychologist Carsten Wrosch and colleagues found that people who maintain meaningful personal goals show lower rates of depression, better physical health outcomes, and greater life satisfaction than those without such goals. Critically, the benefits come not only from achieving the goals but from actively pursuing them. Progress toward something meaningful is itself the source of well-being, not the arrival.

Try This Today

- Ask honestly: *is there something I'm building, pursuing, or becoming that feels worthy of my sustained effort?* If the answer is no, that's the most important information you have right now.
- If you have a meaningful goal, identify one specific thing you can do today, however small, that moves you toward it.
- If you don't have one, return to your Core Four: what goal, pursued over the next year, would most reflect the values you identified?
- Write down your goal, your why, and one concrete next step.

What If the Goal Feels Too Big?

Break it down until a meaningful next step is visible, then take it. Teresa Amabile's Progress Principle shows that small daily progress toward a meaningful goal is one of the most powerful drivers of positive inner experience available. You don't need to see the whole staircase. Just take the next step.

Bottom Line

Find your worthy goal. Work toward it today, even by one small step. And trust that the working itself is most of the point.

82. Practice Faith or Spirituality in Your Own Way

You were made for more than comfort and convenience. Tend the part of you that reaches toward something larger.

What It Is

My faith, instilled in me by two faithful parents, has been one of the genuine anchors of my life. It affects everything—bringing comfort during times of sorrow and grief, helping me see things with a broader eternal perspective, and filling me with a steady sense of hope and happiness that I honestly don't know how I'd navigate life without. I'm not here to prescribe any particular path for you. But I'd be leaving something essential out of this book if I didn't include this.

This entry is not an argument for any particular tradition, theology, or practice. It is an honest acknowledgment of what the research consistently shows: that human beings who cultivate some form of spiritual or religious life tend to be measurably happier, healthier, more resilient, and more connected than those who don't. The particular form that practice takes matters far less than the sincerity and consistency with which it is pursued.

For some people, faith means a specific religious tradition, a community of worship, a relationship with God that orients everything else. For others, spirituality means something quieter, meditation, time in nature, contemplative reading, a sustained sense of connection to something larger than the self. What matters is not the label. What matters is the regular, intentional turning toward whatever reminds you that your life is part of something larger and that you are not alone in the deepest sense of that word. The happiest people across decades of research tend not to be those with the most sophisticated theology, but those with the most genuine relationship with whatever they understand to be the source of meaning and goodness in the world.

Why It Works

Harold Koenig at Duke University, whose research group has produced some of the most comprehensive reviews of religion and health, found that people with active religious or spiritual lives show lower rates of depression, anxiety, and suicide, higher rates of life satisfaction and meaning, stronger immune function, and significantly greater longevity than those without such practices. The effects hold across age groups, cultures, and specific traditions.

Research by Kenneth Pargament on spiritual coping shows that people who draw on spiritual resources during hard times show significantly greater psychological resilience and post-traumatic growth than those who rely on secular coping alone. Faith doesn't prevent hardship. It changes what hardship does to a person, providing a framework of meaning that allows difficulty to be integrated rather than simply endured.

Try This Today

- If you have a faith tradition, show up for it this week with genuine intentionality rather than habit.
- If formal religion isn't your path, identify what connects you to something larger than yourself and build fifteen minutes of that practice into your daily rhythm.
- If you've drifted from a practice that once nourished you, consider returning, not out of obligation but out of

honest recognition that something important was present that has been missing since.

What If You Don't Consider Yourself Religious or Spiritual?

The research doesn't require a particular label. It simply shows that human beings have a deep need for self-transcendence—the experience of being connected to something larger and more meaningful than the individual self. Find what produces that feeling for you. Tend it consistently.

Bottom Line

The part of you that reaches toward meaning and connection to something larger than yourself is not a luxury feature of human experience. It's one of its most essential dimensions. Tend it. In your own way. Consistently.

83. Experience Awe as Self-Transcendence Seek the experiences that make you feel small in the best possible way.

What It Is We touched on awe earlier in Chapter 4. That entry was about noticing sensory beauty and wonder in ordinary experience—the light through a window, a moment of unexpected loveliness close at hand. This entry is about something larger and more specifically self-transcendent: the experiences that briefly dissolve the boundaries of the self entirely.

Astronauts have a name for this. When they look back at Earth from space—fragile, borderless, suspended in darkness—they often describe a profound psychological shift called the overview effect. Petty concerns fall away. Divisions feel artificial. What remains is a deep sense of connection, humility, and reverence for life itself. Many return changed, with a renewed commitment to what matters most.

You don't have to leave the planet to experience something similar. A few years ago I joined a group of adults from our church who took a group of young men on a 21-mile hike through the Tetons. When we finally reached the top, something happened that I didn't quite expect. It went almost silent. Nobody said much. We just stood there looking out for miles in every direction, breathing hard, taking it in. We had earned those views, and they were breathtaking in the truest sense of that word. That's the kind of awe this entry is about.

A night sky far from city lights. A cathedral. A forest of old-growth trees. An act of extraordinary human courage witnessed up close. The particular silence that settles after something genuinely beautiful has happened. Awe at this scale produces a rare and specific sensation—feeling small and expanded at once—that turns out to be one of the most psychologically significant emotional experiences available to human beings. This isn't just about feeling good. It's about being briefly reminded of what you are part of.

Why It Works

Research by Patty Van Cappellen and colleagues shows that awe reliably activates self-transcendent positive emotions—those that shift attention from the self toward something larger—and that these emotions are uniquely associated with increased sense of meaning, spiritual feeling, and connection to something beyond the individual. Awe doesn't just feel good; it reorients you.

In many ways, awe is the ground-level version of the overview effect. You may not be looking at Earth from space, but your mind and body respond in strikingly similar ways when you encounter vastness—whether physical, emotional, or spiritual.

Building on the power of small joys covered in Chapter 4, awe experiences at this larger scale produce additional effects worth noting here. Studies show that vast awe experiences produce increased feelings of connectedness to others, greater generosity and prosocial behavior, enhanced creativity, reduced inflammatory stress markers, and a significantly expanded sense of available time—the feeling that life is larger and less rushed than ordinary preoccupation normally makes it feel.

Try This Today

- Identify what has produced genuine awe in your life before and plan to encounter it deliberately rather than waiting for it to happen accidentally.
- Go somewhere with scale: a mountain, a canyon, an ocean, a cathedral, a forest of old trees. Let the scale do its work rather than documenting it for social media before you've actually felt it.
- Look up. Spend a few minutes with the night sky or even images of Earth from space. Let yourself consider, even briefly, your place in something vast.
- Find a piece of music or a work of art that has previously produced the chest-opening quality of genuine awe and give it your full undistracted attention.

What If You Rarely Experience Awe?

You may be moving too fast for it. Awe requires open, unhurried attention that the pace of modern life actively resists. The night sky has always been there. The old trees have always been there. The music that opens something in you has always been there. Slow down enough to let them work.

Bottom Line

We live in an extraordinary universe, and most days the smallness of ordinary preoccupation makes it impossible to feel that. Seek the experiences that briefly dissolve the small self. Let yourself feel small in the way that only awe produces, small and connected and part of something vast. That feeling is not an escape from your life. It is a reminder of what your life is actually embedded in.

84. Find the Glory in Your Life Story

You've survived every hard chapter so far. That's worth looking at.

What It Is

Most of us move through our lives head down, focused on what's next, managing the immediate and the urgent, without ever pausing to look back at the full arc of what we've already lived. When we do pause and look back honestly, what most people find surprises them. Not a perfect story. Not an easy one. But a richer, more meaningful, more resilient story than the daily press of ordinary life allows them to see.

Step back from the daily accumulation of events and look at your life as a whole. A real story with a beginning that shaped you in ways you're still discovering, a middle full of chapters you didn't plan and wouldn't have chosen, and a continuing narrative whose best chapters may still be ahead. The glory isn't only in the triumphant chapters. It's in the survived ones. The rebuilt ones. The ones where you didn't know how you were going to get through and then somehow did. The ones where something was lost and you discovered, eventually, that you were still standing. Your life story, the whole of it, not just the parts you're proud of, is more glorious than you think. And even the painful chapters carry seeds of meaning that only become visible from a longer view.

Why It Works

Psychologist Dan McAdams has spent decades studying what he calls narrative identity, the internalized story each person constructs about their own life that gives it coherence, meaning, and direction. His research consistently shows that the way we story our lives, the themes we identify, the meaning we make from difficulty, the arc we understand ourselves to be living, is one of the most powerful predictors of psychological well-being, resilience, and sense of purpose.

Critically, McAdams identifies what he calls redemptive sequences, narrative patterns in which a difficult chapter is followed by something positive that grew from it, as the single most important feature distinguishing the life stories of flourishing adults from those who feel stuck or diminished. People whose stories contain redemptive sequences don't have easier lives. They have a different relationship to the difficult chapters, one that finds meaning in them rather than simply enduring them.

Try This Today

- Write a brief outline of your life in chapters, not events but themes. What has each major season been about? What was being built, lost, or learned?
- Identify three experiences that were genuinely hard and ask: *what did each one produce in you that wouldn't exist without it?*
- Ask the McAdams question: *what is the overall theme of my life story so far?* Not what happened, but what has it been about?
- Share a chapter of your story with someone who will listen well. The telling of it, witnessed by another person, often reveals meaning that private reflection alone doesn't reach.

What If Your Story Contains Chapters You'd Rather Not Look At?

The stories we avoid integrating don't disappear. They operate below the surface, shaping our present in ways we don't fully understand until we bring them into the light. If certain chapters carry significant trauma, a skilled therapist can be an invaluable guide. The story deserves to be told fully.

Bottom Line

Step back. Look at the whole arc. Find the glory. It's there in the survived chapters as much as the triumphant ones.

85. Find the Plot Twist—Reframe Painful Chapters With a Growth Lens

The hard chapters are often where the most important becoming happened.

What It Is

My wife and I were barely 21 when we married and just a couple years into marriage she began feeling numb and tingly on the right side of her body and started having painful headaches. After what felt like endless tests, doctors told us she needed brain surgery. I remember those scary, painful days vividly. We were newly married, young, and completely unprepared for something like that. But looking back now, those hard months also produced something real and lasting, a deeper sense of meaning, a greater love and appreciation for her, and a closeness between us that I'm not sure we would have found any other way or any other time.

That's what this entry is about. Take one of the hard chapters of your life and look at it again through a different lens. Not a denial lens. Not toxic positivity that insists everything happens for a reason. A growth lens, the honest recognition that difficult experiences, when processed with intention, frequently produce qualities and depths of character that easier lives simply don't generate.

The plot twist isn't that the hard thing wasn't hard. It was. The plot twist is what happened in you because of it. The courage you didn't know you had until you needed it. The compassion that only arrived after you'd needed compassion yourself. The person you became in the rebuilding that you could not have become any other way.

Why It Works

Psychologists Richard Tedeschi and Lawrence Calhoun developed the concept of post-traumatic growth, the well-documented phenomenon in which people who navigate significant adversity report meaningful positive changes as a result of the struggle. Their research identified five consistent domains: greater personal strength, new possibilities and paths, deeper relationships, greater appreciation for life, and spiritual or existential deepening.

Post-traumatic growth is not the same as resilience, bouncing back to where you were before. It is growth beyond the previous baseline, becoming more than you were before the difficulty. And it occurs not despite the pain but through the deliberate processing of it. The growth doesn't come from the trauma. It comes from the meaning made in its aftermath.

James Pennebaker's research on expressive writing shows that writing about difficult experiences, specifically about both the emotional content and the meaning gained, produces significant improvements in psychological and physical health. The plot twist isn't just a reframe. It's a genuine reorganization of how a painful experience is stored and processed in the mind.

Try This Today

- Write for twenty minutes about a hard experience: what happened, how it felt, and what you understand now that you didn't then.
- Ask the five post-traumatic growth questions: *Did this make me stronger? Did it open new paths? Did it deepen relationships? Did it change what I appreciate? Did it change how I understand my life's meaning?*
- Identify one quality you possess today that you can honestly trace back to a hard chapter. Name the chapter. Name what it grew in you.

What If It's Too Raw?

Don't force the lens. Be in the pain first, fully and honestly, without rushing toward the lesson. The plot twist will be there when you're ready to find it.

Bottom Line

Ask what the hard thing produced in you. Find the plot twist. It won't erase what the chapter cost, but it will change what it means. And meaning, more than almost anything else, is what makes a life feel worth living.

86. Identify Your Strengths and Use Them

You were built with specific strengths. Find them, name them, use them.

What It Is

This is one of my favorites, and I share it with everyone I know—in workshops, with students, with family and friends. I've come to believe that some of the happiest people on this planet are those who have discovered their strengths, gifts, and talents and find regular ways to use them. If you take nothing else from this chapter, take this.

Discover what you're genuinely good at, the qualities and capacities that feel most naturally and energetically yours, and find more ways to use them. Not the things you're competent at out of necessity. Your actual strengths, the ones that when you're using them produce a particular quality of engagement and aliveness that other activities simply don't generate.

Strengths feel different from competencies. When you're using a genuine strength, time moves differently. The work feels less like work. You bring more energy to it than it costs you and often leave with more than you arrived with. The research has a specific term for this: signature strengths, the character strengths that are most essentially yours, that feel authentic rather than performed, and whose use produces both high performance and genuine well-being simultaneously.

Martin Seligman and Christopher Peterson spent years developing the Values in Action classification of character strengths, a taxonomy of twenty-four strengths organized into six broad virtues, from creativity and curiosity through kindness and love to fairness, humility, and spirituality. Their research consistently shows that people who know their signature strengths and find regular opportunities to use them report significantly higher levels of well-being, engagement, meaning, and life satisfaction than those who don't. The question isn't whether you have strengths. You do. The question is whether you know what they are and whether you're living in a way that makes regular use of them.

Why It Works

Seligman's strengths intervention, asking people to identify their top five signature strengths and use one in a new way each day, produced some of the largest and most lasting well-being effects of any intervention tested in the original positive psychology studies. Participants showed significant increases in happiness and decreases in depression that persisted for six months after the one-week intervention ended.

The mechanism involves what Csikszentmihalyi calls the optimal challenge-skill balance, the sweet spot where task demands are well-matched to your genuine capabilities. When you use your signature strengths you're most likely to operate in this zone, engaged rather than bored, stretched rather than overwhelmed, producing your best work with the least psychological friction.

Try This Today

- Take the free VIA Character Strengths survey at viacharacter.org. It takes fifteen minutes and produces a ranked profile of your twenty-four character strengths. Pay particular attention to your top five.
- Think of three times in your life when you felt most fully yourself and most energetically engaged. What were you doing? What strengths were in use?
- Choose one signature strength and find one new way to use it today.
- Ask someone who knows you well: *when do you think I'm most fully myself?* Their answer will often surface strengths you've stopped noticing because they've always been there.

What If Your Current Life Doesn't Have Much Room for Your Strengths?

Start by finding small windows rather than waiting for large ones. A strength used briefly and genuinely is worth more than the same strength entirely suppressed while you wait for better conditions.

Bottom Line

You were not built for generic existence. You were built with specific strengths that when regularly used make you more alive, more effective, and more genuinely yourself. Find them. Name them. Use them. That's not self-indulgence. It's what flourishing looks like.

87. Engage in Flow-Work—Purposeful, Strength-Using Engagement

Find where challenge, strength, and meaning converge. That's where the best of your work lives.

What It Is

Back in Chapter 4 we talked about flow in the context of creative, hands-on activities—drawing building, making something with your hands. That entry was about the restorative, joy-generating qualities of absorbing leisure activity. This entry is about something distinct: flow-work, the purposeful, strength-using engagement that happens when your best capacities are directed toward something that genuinely matters. Same psychological state, different stakes. And the well-being benefits, it turns out, are even larger.

Find the work, paid or unpaid, professional or personal, that absorbs you so completely that time disappears, self-consciousness evaporates, and you emerge from the doing feeling more alive than when you entered it. Csikszentmihalyi called this state flow and spent decades studying the conditions that produce it. Flow is not relaxation. It's not passive enjoyment. It's the state of complete absorption in a challenging, meaningful activity that matches your skills so precisely that the boundary between you and the work temporarily dissolves.

Flow-work is what happens when what you do and who you are converge in the same activity. That convergence, experienced regularly, is one of the most profound sources of meaning available in a human life.

Why It Works

Csikszentmihalyi's research across cultures, professions, and age groups consistently found that the flow state is associated with the highest reported levels of engagement, meaning, and positive experience available in human life. People in flow report greater well-being than people in leisure, rest, or even social interaction, which challenges the common assumption that happiness comes primarily from comfort and pleasure.

The mechanism is neurological as well as psychological. Flow states are associated with reduced activity in the prefrontal cortex, the seat of self-monitoring, self-criticism, and rumination. The inner critic goes quiet. The self-consciousness that makes most activities feel observed dissolves. What remains is pure directed engagement with something genuinely worth doing.

When flow-work is combined with strengths use and meaningful contribution, the well-being benefits compound. Seligman's PERMA model identifies both engagement and meaning as independent contributors to flourishing, and flow-work is the activity most reliably capable of satisfying both simultaneously in a single experience.

Try This Today

- Think of the last time you lost track of time while doing something meaningful. What were you doing? How could you create more conditions for that experience?
- Identify one activity that combines three things: genuine challenge, use of your signature strengths, and connection to something you care about. Protect time for it this week.
- Remove one source of fragmentation from your next significant work session, phone, notifications, competing tasks, and give yourself the conditions flow requires: uninterrupted, single-focused engagement with something that stretches you.

What If You Can't Find Flow in Your Current Work?

Look for it at the edges first. Flow doesn't require a perfect job. It requires the right match between challenge and skill applied to something meaningful. But if flow is entirely absent from your working life, that's worth more than minor adjustment. Chronic disengagement from meaningful work is one of the most significant well-being deficits available to a human life.

Bottom Line

There is a version of your work that absorbs you completely, uses what's most essentially yours, and produces something beyond yourself. Find it. Protect time for it. Flow-work is available in some form to anyone willing to look for the convergence of challenge, strength, and meaning in what they do.

88. Anchor Yourself to Something That Outlasts You

What you build for the future is also what gives the present its meaning.

What It Is

One of the questions I return to often is this: what am I building that will still matter after I'm gone? It's not a morbid question. It's one of the most clarifying ones I know. Invest your time, energy, and care in something whose significance extends beyond the boundaries of your own life—a cause, a family culture, a community, students whose lives you've shaped, a body of work that outlasts the working.

Erik Erikson identified generativity, the concern for contributing to something that will outlast oneself, as the defining developmental task of midlife and one of the primary sources of meaning available to human beings. Its opposite, he suggested, was stagnation, the self-absorption that results when energy remains entirely directed toward one's own comfort and immediate experience. Generativity is not a personality trait. It is a choice, available to anyone willing to ask what they are building that will outlast them.

Why It Works

Research by Dan McAdams shows that adults oriented toward contributing to the next generation report significantly higher levels of life satisfaction, meaning, and psychological well-being. The benefits aren't limited to dramatic contributions. Ordinary consistent investment in something beyond yourself, raising children intentionally, mentoring youth, volunteering in a community organization, produces the same generativity benefits as more visible forms of contribution.

Patricia Boyle's research on purpose and longevity adds a biological dimension: people with a strong sense of purpose extending beyond their own lifetime show significantly lower rates of cognitive decline and meaningfully greater longevity. Anchoring yourself to something that outlasts you isn't just meaningful. It is, in the most literal sense, life-sustaining.

Try This Today

- Ask honestly: *what am I building or contributing to that will still matter after I'm gone?* If the answer is nothing, that's the most important information you have right now.
- Identify one relationship where you have a genuine opportunity to invest in someone's growth and take one intentional step toward that investment this week.
- Consider the family culture you are creating. Is it being built deliberately or by default?

What If You're Young and This Feels Premature?

It isn't. The habits of outward investment are most sustainably developed early rather than discovered late. Start now. The investment compounds.

Bottom Line

A life anchored only to itself is a life whose significance ends at its edges. Invest in something that outlasts you. The anchor holds you now as much as it holds what comes after

89. Think About Legacy, Not Just Success

Success asks how am I doing. Legacy asks what am I building. Only one of them will still matter at the end.

What It Is

I've spent a good portion of my career chasing things that looked like success—publications, promotions, grants, recognition, and checking boxes that the academic world said mattered. And those things aren't meaningless. But somewhere along the way I started asking a different question. Not how am I doing, but what am I leaving? That shift changed how I think about almost everything.

Legacy thinking doesn't replace ambition. It gives ambition somewhere worth pointing. Not what will people think of me, but what will remain of me? Not what have I accomplished, but what have I contributed, to the people I love, to the work I care about, to the world that will continue after I'm gone?

Success without legacy thinking produces a particular restlessness, the experience of reaching destinations that don't feel as significant as the pursuit suggested they would. The promotion achieved and quickly normalized. The recognition received and almost immediately followed by anxiety about the next level. Success measured only by its own standards tends to raise the bar faster than the achiever can clear it. Legacy thinking interrupts that cycle by asking what you're building rather than only what you're accumulating.

Why It Works

Psychologist Tim Kasser's research on intrinsic versus extrinsic goal orientations shows that people who organize their lives primarily around extrinsic goals, wealth, status, image, and recognition, consistently report lower well-being, greater anxiety, and less life satisfaction than those oriented toward intrinsic goals, personal growth, meaningful relationships, community contribution, and purpose. The correlation holds across cultures and income levels. It's not that achievement is bad. It's that achievement pursued as an end in itself, without the larger frame of meaning and contribution, reliably underdelivers on the happiness it promises.

Legacy thinking is the reorientation from extrinsic to intrinsic that the research consistently identifies as the more sustainable path to genuine well-being. When you ask what you're leaving rather than only what you're achieving, you naturally shift your investment toward the relationships, contributions, and values-aligned work that produces durable meaning rather than hedonic adaptation.

Try This Today

- Ask: *if I were at the end of my life looking back at this current season, what would I want to have been doing with it?* Let the answer evaluate how you're currently spending your time.
- Write a brief answer to this question: what do I want to have stood for? Not what you want to have accomplished. What you want to have stood for. Notice the difference.
- Think about the people closest to you and ask: *what am I leaving in them?* Not what you've given them materially. What you've deposited in who they are.

What If Legacy Thinking Feels Grandiose?

Reduce the scale until it feels true. The most enduring legacies are almost always the quietest ones—the parent who raised children of character, the teacher who believed in students who went on to believe in others, the friend who showed up consistently for decades. Legacy at any scale is simply the answer to: what did I leave in the world that wasn't there before I came?

Bottom Line

Think about what you want to have stood for in your relationships, your work, your community, and the quiet corners of your life that no one evaluates but you. Then live backward from that answer. That is what a life of meaning looks like from the inside.

8.

HARD THINGS DON'T CANCEL HAPPINESS

Nobody arrives at the end of a happy life having avoided difficulty. That's worth saying plainly at the beginning of this final chapter, because one of the most persistent and damaging myths about happiness is that it belongs primarily to people whose lives have been spared the hardest things. That the people who seem most genuinely at peace have simply been luckier, less tested, more protected from the losses and failures and griefs that visit everyone eventually.

The research tells a different story. And so does my own life. I've sat with a widow and listened as she shared about her husband who died from a sudden heart attack, leaving her alone without warning on an ordinary day. I've mourned with a brother-in-law who faced multiple heart surgeries. I've watched a young nephew, a sister-in-law, a next-door neighbor, and my own mother battle cancer. I have a sister who lost a baby girl at birth and nearly died herself from loss of blood, siblings who have been through painful divorces, and our family has had our own scary moments in car accidents and surgeries, including holding my wife's hand through brain surgery when we were barely into our twenties, scared and completely unprepared for what we were facing.

I don't share any of that to compare suffering. Everyone's hard is hard. I share it because I've had a front-row seat to what difficulty actually does to people, and what I've observed again and again is this: the difference between those who are broken by hard things and those who are deepened by them is rarely a matter of what happened. It's almost always a matter of how they responded. The resources they drew on. The meaning they made. The support they accepted. The small daily practices of resilience that were either in place before the difficulty arrived or developed in its aftermath.

I've also watched my mom face her liver cancer diagnosis with a grace and groundedness that has taught me more about happiness than almost anything I've ever read in a research paper. I've sat with couples who rebuilt something after it broke and found, to their own surprise, that what they rebuilt was stronger than what preceded it. I've watched students navigate losses that seemed unsurvivable and emerge with a clarity and compassion they didn't have before.

Psychologist Kelly McGonigal's research on stress reappraisal shows that stress itself is not the enemy. The belief that stress is harmful is the enemy. People who understand stress as a natural, mobilizing response to things that matter to them show measurably different cardiovascular and hormonal profiles than those who treat the same stress as a threat to be escaped. Same stress. Different story. Profoundly different outcomes.

Ann Masten, one of the foremost resilience researchers in the world, describes resilience not as a rare and heroic quality possessed by exceptional people but as what she calls ordinary magic, the natural capacity for recovery and growth that most human beings possess and that is activated and strengthened by the right conditions and practices. Resilience isn't something you either have or don't have. It's something you build, before you need it, during the hard thing, and in the reflection that follows.

Two other bodies of research have shaped how I think about this, and they belong here. The first is Carol Dweck's work on growth mindset. Dweck spent decades studying how people respond to difficulty, failure, and the limits of their current ability. What she found is that the story you tell yourself about struggle changes everything. People who believe their capacities are fixed, that talent is something you have or you don't, tend to avoid difficulty, hide their failures, and interpret setbacks as evidence of inadequacy. People who believe their capacities are developable, that effort and persistence actually change what they're capable of, respond to the same difficulty with curiosity, persistence, and a willingness to try again differently. Same obstacle. Entirely different response, based entirely on the story being told about what the obstacle means. And critically, that story is not fixed. It can be changed. The practices in this chapter are partly about building exactly that orientation before difficulty arrives.

The second is Angela Duckworth's research on grit—the combination of passion and perseverance for long-term goals that she found to be one of the strongest predictors of achievement and well-being across every domain she studied, from West Point cadets to spelling bee finalists to teachers in challenging schools. Duckworth's research shows that grit isn't a personality trait you're born with. It's built through the repeated experience of staying in hard things long enough to discover you can. Every time you press through difficulty rather than around it, you are depositing into a psychological account that will be available to you the next time something hard arrives. Grit, in other words, is not what you have before the hard thing. It's what the hard thing builds in you, if you let it.

Together, Dweck's growth mindset and Duckworth's grit research point toward the same conviction: difficulty is not the opposite of flourishing. Engaged, supported, and oriented correctly, it is frequently the mechanism of it.

This is the final chapter of happy hacks, and in some ways the most important one. Not because stress and difficulty are more significant than joy, connection, or meaning. But because the capacity to navigate hardship well is the foundation that everything else in this book is built on. The gratitude practices of Chapter 5 work better when you've developed the resilience to practice them on hard days. The meaning-making of Chapter 7 reaches its full depth when tested by real adversity. The connections of Chapter 6 become something entirely different, something lifesaving, when difficulty arrives and those connections are strong enough to hold you.

Happiness is not the absence of hard things. It is what becomes available to you, in you, through you, and sometimes because of the hard things, when you've developed the orientation, the practices, and the support to meet difficulty without being defined by it.

The thirteen practices that follow are about building that capacity. Some address the moment of acute stress. Some address the long arc of recovery and growth. All of them are oriented toward the same conviction that has animated this entire book from the beginning: Hard things don't cancel happiness. They can deepen it.

90. Reframe Stress as a Challenge, Not a Threat

Your racing heart is not a warning. It is your body showing up for something that matters.

What It Is

I used to think the goal was to eliminate stress. Get through the hard thing, reduce the pressure, return to calm. What the research taught me, and what I've come to believe from experience, is that this is exactly the wrong goal. The goal isn't to escape stress. It's to change the story you're telling yourself about what it means.

When stress arrives, here's the default story most people tell: something is wrong. I need to escape this as quickly as possible. This threat response made excellent evolutionary sense when stressors were predators and physical danger. It makes considerably less sense when the stressor is a difficult conversation, a demanding deadline, or a hard season of life that requires sustained engagement rather than flight.

Here's the alternative story, and the research suggests it's not just more useful but more accurate: something important is happening. My body is mobilizing to meet it. The energy I'm feeling is preparation, not warning. That reframe, from threat to challenge, changes not just how stress feels but what it does to your body, your brain, and your performance. Same racing heart. Same heightened alertness. Entirely different meaning and entirely different outcomes.

Why It Works

Kelly McGonigal's research on stress mindset shows that people who believe stress is harmful experience measurably worse health, performance, and well-being outcomes than people who believe stress is a natural mobilizing response to things that matter. Across large population studies, the most harmful thing about stress was not the stress itself but the belief that stress was harmful. That belief, held consistently, transformed a neutral or even beneficial physiological response into a genuine health risk.

Psychologist Jeremy Jamieson and colleagues studied the challenge versus threat distinction in high-pressure performance contexts and found that people who reappraised their pre-performance anxiety as excitement and preparation showed significantly better cardiovascular profiles, greater cognitive flexibility, and stronger performance outcomes than those who tried to calm down or suppress the arousal. The reframe works not by reducing the stress but by changing its meaning, which changes its biology.

Try This Today

- Name what your body is doing and reinterpret it deliberately: my heart is racing because something important is happening and my body is getting ready. This is preparation, not danger.
- Ask the challenge reframe question: what would it look like to meet this rather than escape it?
- Identify what the stress is telling you matters. Stress is almost always attached to something you care about. Name what that something is and let the caring reframe the stress.
- Say out loud: *I can do hard things*. Research on self-talk consistently shows that direct self-encouragement produces measurable improvements in stress response and resilience.

What If the Stress Feels Genuinely Overwhelming?

The challenge reframe works best for moderate, everyday stress. For acute crisis or traumatic events, safety, support, and stabilization come first. This reframe is not a demand that you be stronger than your circumstances. It's an invitation to approach them with more of your actual capacity than the threat response allows you to access.

Bottom Line

The story you tell yourself about stress changes what stress does to you. Meet it like a challenge and discover that you are more capable of meeting it than the threat response ever allowed you to believe.

91. Normalize Struggle as Part of Growth

Everyone who has ever grown into someone worth admiring has passed through difficulty to get there.

What It Is

One of the most quietly damaging beliefs in contemporary culture is that a good life should be relatively smooth, that struggle signals failure or inadequacy rather than the ordinary, inevitable texture of a life being genuinely lived. It turns normal human difficulty into a source of shame. It makes people hide their struggles rather than process them. It produces the exhausting performance of fine-ness in a world where almost nobody is entirely fine and everyone is pretending otherwise.

Stop treating difficulty as evidence that something has gone wrong and start recognizing it as evidence that something is happening. The research on human development is unambiguous: struggle is not a detour from growth. It is the primary mechanism of growth. Every person you admire for their character, their resilience, or their depth of compassion has been shaped by difficulty. Not despite their hard chapters. Because of them.

This doesn't mean all suffering is useful or that difficulty should be romantically embraced. It means that when struggle arrives, as it will for every human being regardless of circumstance, the most productive response is neither denial nor despair but honest acknowledgment and the willingness to ask: *what is this making possible in me?*

Why It Works

We covered Carol Dweck's growth mindset research earlier in this chapter and in Chapter 7, and it applies directly here. People who believe their capacities are developable respond to difficulty with engagement and persistence rather than shame and withdrawal. Same obstacle. Entirely different response, based entirely on the story being told about what the obstacle means. And that story, the research consistently shows, can be changed.

Research on what psychologist Susan David calls emotional agility, the capacity to relate to difficult emotions with curiosity and openness rather than avoidance or suppression, adds another dimension. David's work shows that people who normalize their difficult emotions, acknowledging them without being controlled by them, show greater resilience, more flexible thinking, and better long-term well-being than those who either suppress difficulty or are overwhelmed by it. The normalization itself, simply recognizing that struggle is universal, expected, and navigable, is a meaningful psychological intervention.

Try This Today

- The next time you encounter difficulty, try replacing why is this happening to me with this is hard and I'm still here. The second statement is both more accurate and more useful.
- Think of one person currently struggling and reach out with the specific message that struggle is normal, their difficulty makes sense, and they are not failing at life. That message is rarer and more nourishing than most people realize (be sensitive and wise with this one).
- Try the single word reframe: I can't do this yet rather than I can't do this. Research consistently shows that one word changes the subsequent behavior.

What If Normalizing Struggle Feels Like Lowering the Bar?

It's the opposite. Normalizing struggle removes the shame that keeps people stuck, the extra layer of suffering added to genuine difficulty by the belief that difficulty shouldn't be happening. When struggle is normalized, energy that was going into hiding it becomes available for actually navigating it. The bar isn't lowered by acknowledging that things are hard. It's made reachable.

Bottom Line

Struggle is not a sign that you're falling behind. It's a sign that you're in the process of becoming something you haven't been yet. Keep going. This is what growth feels like from the inside.

92. Build a Support Plan Before You Need It

The best time to tend your support network was years ago. The second best time is today.

What It Is

When COVID-19 hit, researchers and clinicians observed something consistent across thousands of families navigating the same crisis: outcomes varied wildly, and the difference wasn't primarily about what happened to people. It was about what they had in place when it did. The families who fared best weren't necessarily the strongest or the luckiest. They were the ones who already had resources, relationships, and a perspective that helped them make sense of what they were facing.

This is essentially what family stress researchers have known for decades through what's called the ABC-X model, one of the foundational frameworks in family science. In its simplest form: A is the stressor, B is the resources you bring to it, and C is how you perceive and make meaning of it. And X is the outcome. The stressor itself, the A, is often outside your control. But your resources and your perspective, the B and C, are buildable. And they make an enormous difference in what the X ends up being.

This happy hack is about building the B before you need it. Identify your people, know your resources, and have a basic plan for hard times before the hard times arrive. Not in a fearful way. In the same practical way you keep a first aid kit in your home, not because you expect an emergency but because emergencies don't announce themselves in advance.

A support plan is really just honest answers to a few simple questions: Who are the people I can call when something is genuinely wrong? What community, faith, or professional resources could I access if I needed them? What practices, exercise, prayer, journaling, time in nature, have helped me navigate difficulty before, and am I keeping them alive? Is there a therapist or counselor whose relationship I could develop now, before crisis, so the relationship is already real when it matters?

Why It Works

Research on social support and stress buffering, one of the most consistently replicated findings in health psychology, shows that strong social support doesn't just make difficulty more bearable. It changes its physiological and psychological effects. People with robust support networks show lower cortisol responses to stressors, faster cardiovascular recovery, lower rates of depression and anxiety, and significantly better long-term health outcomes than those who face difficulty without adequate support.

Critically, the research distinguishes between support that exists in principle and support that is genuinely accessible in practice. A network that hasn't been tended is far less effective when genuine need arrives than one built through consistent relational investment. The support plan works because it makes the support real before the need is acute.

Try This Today

- Write down the names of 3-5 people you could genuinely call in a crisis. If the list is shorter than you'd like, that's important information about where to invest relationally right now.
- Identify one professional resource, a therapist, a counselor,

a support group, that you could access if needed. You don't have to use it now. Just know it exists.

- Inventory the practices that have helped you navigate difficulty before and ask honestly: *are they currently active in my life?*

What If You Don't Feel Like You Have Enough People?

Then building the support plan reveals the most important work to do right now, before a crisis, not during one. Start with one relationship worth deepening. Build from there.

Bottom Line

You will face hard things. Everyone does. The difference between being broken by them and being held through them is often not about what the hard thing is. It's about what's already in place when it arrives. Build your support plan now. So that when the hard thing comes, you don't face it alone.

93. Ask for Help Early

The most capable people you know are not the ones who never need help. They are the ones who ask for it early enough that it actually helps.

What It Is

A few years ago our family took a trip to Hawaii and I had a great time learning to boogie board. On one wave the ocean had other plans and smashed me headfirst into the sand. I hurt my shoulder badly enough that it bothered me for more than eighteen months afterward. Finally, I reached out to a neighbor who happened to be a physical therapist. He had me get an X-ray, gave me some simple exercises to do at home, and within a few weeks my shoulder felt completely normal again.

I remember thinking afterward: why did I wait so long? What was I waiting for? That question applies to a lot more than shoulders. When something is genuinely hard, ask for help before you absolutely have to. Not after you've exhausted every independent option. Not when the crisis has fully arrived and the weight has become impossible to carry alone. Early, when help would still be most effective and the ask is still relatively small.

This sounds straightforward. It isn't. Asking for help is wrapped in layers of cultural messaging about self-sufficiency and what it means to be capable. Most people carry a deep and largely unexamined belief that needing help is a form of weakness, that asking imposes on others, and that the admirable response to difficulty is to manage it independently for as long as possible. That belief has a cost, and the research quantifies it.

Why It Works

Research by Francis Flynn and Vanessa Lake found that people underestimate others' willingness to help by as much as 50%. The anticipated social cost of asking is roughly double the actual cost. We talk ourselves out of asking based on a fiction.

The timing dimension is equally well-supported. Research on intervention effectiveness across mental health, medical, and interpersonal domains consistently shows that early help-seeking produces significantly better outcomes than delayed help-seeking, not because the problems are smaller early on, but because early intervention catches difficulty before it compounds. A conversation with a therapist during a hard season is far more effective than the same conversation during a crisis. A request for support from a friend early in a difficult period is far more sustainable for both parties than a desperate reach at the point of exhaustion.

The people who navigate hard things most effectively are almost never the most self-sufficient ones. They are the most willing to say early and honestly: *I need help with this.*

Try This Today

- Think of something you're currently managing alone that is harder than it needs to be. Identify one person who could help and reach out before the day ends.
- Practice the sentence out loud: *I'm struggling with this and I could use some support.*
- If professional support would be genuinely useful, make one call or send one email today. Not someday. Today, while the window is still open.

What If Asking Feels Genuinely Impossible?

Start very small. A tiny ask, to the safest person you know, about something genuinely minor. Let the response inform whether the belief that asking is dangerous is as accurate as it feels.

Bottom Line

You were not built to carry everything alone. Nobody is. Ask before you have to. While there's still time for the help to matter. Don't wait eighteen months.

94. Use Movement to Process Stress in the Moment

Move first. Then think. You'll think better for having moved.

What It Is

A few years ago I got some difficult news mid-afternoon and my first instinct was to sit at my desk and think my way through it. I stewed. I ruminated. I checked my email three times without reading anything. Finally, I got up and walked the 124 stairs up Old Main Hill across from my office on campus, and something shifted within the first ten minutes that an hour of desk-sitting hadn't produced. I've trusted that instinct ever since.

This entry is different from the exercise entries in Chapter 2, which focused on the baseline mood and neurological benefits of consistent daily movement. This is about something more immediate: using acute physical movement as a real-time stress processing tool in the moment stress arrives. Not later. Not after you've thought it through. Now, with whatever movement is available to you.

A brisk walk around the block. A run that matches the intensity of what you're feeling. Fifteen minutes of physical effort that gives your body something to do with the energy stress has flooded it with. Stress is a physical event before it's a psychological one. Movement is the most direct response to a physical event.

Why It Works

When you perceive a stressor, your body floods with cortisol and adrenaline. Your heart rate elevates. Your muscles tense. Blood flow redirects toward large muscle groups. Your body, in short, prepares to physically respond to a threat. The problem is that most modern stressors don't permit physical response. The difficult conversation ends and you sit back down at your desk. The stress response activates fully and then has nowhere to go, leaving cortisol circulating and your nervous system in a state of activation that cognitive processing alone rarely resolves.

Andrew Huberman's research on stress and physical movement shows that vigorous exercise following acute stress accelerates the metabolic clearance of stress hormones and restores the nervous system baseline more effectively than rest, distraction, or cognitive reappraisal alone. Movement completes the stress response cycle that the original stressor initiated, giving the body the physical resolution it physiologically prepared for.

Research by Bessel van der Kolk, whose work on trauma and the body has transformed clinical understanding of how stress is stored, shows that unprocessed stress is held in physical tension in ways that talk and thought alone don't fully reach. Rhythmic whole-body movement is one of the most direct pathways to releasing what the body has been holding.

Try This Today

- Go for a walk brisk enough to match your current internal intensity. Not a stroll. A walk with enough physical demand to engage your body rather than simply relocate your rumination.
- If the stress is high, run, or do any vigorous movement that drives your heart rate up and interrupts the cognitive loop with genuine exertion.
- If leaving isn't immediately possible, find the first available moment afterward to move before doing anything else. Move first. Then think.

What If You Don't Feel Like Moving When Stressed?

You probably won't. Move anyway. The motivation to exercise almost never precedes exercise during periods of stress. It follows it. A ten-minute walk counts. Around the parking lot counts. The specifics matter far less than the decision to move rather than sit with it. Moving your body moves your brain.

Bottom Line

Stress is a physical event. Your body prepared to move in response to it. Give it the movement it was preparing for, not as a distraction from what's hard, but as a direct physiological response to it. Move first. Then think.

95. Practice Meaning-Making During Adversity — In Real Time

Suffering without meaning is simply loss. Suffering with meaning, chosen in the middle of the hard thing, is something else entirely.

What It Is

We've covered related ground in earlier chapters. Happy hack 58 focused on practicing gratitude during hard moments. Hack 85 was about retrospectively reframing painful chapters with a growth lens. This entry is about something distinct from both: the real-time, active construction of meaning while adversity is actually happening. Not looking back. Not finding silver linings. Asking, in the middle of the hard thing, what it is for: *What meaning can I make from this, right now, with what I have?*

When I was serving a two-year church mission as a young man at age 19, my sister wrote me letters regularly. She ended every single one the same way, with a line I've carried with me ever since: pain is inevitable, but misery is optional. I didn't fully understand it at the time. I've spent the rest of my life learning what she meant. The pain of hard things is rarely in our control. The meaning we make of them is.

Viktor Frankl described this as the fundamental human capacity, the ability to find meaning not just after suffering but within it. He watched people transform unavoidable suffering into something bearable, not by denying it, not by bypassing it, but by standing inside it and choosing to give it meaning rather than letting it remain simply loss. That capacity, he insisted, is available to everyone. Not easily. But genuinely.

This is harder than retrospective reframing because there's no distance yet. The dust hasn't settled. The outcome isn't known. You're being asked to construct meaning from inside the storm rather than after it has passed. And yet that is precisely when it matters most, because the frame you bring to difficulty while you're in it shapes what the difficulty does to you.

Why It Works

Crystal Park's research on meaning-making coping identifies the active, real-time process of constructing significance from difficult events as distinct from both problem-focused and emotion-focused coping, and as producing unique resilience benefits that neither of those approaches fully generates. Meaning-making coping doesn't reduce the difficulty. It changes the person moving through it, providing a psychological frame that makes the difficulty navigable rather than simply endurable.

Research consistently shows that the ability to construct a narrative that gives difficulty a purpose or context larger than the suffering itself is one of the strongest predictors of post-traumatic growth and well-being during hard seasons. The meaning doesn't have to be complete or certain. It just has to be present enough to provide direction.

Try This Today

- Ask Frankl's question directly: *if I cannot change this, how can I choose my attitude toward it?* Let the question open something rather than demand an immediate answer.
- Identify what the hard thing is connected to that matters. Struggle almost always arrives in the vicinity of something you deeply care about. Naming what you care about gives the difficulty a frame larger than the pain itself.
- Ask: *who is watching how I handle this?* Not for performance, but because the way you navigate difficulty is one of the most powerful things you can model for your children or anyone paying close attention.
- Write for 10 minutes about what the current difficulty might be producing in you, not what you wish it wasn't costing, but what it might be building.

What If It's Too Acute Right Now?

Then tend to the acute need first. Meaning-making is most accessible when the immediate crisis has stabilized enough for reflection to be possible. The meaning doesn't have to be made in the first hours. It has to be made before the story about what happened hardens into something that forecloses it entirely. When you're ready, even partially, ask the question.

Bottom Line

Pain is inevitable. Misery is optional. Ask the question while you're still in it: *what can I make of this, right now, with what I have?* The answering itself, the refusal to let difficulty be only loss, is one of the most profound acts of resilience available to a human being.

96. Focus on What You Can Control

You can't control everything that matters. But you can always control more than anxiety allows you to believe.

What It Is

When life gets hard, narrow your focus to the one territory where your effort actually produces results: what you can control. I use two overlapping circles in my presentations to illustrate this. One circle is labeled Things That Matter. The other is labeled Things I Can Control. Most people, when stressed and struggling, spend the majority of their mental and emotional energy in the parts of those circles that don't overlap, worrying about things that matter but that they cannot control, or controlling things that don't particularly matter. The sweet spot, the place where focused energy actually produces both results and peace, is where the circles overlap. That's where your attention belongs.

I also use what I call the Triangle of Tough Times. Picture a triangle. Each bottom corner represents something you have very little control over: the Circumstances of your life—illness, loss, the unexpected things that arrive without invitation, and Other People's Choices—what the people around you decide to do, how they treat you, whether they show up the way you need them to. Both bottom corners are largely outside your control.

But the top corner of the triangle is yours entirely. Your Choices. How you respond. What you decide to do next. The attitude you bring. The meaning you make. The person you choose to be in the face of what you cannot change. That top corner is where your power lives. And the difference between responding from that top corner versus reacting from the bottom ones is one of the most important skills available during hard times.

Why It Works

Martin Seligman's foundational research on learned helplessness shows that people who believe their actions can influence their outcomes show dramatically better resilience, health, and well-being than those who believe outcomes are entirely beyond their control. The perception of control, even partial control, is one of the most powerful psychological resources available during adversity.

Research by Steven Hayes on Acceptance and Commitment Therapy adds the essential complement: the willingness to accept what genuinely cannot be controlled is not resignation. It is the psychological move that frees up the cognitive and emotional resources currently consumed by fighting the uncontrollable. Accept what's outside the circles' overlap. Act decisively within it.

Try This Today

When stress arrives, use SNAP before reacting:

Stop—pause before the automatic reaction takes over. Breathe and get curious rather than furious.

Notice and Name—identify the emotion rising in you without

letting it drive. Simply naming what you're feeling activates the thinking brain and reduces the emotional hijack.

Assess and Ask—apply the Law of 3s: *Will this matter in three hours? Three days? Three months? Three years?* Most situations that generate intense reactions don't survive honest contact with that question.

Ponder and Plan—decide deliberately how to respond rather than letting the reaction decide for you.

Then apply the two circles and the triangle: identify specifically what falls in your controllable territory right now and put your energy there.

What If Everything Feels Outside Your Control?

Look more carefully. There is almost always something in the top corner. Even in the most constrained circumstances, something remains yours. Your attitude. Whether you ask for help. How you treat the people around you. What meaning you make. What you do in the next hour. That corner is always yours. Even when everything else isn't.

Bottom Line

You cannot control everything that matters. But you can control more than anxiety allows you to believe. Draw the circles. Use the triangle. SNAP before you react. Find your top corner and put your energy there.

97. Build Structure When Life Feels Structureless

When everything feels uncertain, structure is the message your nervous system needs most.

What It Is

Not long ago my wife and I decided to remodel our kitchen. What started as a kitchen project expanded into replacing all the floors on the main level of the house and repainting several rooms. We knew it would be disruptive. We did not know it would be as genuinely miserable as it turned out to be.

For several weeks the floors were torn up, the air was dusty and hard to breathe, and our bedroom and basement were piled high with everything we'd cleared from the main level. At one point the entire kitchen was taped off and covered in plastic and we couldn't get to our refrigerator, our food, or any kitchen essentials. We cooked in our small basement kitchen when we could. Our routines fell apart completely. Our son, who was a senior in high school at the time, felt it too. Everyone was irritable and edgy in ways that were hard to explain until we realized the explanation was simple: nothing was where it belonged, nothing happened when it was supposed to, and the baseline predictability that makes a home feel like a home had completely disappeared. We basically retreated to our bedroom and shut the door for weeks. We took for granted our ability to have a calm morning or sit on the living room couch. All of it was covered in plastic and dust.

We knew there would be an end. That knowledge helped. But knowing there's an endpoint doesn't make the messy middle any less disorienting. And what that experience clarified for me was something the research had already established: the loss of daily routine and structure is itself a significant source of stress, separate from whatever caused the disruption in the first place. It's not just the hard thing. It's what the hard thing does to the architecture of your days.

I've seen this in more serious forms too. A close friend going through a painful divorce stopped sleeping at consistent times, stopped eating regular meals, stopped exercising. The loss of the relationship had taken out the structure of his life along with it, and the structurelessness was making everything harder than it needed to be. When he finally started rebuilding simple daily rhythms, even small ones, something shifted. Not because the pain was gone. Because some things were reliable again.

When difficulty arrives and disrupts the ordinary rhythms of your life, build something to replace them. Deliberately. Even imperfectly. Grief disrupts structure. Job loss disrupts structure. Illness, divorce, a home renovation that spirals, unexpected crisis, major life transition, all of them share a common feature: the daily architecture you were living inside suddenly doesn't fit the life you're now in. And that structurelessness is itself a significant source of distress that most people never fully identify or address.

Here's why this matters so much. The brain and body do best with predictability. Stability, routine, and consistent rhythm are not just comforting preferences. They are biological needs. When your daily structure is intact, your nervous system operates from a baseline of safety, which makes clear thinking, emotional regulation, and genuine resilience all more accessible. When structure collapses, the nervous system loses those anchoring signals and stress hormones fill the gap. In the absence of predictability, the brain essentially stays on alert, scanning for what comes next because nothing reliable is telling it.

Structure sends the signal the stressed brain is desperately waiting for: some things are still stable. Some things still happen. You know what comes next. A consistent wake time. A simple morning practice. A regular meal. A predictable evening rhythm. These things sound small. Their absence during hard times is anything but.

Why It Works

Research on behavioral activation, the evidence-based approach to depression and stress that focuses on restoring structured activity rather than waiting for motivation to return first, consistently shows that rebuilding routine during hard times produces significant improvements in mood, resilience, and sense of agency. The structure doesn't wait for you to feel better. It creates the conditions in which feeling better becomes possible.

Ann Masten's research on resilience identifies routine and predictable daily structure as one of the most powerful ordinary resources that sustain people through adversity. The routine itself, however modest, communicates stability and continuity in the face of circumstances that feel neither stable nor continuous. Predictability, it turns out, is one of the brain's most powerful forms of comfort.

Try This Today

- Identify three non-negotiable daily anchors you will maintain regardless of what the day brings: a consistent wake time, a brief morning practice of any kind, and one reliable evening rhythm. These three alone provide more structural stability than most people realize.
- If your structure has recently collapsed through loss or crisis, don't wait until you feel ready to rebuild it. Start with one anchor. One consistent practice. Build from there.
- When stress hits and clear thinking feels out of reach, try a simple breathing reset: five slow breaths, in through the nose, out through the nose, counting each one. Ninety seconds. Your nervous system will respond before your mind believes it should.
- Protect your most stabilizing practices specifically during hard seasons, when the temptation to abandon them is strongest and the need for them is greatest.

What If Building Structure Feels Impossible?

Start smaller than feels meaningful and trust the research rather than your current motivation. You don't have to feel like building structure for structure to work. You just have to build it. One anchor. Today. The nervous system responds to consistency before the mind believes in it.

Bottom Line

The brain and body do best with predictability. In the middle of what you can't control, structure is something you can. Build the anchors. Maintain them even imperfectly. That small daily act of building, repeated through the hardest days, is what keeps you oriented until the ground steadies beneath you again.

98. Allow Rest Without Guilt

Rest is not a reward for sufficient productivity. It is the condition that makes everything else sustainable.

What It Is

This one is especially for the tired, overwhelmed mom who hasn't sat down without a to-do list running in the background since she can remember. Who feels vaguely irresponsible the moment things go quiet. Who rests, when she rests at all, with one eye on what still needs doing and a low hum of guilt that never quite turns off. You are not alone, and this entry is for you. But honestly, it's for all of us.

We have collectively developed a profound ambivalence about rest, knowing we need it, resenting that we do, and undermining it with guilt even when we manage to take it. We wear packed schedules like badges of importance. We apologize for taking time off. Busyness has become a virtue and exhaustion a status symbol, and the result is a particular kind of modern depletion, not just physical tiredness but the accumulated drain of a nervous system that never fully recovers because rest, when it happens, is spent half-present and half-guilty rather than fully received.

Rest is not the opposite of productivity. It is the condition that makes sustained productivity possible. Rest is not the absence of contribution. It is the replenishment of the capacity to contribute. And rest taken without guilt, fully and genuinely, is a fundamentally different physiological and psychological experience than rest taken while mentally still at work.

Why It Works

This entry isn't about sleep specifically, that was covered in Chapter 2. This is about the broader practice of genuine psychological rest, the deliberate, guilt-free disengagement from demands that allows the nervous system to actually recover.

Sabine Sonnentag's research on psychological detachment from work stress consistently finds that people who fully detach during rest periods, who are genuinely present in their rest rather than partially still at work, show significantly better next-day energy, mood, performance, and resilience than those who rest physically while remaining mentally engaged with demands. The guilt that prevents full detachment doesn't just feel bad. It actively undermines the recovery it's interrupting.

For overwhelmed parents especially, research consistently shows that parental depletion, the chronic exhaustion that comes from giving without replenishing, reduces the very qualities, patience, presence, warmth, and attunement, that make for the parent you most want to be. Rest isn't selfish. It's how you show up better for the people who need you most.

Try This Today

- Identify what genuine rest actually looks like for you specifically, not what you think it should be, but what actually replenishes you. Know what yours is and stop apologizing for needing it.
- Schedule one period of genuine rest this week and treat it with the same commitment you give your most important obligations.

- When the guilt arrives, reframe it honestly: *this rest is not a withdrawal from my responsibilities. It is an investment in my capacity to meet them.*
- Practice a simple transition into rest: five slow breaths, eyes closed, deliberately setting down whatever you were carrying. Let your body know it's allowed to stop.

What If You Genuinely Can't Rest Right Now?

Find the smallest possible recovery window and use it fully. Five minutes of complete mental disengagement is worth more than an hour of guilty half-rest. Rest is not waiting for permission. It is recognizing that you are not a machine, and that even machines require maintenance.

Bottom Line

You were not built for perpetual output. Rest fully, without guilt, not because you've earned it, but because you need it. And needing it doesn't make you weak. It makes you human.

99. Practice Courage in Small Ways

Courage is not a personality trait you either have or don't. It is a practice, built one small act at a time.

What It Is

A few years ago one of my students stayed after class looking uncomfortable. She finally said she needed to tell me something hard. She had been struggling with anxiety for months and hadn't told anyone, not her roommates, not her parents, not her advisor. Coming to talk to me that day was, for her, an act of genuine courage. It wasn't dramatic. Nobody else would have noticed. But it changed the trajectory of that semester for her, and probably more than that.

That's the kind of courage this entry is about. Not a dramatic act of heroism. Not a public declaration or a life-altering leap. A small, specific, ordinary act that requires you to move toward something that matters past the fear, the discomfort, or the self-doubt that is trying to keep you exactly where you are.

Make the phone call you've been avoiding. Say the true thing in the meeting where you've been staying quiet. Ask for help before you're desperate. Set the boundary you've been unable to hold. Start the thing you've been waiting until you're ready to start, knowing that ready precedes action far less reliably than it follows it. Tell someone what they mean to you before the occasion that would make it feel less vulnerable.

C.S. Lewis called courage not merely a virtue among others but the form of every virtue at its testing point, the quality that allows all the others to become real rather than theoretical. Kindness when kindness is costly. Honesty when honesty is risky. Love when love might not be returned. Without courage at the testing point, every other value remains aspiration rather than action.

Why It Works

Brenй Brown's research on courage and vulnerability shows that the willingness to act despite uncertainty and emotional risk is not a fixed personality trait but a practiced behavior that develops with use. People who practice vulnerability and courage in small everyday ways develop greater resilience, deeper relationships, stronger sense of meaning, and higher overall well-being than those who habitually choose the safe and comfortable option.

Research consistently shows that approach-oriented coping, moving toward challenges rather than away from them, produces significantly greater resilience, lower rates of depression and anxiety, and higher well-being than habitual avoidance. Small daily courage is approach-oriented coping practiced as a lifestyle rather than deployed only in crisis.

Try This Today

- Think of one thing you've been avoiding because it feels uncomfortable or vulnerable and ask honestly: *is this worth the cost of continuing to avoid it?* Take one step toward it today.
- Start something you've been waiting to feel ready for. Write the first paragraph. Make the first call. Readiness is almost never a prerequisite for beginning. It is almost always a consequence of it.
- At the end of today ask: *did I do one thing that required genuine courage, however small?* If yes, notice it and let it build. If no, identify what tomorrow's small courageous act will be.

What If the Fear Feels Too Big?

Then the small steps are exactly right. Courage is built by acting while the fear is present and discovering, repeatedly, that the action was survivable and something on the other side was worth the cost of getting there. The larger courage you'll need for the larger moments is being built right now, in the small ones.

Bottom Line

Do one small courageous thing today. Not because it's easy. Because the person you most want to become is built, one small act at a time, in exactly these ordinary moments.

100. Look for One Unexpected Gain—Practice Benefit-Finding

Hard things, met with honesty and intention, almost always produce something real alongside what they cost.

What It Is

When my wife and I were on the other side of her brain surgery, young and relieved and exhaling for what felt like the first time in months, I remember noticing something unexpected. We were closer. Not just grateful to be through it, but genuinely closer in a way that I'm not sure we would have been without it. The fear and the uncertainty and the showing up for each other through something neither of us had chosen had produced something between us that easier circumstances hadn't yet built. That was an unexpected gain. And naming it mattered.

In the middle of something difficult, or just on the other side of it, look carefully for one thing that wouldn't exist in your life without it. Not the silver lining that minimizes the cloud. Not a forced positive reframe. One genuine, specific, honest gain, something that grew in you, or around you, or because of you during the hard thing, that you can identify and name with real precision.

The relationship that deepened because the crisis required both of you to show up. The strength you discovered only because the circumstances demanded it. The clarity about what actually matters that arrived only after something you thought mattered turned out not to be worth what it cost. The compassion for other people's suffering you couldn't have developed without your own.

This entry is distinct from happy hack 85 on reframing painful chapters, which was about the broader narrative work of finding a growth story in a past experience. This is more immediate and targeted: the specific practice of looking for one unexpected gain in a current or recent hard experience. Not the whole story rewritten. Just one genuine benefit found and named. One is enough. One is where it starts.

Why It Works

Research by Suzanne Folkman on benefit-finding, the deliberate identification of positive outcomes within negative experiences, shows that this practice produces significant improvements in psychological well-being, immune function, and stress resilience during and after adversity. People who actively engaged in benefit-finding during sustained hardship maintained meaningfully better psychological health than those who didn't, not because their circumstances were easier but because their relationship to those circumstances included an active search for what the difficulty was also producing.

Martin Seligman's research on benefit reminding, actively rehearsing the gains produced by adversity rather than simply identifying them once, shows that the practice's well-being benefits increase with repetition. Finding the benefit once opens the door. Returning to it regularly consolidates the gain into something that genuinely reorients your relationship with the difficulty over time.

Try This Today

- Ask the benefit-finding questions: *what did this require of me that I didn't know I had? What relationship deepened because of it? What do I value now that I didn't before?*
- Write the benefit down specifically, with honest acknowledgment of both what the difficulty cost and what it also produced. Specificity matters more than you'd expect.
- Return to the gain you identified at least once more this week. Rehearsing the benefit, not just finding it, is where much of the well-being return lives.

What If You Can't Find a Genuine Benefit?

Don't force one. If a genuine benefit isn't visible yet, it may simply be too soon. Be honest first. The benefit, if it's there, will surface when the emotional ground is ready for it.

Bottom Line

Hard things almost always cost something real. And hard things, met with honesty and intention, almost always produce something real too. Look for the one unexpected gain, not to replace the cost, but to complete it. Name it. Write it down. Return to it.

101. Write a Letter to Your Future Self

Somewhere in your future is a person who will read what you write today and be moved by the distance traveled.

What It Is

We've arrived at the final happy hack. One hundred and one practices, all pointing toward the same thing: a life that is richer, more connected, more meaningful, and more genuinely yours. And I can think of no better way to close than with this.

Sit down, unhurried and honestly, and write a letter to the person you will be one year, five years, or ten years from now. Not a goal list. Not a performance of who you think you should be becoming. A genuine letter from the person you are today, in the middle of whatever you're currently living, to the person you will be when you read it.

Tell yourself what's hard right now. What you're hoping for. What you're afraid of. What you're working toward. What you want your future self to know about who you actually were in this particular chapter, not who you aspired to be, but who you were. Tell yourself what you hope is true by the time you read it. What you hope has changed. What you hope has stayed. What you hope you had the courage to do. Then seal it. Put it somewhere you'll find it, or use FutureMe.org, a free site that delivers your letter to your email inbox on any future date you choose.

What happens when you read it is difficult to fully anticipate and worth experiencing firsthand. Most people are surprised by what past-you knew, feared, hoped, and carried. Most are moved by the distance traveled. Many discover that the person who wrote the letter was wiser and braver than you gave yourself credit for at the time. The letter is a gift in both directions. Writing it clarifies the present. Reading it illuminates the past and measures the growth.

Why It Works

Psychologist Hal Hershfield's research on future self-continuity, the degree to which people feel psychologically connected to the person they will become, shows that people with stronger future self-continuity make significantly better long-term decisions, show greater self-regulatory capacity, and report higher levels of meaning and life satisfaction. Writing a letter to your future self is one of the most direct ways to strengthen that continuity, to make your future self real enough to care about and specific enough to write to.

Dan McAdams' narrative identity research adds the second dimension. Writing to your future self requires you to locate yourself in your own ongoing story, to identify where you are in the arc, what chapter you're currently living, and what you imagine comes next. That narrative self-placement is itself a meaning-making act. It gives the present moment its context and its significance.

Try This Today

- Begin with where you are right now. Not the polished version. The honest one.
- Tell your future self what you most want yourself to remember about who you were at this moment, the things that daily life will blur and time will soften if you don't name them now.
- Name what you're hoping for specifically. Not "I hope things are better" but the particular hopes that are alive in you right now, for your relationships, your work, your health, your character, your unfinished becoming.

- Seal it and schedule its reading. One year is a meaningful interval. Five or ten produces a different and equally profound experience.

What If You're Not Sure What to Say?

Start with the truth of right now and trust that it's enough. Your future self doesn't need inspiration or polished wisdom from the past you. You need to know who you actually were. Tell the truth. In as much detail as possible. The rest takes care of itself.

Bottom Line

101 hacks. All of them pointing toward a life that is happier, more meaningful, and more fully yours. But none of them matter as much as this final truth: your life, right now, in this chapter, with all its difficulty and beauty and unfinished becoming, is worth documenting. Worth reflecting on. Worth sending forward.

Write the letter. Tell the truth about where you are. Tell yourself what you're hoping for. And trust that the distance between the writing and the reading, filled with choices, growth, difficulty, and becoming, will be one of the most meaningful journeys you'll ever make.

The letter is waiting. So are you.

9.

THE EMERGING EDGE: HAPPY HACKS WORTH WATCHING

I want to be up front with you before we begin this chapter. Everything in the previous eight chapters rests on a foundation of well-replicated, peer-reviewed research. The practices I've shared with you have been studied across hundreds, even thousands of participants, refined over decades, and confirmed by independent researchers in studies and labs around the world. When I told you that gratitude journaling works, or that strong relationships are the single greatest predictor of happiness, I was standing on solid ground.

This chapter is different. I'll tell you what prompted it. My wife and I use essential oils in our home. We have a red light therapy panel in a spare bedroom in our basement. We own a vibration plate that we both step on regularly, not because we've read compelling peer-reviewed trials about it, but because it feels good, it wakes us up, and we've decided that sometimes that's enough of a reason. And my wife, who lives with an autoimmune disease that brings real and persistent joint pain, has found genuine relief in salves made from dandelion, frankincense, lavender, and dozens of other plant-based remedies that her rheumatologist didn't prescribe and her insurance doesn't cover.

Do they work? She would tell you absolutely yes. Can I point you to a robust body of peer-reviewed clinical trials? Not always. Both of those things are true at the same time, and I think that tension deserves an honest conversation rather than a dismissive eye roll from either direction.

Here's something worth understanding about how science actually works. It moves in phases. First come observations, the people who notice that something seems to help and start talking about it. Then come early studies, small and imperfect but pointing in an interesting direction. Then come replications, larger trials, independent confirmation, and eventually the kind of settled consensus that earned a place in the previous eight chapters. The practices in this chapter sit somewhere in those earlier stages. They are not settled science yet. But they are interesting enough, and in many cases promising enough, to pay attention to. Dismissing them entirely because they haven't completed the full journey would mean ignoring something that may genuinely matter. Overselling them as proven would mean misleading you. This chapter tries to do neither.

Are we biased? Probably. Are we alone? Definitely not. Millions of people are using practices like these and reporting real benefits, and I've come to believe they deserve to be taken seriously rather than simply sorted into proven or pseudoscience and left there. The history of medicine is genuinely full of practices that were considered fringe until the research caught up. Willow bark was folk medicine before it became aspirin. Handwashing was considered unnecessary before germ theory. Mindfulness was dismissed as wishful thinking before decades of neuroscience validated what practitioners had known for centuries.

At the same time, I care too much about you to oversell what the science currently supports. Some of what follows has small but promising research bases that are growing quickly. Some has plausible biological mechanisms that scientists are still working to fully understand. Some, like our vibration plate, has almost no mood-specific research (yet) but enough anecdotal support and low enough risk that it seems worth mentioning. And some, like the plant-based salves my wife swears by, operates in the complicated space where personal experience is real and consistent even when the clinical trial literature is thin.

I'm also aware that some of you came to this book already using practices that fall outside conventional medicine, whether that's essential oils, herbal remedies, earthing, homeopathic treatments, or other approaches your doctor might raise an eyebrow at. I don't want to dismiss what you've experienced. Personal experience is data too, even when it's hard to study. And I've watched my wife find relief that prescription medications didn't fully provide through approaches that conventional medicine hasn't fully investigated. That matters to me. It's part of why this chapter exists.

So, here's my promise for this chapter: I'll tell you what the research actually shows (as of the writing of this book), where it's strong, where it's thin, and where we genuinely need more. This certainly isn't an exhaustive list. But, I'll be honest about what my wife and I do ourselves and why. I'll respect both the science and the lived experience of people who have found real benefit in practices that science hasn't fully caught up with yet. And I'll trust you, as I have throughout this entire book, to take what's useful, leave what isn't, and keep paying attention as the science develops.

These are the emerging edges worth watching. Let's look at them together.

Red Light Therapy:
More Science Than You Might Think

The mood claims are getting ahead of the science. The recovery and sleep research, however, is genuinely interesting.

We have a red light panel in a bedroom in our basement and we use it often. I'll be honest about how it started: my wife tried it first, reported feeling better and sleeping more soundly, and that was enough to get me on board. Rigorous? No. Relatable? I suspect yes.

But here's what surprised me when I actually went looking at the research: there's more there than I expected, particularly around physical recovery and sleep. On the recovery side, the evidence is the strongest. A review of 46 studies involving over 1,000 participants found that red and near-infrared light therapy can reduce inflammation, decrease delayed onset muscle soreness, and lower markers of muscle damage after exercise. My wife and I both use ours after hard workouts or when something is sore, and the research at least gives us reason to think we're not just imagining the relief. One study on university athletes found that those using red light therapy returned to play from sports injuries in an average of about 9 days compared to an anticipated 19 days. That's a meaningful difference if it holds up in larger studies.

Then there's the BYU connection that I find particularly fascinating as an academic living in Utah. A study funded in part by BYU and conducted by Lindsey and colleagues, published in the Journal of Neurotrauma, followed collegiate football players across a full season. Players using near-infrared light therapy showed significantly reduced brain inflammation compared to those in the placebo group, whose brain inflammation increased measurably over the season. Preliminary results also showed increases in grip strength, sustained attention, mental speed, and reaction time in the treatment group. The lead researcher's first reaction to the findings was reportedly that there was no way it could be real. That's how striking the results were.

On sleep, the evidence is also real. Red and near-infrared light wavelengths in the evening don't suppress melatonin production the way blue light from screens does, and some studies suggest they may actively support the body's natural wind-down process. Given everything we know about sleep's relationship to mood, energy, and well-being, that matters.

The honest caveat: direct mood enhancement claims from red light therapy are still getting ahead of the science. The biological mechanism involving mitochondrial function is plausible, but plausible doesn't always equal proven. And consumer-grade panels are generally less powerful than the medical-grade devices used in research settings, so results may vary.

My take: think of red light therapy as a recovery and sleep tool first, a possible mood tool second. The research in those first two categories is real enough to take seriously. Just don't spend a fortune based on claims the science hasn't fully earned yet.

Essential Oils: What We Actually Know

The research is limited. The experience is real. Both things can be true.

My wife has diffused lavender in our bedroom for years. It's part of our wind-down routine, along with dimming the lights and putting phones away. Does lavender specifically account for better sleep? Honestly, I can't say for certain. But here's what I can say: the research on aromatherapy, while far from conclusive, is more interesting than most scientists will admit at a dinner party.

Several small studies have found that lavender oil, specifically its primary compound linalool, produces measurable reductions in anxiety and cortisol levels, with some studies showing effects comparable to low-dose anti-anxiety medication. Peppermint has shown some evidence for alertness and cognitive performance. Citrus scents have been linked in small trials to mood elevation and reduced stress markers.

The truthful caveat: most of these studies are small, poorly controlled, and difficult to replicate. The placebo effect in aromatherapy research is notoriously hard to account for, since you can't exactly give someone a fake smell. We genuinely need larger, better-designed studies before making strong claims.

What I believe, based on the evidence and our own experience: scent is one of the most direct pathways to the brain's limbic system, the emotional processing center, which is why a smell can transport you instantly to a memory or a feeling. That connection is real and well-established even if the specific therapeutic claims need more research. If a scent reliably signals safety, calm, or comfort to your nervous system, that signal has value. Just don't pay $80 for a bottle based on claims science hasn't yet earned.

Breathwork:
The One That Almost Made the Main Book

Five minutes. One simple pattern. Real, peer-reviewed data.

Most of us know that slow, deep breathing calms the nervous system. That's not emerging science, it's well-established. What is newer is the precise identification of specific breathwork protocols and their measurable effects on mood, anxiety, and stress in real time.

Stanford neuroscientist Andrew Huberman and colleagues published a randomized controlled trial comparing several breathwork protocols against mindfulness meditation. The winner, and it wasn't close, was something called cyclic sighing: a double inhale through the nose followed by a long, slow exhale through the mouth, repeated for five minutes. Participants who practiced cyclic sighing daily reported the greatest reductions in anxiety, the greatest improvements in mood, and the strongest physiological markers of nervous system regulation of any group in the study, including the mindfulness group.

Five minutes. One simple pattern. Real randomized controlled trial data from Stanford. This one is strong enough that it almost landed in the main book, and it may well belong there by the time the research continues to accumulate.

Try it now: set a five-minute timer. Double inhale through the nose, filling the lungs completely on the second inhale, then a slow full exhale through the mouth. Repeat until the timer ends. Most people notice something real within the first two or three minutes. Your nervous system will respond before your skeptical mind catches up.

Grounding and Earthing: Ancient Practice, Emerging Science

Walking barefoot in the grass sounds too simple to work. The research says maybe don't dismiss it quite yet.

I'll admit I raised an eyebrow the first time a student brought this one to my attention. The idea that walking barefoot on the earth could meaningfully affect your stress levels sounded more like wellness marketing than science. Then I looked more carefully. The proposed mechanism is this: the earth's surface carries a mild negative electrical charge, and direct physical contact with it allows free electrons to transfer into the body. Those electrons, the hypothesis goes, act as natural antioxidants, reducing inflammation and potentially influencing cortisol levels and mood.

It sounds unusual. But a small and growing body of research has found measurable reductions in cortisol, improvements in sleep quality, reductions in self-reported stress, and in some studies mood improvements in participants who practiced regular grounding compared to controls. A study published in the Journal of Inflammation Research found that grounding affected multiple markers of inflammation and immune response in ways consistent with the proposed mechanism.

The important caveat: most studies are small and independent replication is limited. We cannot say with confidence that grounding works the way proponents claim. What we can say is that the mechanism is plausible, the early findings are interesting and walking barefoot in the grass on a warm morning costs you nothing. It also gets you outside, slows you down, and connects you to the natural world in ways that are probably beneficial regardless of the electron theory.

If you already do this and love it, the science is at least beginning to catch up. If you've never tried it, it's about as low-risk an experiment as exists.

Cold Water Immersion: The Dopamine You Didn't Expect

This one has more science behind it than the trend would suggest.

Cold showers are familiar enough. This entry goes further because the research on deliberate cold water immersion, cold plunges, ice baths, or cold open water swimming, is stronger and more interesting than the wellness industry hype might suggest.

Research has found that a single cold water immersion session can produce a substantial and sustained increase in dopamine levels lasting several hours afterward, larger and more sustained than almost any other non-pharmacological intervention studied. Participants also reported significant improvements in mood, alertness, and sense of well-being. The physiological mechanism is real: cold exposure activates the sympathetic nervous system, releases norepinephrine, and triggers a cascade of neurochemical responses that affect mood, energy, and focus in measurable ways.

There's also a growing social dimension worth noting. The cold plunge community, whether it's a backyard tub, a local cryotherapy spot, or an open water swimming group, tends to be unusually enthusiastic and connected. Some of the benefit people report may be as much about the shared experience and the sense of accomplishment as the cold itself. That's not a reason to dismiss it. It's actually a reason to find a friend and do it together.

The honest caveat: long-term mood effects need more study, and cold water immersion carries genuine physiological risks for people with certain heart conditions. Start with a cold shower. End your regular shower with 30 to 60 seconds of cold water and work up gradually from there. Talk to your doctor if you have cardiovascular concerns.

Float Therapy: Silence as Medicine

Most people are surprised by what happens when everything external goes quiet.

Floatation therapy involves lying in a shallow pool of skin-temperature water saturated with Epsom salt, in complete darkness and silence, for 60 to 90 minutes. If that sounds either deeply appealing or mildly terrifying, you're in good company. Most people feel both before their first session.

The research is small but surprisingly consistent. Studies from researchers including Justin Feinstein at the Laureate Institute for Brain Research have found significant reductions in anxiety, stress, and muscle tension following float sessions, along with mood improvements that persisted for days afterward in some participants. Brain imaging studies have shown measurable changes in neural activity following floating, suggesting genuine neurological effects rather than simple relaxation.

What most people report afterward isn't dramatic. It's quieter than that. A kind of reset. A slowing down that modern life rarely permits. Several people I know who have tried it describe the same thing: they didn't realize how loud their nervous system had been running until it finally went quiet.

Float spas exist in most mid-sized cities and sessions typically run between $50-$100. It's not an everyday practice for most people, but as an occasional reset during high-stress seasons, the evidence and the anecdotal reports are consistent enough to make it worth trying at least once. Many people who try it once go back.

Psychedelic-Assisted Therapy: The Science You Might Not Expect

I'm not recommending this. I am telling you the research is serious enough to know about.

Let me be careful here, and clear. This is not a hack you can try today in most places, and I am not suggesting you should seek it out. What I am telling you is that some of the most compelling mental health research being conducted anywhere in the world right now involves psilocybin, the active compound in certain mushrooms, and that the findings are serious enough that an honest book about happiness and well-being would be incomplete without acknowledging them.

Research from Johns Hopkins University and NYU, published in peer-reviewed journals including the New England Journal of Medicine, has shown that psilocybin-assisted therapy produces dramatic and sustained reductions in depression and anxiety, including in patients with treatment-resistant depression and in people facing end-of-life anxiety. In some studies, one or two sessions produced effects lasting months or years. Participants consistently report experiences of profound meaning, connectedness, and what researchers describe as increased openness and well-being that persist long after the session itself.

The proposed mechanism is fascinating: psilocybin appears to temporarily increase neuroplasticity and disrupt entrenched patterns of rumination and self-referential thinking, essentially creating a window in which the brain is more open to new perspectives and patterns. Some researchers describe it as a kind of reset for a stuck system.

Microdosing, taking sub-perceptual doses regularly, has a growing observational literature showing self-reported improvements in mood, creativity, and well-being, though controlled trial data is still limited and placebo effects in self-selected populations are difficult to rule out.

Psilocybin remains a controlled substance in most places, though that is changing as research advances and several cities and states have moved toward decriminalization or regulated therapeutic use. The science is real, the effects being documented are significant, and the therapeutic model being developed at major research institutions deserves to be taken seriously. Watch this space closely over the next decade. It may well reshape how we understand and treat depression, anxiety, and end-of-life distress in ways that are genuinely significant.

Social Prescribing: When the Doctor Prescribes Community

Medicine is finally catching up to what happiness research has known for decades.

Here's one that has nothing to do with supplements, technology, or anything you'd find in a wellness store, and everything to do with what this entire book has been saying from the beginning.

Social prescribing is an emerging practice in which healthcare providers, rather than or alongside prescribing medication, formally prescribe community engagement: volunteering, joining a group, spending time in nature, participating in arts or music programs. The United Kingdom has implemented social prescribing at a national level through the National Health Service, with dedicated link workers whose specific job is to connect patients with community resources rather than clinical ones.

The results have been promising. Studies show reductions in doctor visits, improvements in mental health outcomes, and significant improvements in loneliness and sense of belonging among participants. In one large evaluation of the UK program, participants reported meaningful improvements in well-being, with the greatest gains among those who had been most isolated before the intervention.

I find this one particularly exciting because it represents medicine beginning to formally acknowledge what happiness research has known for decades: connection is not a lifestyle preference. It is a health intervention. The fact that doctors are now writing prescriptions for community the same way they write them for medication feels like a genuinely meaningful shift in how we understand what makes people well.

If your doctor hasn't heard of social prescribing yet, that's okay. You can prescribe it for yourself. Join something. Show up consistently. Contribute to a group. The research, and one hundred and one happy hacks, all point in exactly the same direction.

Forest Bathing: The Oldest Medicine You Forgot You Had Access To

Time in nature isn't just pleasant. It's physiological.

I grew up spending time outdoors, and like most people I've always felt better after time in the woods or mountains than before it. I assumed that was about the exercise, or the change of scenery, or just getting away from the screens. What research has revealed is that something more specific may be happening, and it's interesting enough to take seriously.

Forest bathing, or shinrin-yoku as it's called in Japan where much of the research originated, doesn't require hiking or exercise. It simply means being present in a forested environment, walking slowly, breathing deeply, and letting the senses take in what's around you. That's it. And the physiological responses that simple practice produces are striking enough that Japan and South Korea have incorporated forest bathing into their national public health programs.

Studies measuring people before and after time in forests have found measurable reductions in cortisol, lower blood pressure, reduced heart rate, improved mood, and increased activity of the parasympathetic nervous system, the branch responsible for calm and recovery rather than stress and alertness. Some studies have found increases in natural killer immune cell activity that lasted for days after a single forest exposure. The proposed mechanism involves phytoncides, the aromatic organic compounds released by trees, which appear to have direct biological effects when inhaled, along with the sensory quiet and what attention restoration researchers describe as the effortless, replenishing quality of natural environments.

Of everything in this chapter, the forest bathing research is among the strongest. The studies are well-designed, the physiological mechanisms are plausible and increasingly supported, and the practice itself costs nothing and is available to most people within reasonable distance of a park, a trail, or any patch of trees.

The truthful caveat: most of the research comes from Japan and South Korea, and replication in Western populations is still growing. We don't yet know the optimal dose, how long effects last, or how much of the benefit comes specifically from forests versus any natural environment. But the risk-benefit calculation here is about as favorable as it gets. Go outside. Find some trees. Move slowly. Breathe. The research suggests your body already knows what to do with that.

Sauna: Heat as Medicine

The Finnish have been onto something for a very long time.

I have a confession: before I looked at this research, sauna felt to me like a luxury, something you did at a nice hotel or after a ski trip, pleasant but not particularly meaningful for health or happiness. The longitudinal data from Finland changed my thinking considerably.

Researchers followed more than 2,000 Finnish men for over two decades and found that those who used a sauna four to seven times per week had dramatically lower rates of cardiovascular mortality, significantly reduced risk of dementia, and meaningfully lower rates of depression compared to those who used one once a week or less. Those are striking findings across a long follow-up period in a large sample. You can't dismiss them easily.

The physiological mechanisms are real and increasingly understood. Sauna use triggers endorphin release, increases growth hormone, reduces inflammatory markers, and stresses the cardiovascular system in ways that researchers have begun describing as exercise mimetic, meaning it produces some of the same adaptations as physical exercise. For people who struggle to exercise intensely due to injury, illness, or chronic pain, that's a meaningful finding. For people who already exercise, it may compound the benefits.

Some researchers have also pointed to the social dimension of sauna culture, particularly in Finland, where sauna is traditionally a communal practice. It's possible that some of what the data is capturing is as much about regular social connection in a relaxed setting as it is about heat exposure specifically. That wouldn't make the finding less interesting. It would make it more consistent with everything Chapter 6 already told us.

The transparent caveat: most of the compelling data is observational, meaning we can't establish definitive causation, and it comes from a specific cultural context where sauna is deeply embedded in daily life. People who use saunas four to seven times weekly in Finland may differ from the general population in other health-relevant ways. We also need more research on women specifically, as most of the landmark studies focused on men. And access is a real limitation. Not everyone has a sauna nearby or can afford frequent visits.

If you have access to one, the research is promising enough to use it intentionally rather than occasionally. If you don't, some gyms, community centers, and spas offer access at reasonable cost. It's worth seeking out, particularly during high-stress seasons or if you're navigating the kind of difficulty Chapter 8 was about.

Time-Restricted Eating: When You Eat May Matter More Than You Think

This one isn't about weight loss. It's about your brain, your mood, and your energy.

Let me say upfront what this entry is not about. It's not a diet recommendation. It's not about weight loss or calorie restriction. It's about something more interesting for our purposes: the emerging evidence that the timing of when you eat may significantly affect your mood, your energy, your sleep, and your emotional regulation.

Circadian biology research, much of it coming from the Salk Institute and other leading institutions, has established that the body operates on finely tuned internal clocks that regulate not just sleep but metabolism, hormone production, inflammation, and even brain function. Cortisol, dopamine, melatonin, and other mood-relevant neurochemicals all follow circadian rhythms. And emerging research suggests that eating patterns either support or disrupt those rhythms in ways that have downstream effects on how you feel.

Time-restricted eating, sometimes called circadian eating, involves consuming all of your daily food within a consistent window of roughly eight to twelve hours during the daytime and allowing the remaining hours to be a fasting period. Early studies suggest this pattern, independent of what or how much you eat, may improve metabolic regulation, reduce inflammation markers, improve sleep quality, and stabilize energy levels throughout the day. Some participants in early trials also report improvements in mood and mental clarity, possibly because steadier blood sugar and better-aligned circadian rhythms reduce the cortisol spikes and energy crashes that affect emotional regulation.

The happiness angle is indirect but real. Better sleep, steadier energy, fewer blood sugar crashes, and lower inflammation all affect how you feel, how you handle stress, and how present you're able to be in your relationships and your life. The honest caveat: human trials are still relatively small and heterogeneous, and the research has not yet established clear optimal windows or protocols that work for everyone. People with histories of disordered eating should approach this one with particular caution and ideally with professional guidance. And I want to be careful not to dress up diet culture in neuroscience language.

The goal here is circadian alignment for mood and energy, not restriction for its own sake.

If you're curious, a reasonable starting experiment is simply to notice your current eating window and consider whether it's consistent and daytime-aligned. Many people find they're eating across a twelve-to-fourteen-hour window without realizing it, including late-night snacking that may be disrupting sleep and circadian rhythms in ways that affect the next day's mood and energy. That's a low-risk observation worth making.

Polyvagal-Inspired Practices: Regulating Your Nervous System From the Inside

The theory is contested. Some of the practices it points toward are genuinely interesting regardless.

I want to be more transparent in this entry than in any other in this chapter, because this one sits in genuinely complicated scientific territory and you deserve to know that upfront. Stephen Porges' polyvagal theory, developed over the past three decades, proposes a specific model of how the autonomic nervous system, and particularly the vagus nerve, regulates our capacity for social connection, emotional safety, and stress response. The theory has become enormously influential in trauma therapy, somatic psychology, and wellness circles, and it has generated a wave of practical interventions aimed at what proponents call vagal toning, using specific practices to regulate the nervous system and increase a person's capacity for calm, connection, and emotional flexibility.

Here's where I need to be totally transparent: the polyvagal theory itself is actively debated among neuroscientists. Some researchers argue that aspects of the theoretical framework don't align with established neuroanatomy and that some of its central claims have been overstated. The wellness industry has, in some cases, run well ahead of what the science actually supports, attaching the polyvagal label to practices and claims that the research doesn't fully warrant.

And yet, some of the specific practices that polyvagal-inspired approaches point toward do have independent research support, even if the theoretical framework underneath them remains debated. Extended exhale breathing, which we already covered in the breathwork entry, has strong RCT data. Humming and gargling, which are thought to stimulate the vagus nerve through vibration, have small but interesting preliminary research. Heart rate variability, or HRV, which is associated with vagal tone and emotional regulation, is a genuinely well-supported biomarker with a robust research literature connecting higher HRV to greater resilience, better emotional regulation, and improved well-being.

I've talked to people who have found polyvagal-informed therapy and practices genuinely transformative, particularly people working through trauma and chronic stress. Their experience is real and worth taking seriously even where the theoretical scaffolding is contested. My wife has found that certain calming practices, slow breathing, gentle humming, deliberate grounding, work for her nervous system in ways that matter, regardless of what we call the mechanism.

My honest take: approach the polyvagal theory with informed curiosity rather than either wholesale adoption or dismissal. The framework may be imperfect. The practices it points toward, breathing with extended exhales, building felt safety in relationships, attending to the body's signals, humming, slowing down, are consistent with a lot of what this book has already established. If they work for you, the theoretical debate is somewhat beside the point. Just hold the claims loosely, be skeptical of anyone selling polyvagal certification courses for $500, and pay attention to your own experience.

If you want to explore: try ending your next exhale a few

seconds longer than your inhale. Try humming a low note for thirty seconds and notice what happens in your chest and your nervous system. Your body will tell you something. Whether Stephen Porges has the mechanism exactly right is a question for the scientists to keep working out.

The Vibration Plate: Almost No Research, Zero Apologies

Sometimes something just feels good. That's worth something too.

I'm going to be more honest in this entry than most wellness books would be: we own a vibration plate and there is almost no peer-reviewed research supporting its use as a mood or happiness intervention. There. I said it.

What there is: some evidence for improved circulation, lymphatic drainage, and muscle activation. A small number of studies suggest potential benefits for balance and bone density in older adults. And one thing I know from personal experience: stepping on it for ten minutes in the morning wakes me up, gets my body moving, and starts the day with a physical jolt that feels genuinely energizing. My wife feels the same way.

Is that the vibration plate specifically? Is it the fact that we're moving our bodies first thing in the morning, which we know from Chapter 2 is beneficial regardless of how you do it? Is it the placebo effect of doing something intentional for yourself before the day takes over? Honestly, I'm not sure. Probably some combination of all three.

Here's what I've come to believe about practices like this one: when something is low-risk, affordable, and consistently makes you feel better, the absence of a peer-reviewed explanation doesn't automatically make it wrong. The research often follows the experience by years or decades. In the meantime, your own body is data too. Just don't buy one expecting it to replace exercise. The research is clear that it won't. Think of it as a complement, a gentle on-ramp for the body in the morning and manage your expectations accordingly.

AI Companionship and Digital Mental Health Tools: A Nuanced Look

Used well, these tools may help. Used as a substitute for real connection, they may quietly make things worse.

I'll end this chapter with the most contested entry and the one I feel most personally uncertain about. AI companions and digital mental health tools, ranging from therapy chatbots to dedicated companionship apps, are being used by millions of people, particularly among those who are lonely, isolated, elderly, or without access to traditional mental health care. Some people report genuine comfort, reduced anxiety, and even therapeutic benefit from these interactions. And given everything we discussed in Chapter 6 about the loneliness epidemic, dismissing any source of perceived connection without careful thought feels both premature and unkind.

The research is genuinely mixed. Some studies show that AI-assisted mental health tools reduce symptoms of depression and anxiety, particularly as supplements to human care. A review of digital mental health interventions found moderate effects on depression and anxiety symptoms, with the strongest results when digital tools were used alongside, rather than instead of, human connection and professional support. Other research raises legitimate concerns about dependency and the risk that artificial connection substitutes for the harder but more nourishing work of building real relationships.

My personal take: I believe human connection is irreplaceable, and I'd be doing you a disservice to suggest otherwise. At the same time, for some people in some circumstances, a digital tool that reduces loneliness or provides a space for reflection is genuinely better than nothing, and that matters. The question worth asking yourself honestly is whether the tool is building your capacity for human connection or gradually substituting for it. If the former, it may have real value. If the latter, it deserves a closer look.

10.

THE FINAL WORD: LOOK HOW FAR YOU'VE COME

I'll be real with you. Writing this book has been one of the most meaningful projects of my career, and one of the more humbling ones. Somewhere around the fiftieth entry I found myself wondering whether I was actually living what I was writing, whether the practices I was describing with such confidence were genuinely woven into my own days or whether I was articulating an ideal I was still working toward. The answer, most days, was both. I'm a family scientist and happiness researcher who still ruminates too long, still gets pulled into busyness as identity, still has to remind myself to put the phone down and be present for the people sitting right in front of me.

I share that not to undermine what I've written but to affirm it. This book was never meant to describe a finished life. It was meant to describe a direction. A set of practices that, taken seriously and returned to consistently, move the needle toward something genuinely better. I need them as much as you do. Probably more, on some days.

So, before you go, I want to ask you to do something. Think about who you were five years ago. Ten years ago. At the hardest chapter you've lived so far. What did that person not yet know how to do that you can do now? What did they carry that you've set down? What were they afraid of that no longer holds the same power? What did they not yet understand about themselves, about other people, about what actually matters, that you understand now, not because someone told you, but because you lived your way to it? Look at what you've survived. What you've rebuilt. What you've lost and grieved and eventually integrated. What you tried and failed at and tried again differently. What you became in the seasons you didn't choose and couldn't control.

You have come further than you know. And I mean that not as a motivational sentiment but as a research finding, one of the most consistent and striking ones in the psychology of human development. People systematically underestimate their own growth. They feel the distance between where they are and where they want to be far more acutely than the distance between where they are and where they were. The gap ahead is vivid. The ground already covered is strangely invisible, present underfoot but rarely examined, rarely acknowledged, rarely given its full weight as evidence of something genuinely significant.

Timothy Wilson's research on the psychological immune system shows that people are consistently better at navigating adversity than they predict they will be before it arrives. We underestimate our own resilience. We underestimate our capacity to grow. We underestimate the degree to which the hard things we've already survived have made us more capable of surviving what comes next. And James Pennebaker's research on expressive processing shows that articulating growth, writing it, speaking it, naming it with specificity, consolidates it in ways that simply having grown does not. Growth that is named becomes a resource. Growth that goes unnamed remains background noise.

Carol Dweck's growth mindset research closes the loop. People who recognize and acknowledge their own growth are significantly more likely to approach future challenges with the orientation that produces further growth. Reflecting on how far you've come is not nostalgia. It is the act of building the psychological foundation from which the next chapter of becoming is launched.

A Few Things Before You Go

If I could leave you with anything, it would be this. Please don't use this book as another way to be hard on yourself. Don't read 101 happy hacks and walk away feeling like you're failing at 87 of them. That's not what any of this is for. Pick one. Practice it until it feels natural. Then pick another. Trust the process and trust yourself.

My sister ended every letter she wrote me during my two-year church mission the same way: pain is inevitable, but misery is optional. I didn't fully understand it at the time. I've spent the rest of my life learning what she meant. The pain of hard things is rarely in our control. What we make of them is. That's been the quiet conviction underneath every page of this book.

I've shared a lot of my own life in these pages. My wife's brain surgery when we were barely into our twenties. My mom's liver cancer diagnosis and the extraordinary grace with which she has faced it. The losses and hard seasons in our extended family that have taught me more about resilience than any research paper. The gratitude letters I wrote years ago that I still think about. The sticky note on my mom's mirror that asked every morning: *And what did you do for someone today?* These weren't illustrations. They were the real material of a real life, shared because I believe deeply that happiness is not an abstract concept or an academic exercise. It gets built and tested and sometimes broken and rebuilt in the middle of real life, with real people, through real difficulty.

The research matters. And so does the living.

The Happy Hack Attacks:
Ten Things Most Likely to Rob Your Happiness

Before we fully close, a word about the other side of the equation. We've spent 101 entries talking about what to do. But happiness isn't just built by adding good things. It's also protected by recognizing and reducing the things that quietly drain it. I call them *happy hack attacks*. This isn't a shame list. Most of us struggle with at least a few of these. Recognizing them is the first step toward doing something about them.

But before we get to the list, I want to share something that has stayed with me for a long time, something I've come to believe is one of the most important insights in this entire book. Earlier I introduced four directions that the happiest, most resilient people tend to move in: Search Inward. Turn Outward. Look Upward. Press Forward. Those eight words have shaped everything in these pages. They reflect what the science consistently points toward: self-awareness that leads to self-giving, a life anchored to something larger than personal comfort, and the willingness to keep moving through difficulty rather than around it.

Here's what I've noticed, though. The recipe for misery is sneakily, almost invisibly close to the recipe for flourishing. It doesn't look dramatically different from the outside. And yet it produces an entirely different life. All you have to do is switch two words. Instead of Searching Inward and Turning Outward, people begin searching *outward* and turning *inward*. Searching outward means measuring your worth by external things, how you look, what you own, how many people follow you, whether others are impressed by you, how you rank compared to everyone else. Turning inward means retreating into self-focus, self-protection, self-promotion, and self-concern as the organizing principle of your daily life. It's a subtle shift. And it leads somewhere very different.

I've seen this pattern in countless forms. The person at the gym who is there not to care for their body but to be *seen* caring for their body, to be admired, to look better than others. The person chasing prestige, popularity, or fame not because those things will help them contribute something meaningful but because the external validation feels, at least temporarily, like proof that they matter. The constant pursuit of what others think, what others have, what others are doing, and how you compare. It all feels like ambition. It all looks like drive. But it's searching in the wrong direction and turning the wrong way, and it leads, reliably and eventually, toward emptiness.

Here's what makes this so hard to see: selfishness rarely announces itself as selfishness. It arrives dressed as motivation, ambition, self-improvement, and self-care. And some of those things genuinely are good. The difference is whether they are serving something larger than yourself or only feeding the self that is doing the searching. External things, status, admiration, possessions, popularity, all have one thing in common. They fade. They require constant replenishment. And they blind you to the things that actually last, the relationships, the meaning, the contribution, the quiet satisfaction of a life pointed outward rather than inward.

I'm confident that the most self-centered and prideful people are not the happiest people. They are, in fact, among the least happy, because the self is simply not a large enough object to sustain a meaningful life. Happiness, as this entire book has tried to show, is not something you find by looking for it directly. It shows up as a byproduct of searching inward honestly, turning outward generously, looking upward humbly, and pressing forward persistently. Switch any of those directions, and the whole system quietly begins to unravel.

The ten happy hack attacks that follow are some of the most common ways that unraveling happens. Some are dramatic and obvious. Some are subtle enough that you might not recognize them in your own life without looking carefully. All of them share a common thread: they redirect your attention away from what actually sustains well-being and toward what merely simulates it.

Recognizing them is the first step. The rest of this book has already given you the antidotes.

Happy Hack Attack #1: Chronic Comparison

Teddy Roosevelt is credited with calling comparison the thief of joy, and the research agrees completely. Social comparison theory shows that upward comparison, measuring yourself against people who appear to have more, do more, or be more, consistently produces feelings of inadequacy and dissatisfaction. Social media has turned this ancient tendency into a relentless, algorithmically optimized assault on contentment. The highlight reels you scroll through are not representative of real life. They're curated performances of carefully selected best moments, and comparing your interior experience to someone else's exterior presentation is a guaranteed path to feeling worse. The antidote is in Chapter 5: gratitude for what is, rather than resentment for what isn't.

Happy Hack Attack #2: Loneliness and Social Disconnection

We covered this extensively in Chapter 6, but it bears repeating here because loneliness is arguably the single greatest threat to happiness and health in contemporary life. Julianne Holt-Lunstad's research places chronic loneliness in the same risk category as smoking fifteen cigarettes a day. The surgeon general of the United States has declared loneliness a public health epidemic. And yet we have collectively normalized a level of social disconnection that previous generations would have found alarming. If there is one area of your life where investment pays the highest happiness return, it is the quality and consistency of your close relationships. Don't let busyness or the illusion of digital connection substitute for the real thing.

Happy Hack Attack #3: Rumination and Overthinking

Your brain is extraordinarily good at one particularly unhelpful thing: replaying difficult experiences, rehearsing future catastrophes, and constructing elaborate narratives about everything that could go wrong or already has. Susan Nolen-Hoeksema's decades of research on rumination show that it is one of the strongest predictors of depression and anxiety, and that people who ruminate don't actually solve their problems more effectively. They just suffer longer. The thinking that feels productive during a rumination spiral almost never is. The antidote is movement, connection, engagement, and the present-moment practices scattered throughout this book. When the loop starts, don't analyze it. Interrupt it.

Happy Hack Attack #4: Sleep Deprivation

We covered sleep in Chapter 2 and it deserves to be on this list too, because sleep deprivation is so normalized in contemporary culture that most chronically under-slept people have lost the ability to accurately gauge how impaired they are. Matthew Walker's research is unambiguous: insufficient sleep compromises emotional regulation, amplifies negative emotion, impairs judgment, reduces empathy, and makes every other happiness practice in this book significantly harder to execute. You cannot gratitude-journal your way out of chronic sleep deprivation. Sleep is the foundation. When it's inadequate, everything built on top of it is unstable. Protecting your sleep is one of the highest-leverage happiness decisions available to you. Period.

Happy Hack Attack #5: Avoidance of Difficult Emotions

One of the most counterintuitive findings in emotion research is that attempting to avoid or suppress difficult emotions doesn't make them smaller. It makes them larger and more persistent. James Gross's research on emotional suppression shows that people who habitually suppress their emotional experience show greater physiological stress responses, worse long-term well-being, and more disrupted social relationships than those who allow and process their emotions more openly. The feelings you push down don't disappear. They go underground and find other ways to surface. The antidote isn't wallowing. It's the honest acknowledgment and processing that Susan David's emotional agility research describes as the path through rather than around difficult emotional experience.

Happy Hack Attack #6: Busyness as Identity

Somewhere along the way many of us absorbed the belief that being busy is the same as being important, productive, or valuable. We wear our packed schedules like badges and apologize for having free time as if leisure were a character flaw. The research tells a different story. The most creative and productive people consistently protect substantial time for rest, reflection, and unstructured thought. Busyness is not the same as meaning. Activity is not the same as progress. And the relentless scheduling that leaves no room for stillness or genuine rest is one of the quieter but more reliable routes to burnout, disconnection, and the nagging sense that your life is happening too fast to actually be lived.

Happy Hack Attack #7: Materialism and Extrinsic Goal Pursuit

Tim Kasser's research on materialism is among the most consistent in happiness science: people who organize their lives primarily around the pursuit of money, status, possessions, and the approval of others report significantly lower well-being than those oriented toward intrinsic goals like relationships, personal growth, and contribution. The painful irony is that our culture is extraordinarily effective at convincing us that the next purchase or the next promotion will finally deliver the lasting satisfaction we're looking for. It won't. The hedonic treadmill is real. You'll never get enough of what you don't need, because what you don't need will never satisfy you. More stuff and more status reliably underdeliver on happiness.

Happy Hack Attack #8: Absence of Meaning and Purpose

Frankl observed that people can endure almost any how if they have a sufficient why. The flip side is equally true: without a sense of meaning and purpose, even comfortable and objectively fortunate lives feel empty in ways that are impossible to shop or scroll your way out of. Michael Steger's research shows that the presence of meaning is one of the strongest independent predictors of well-being, separate from positive emotion, engagement, or achievement. People who haven't connected their daily choices to something larger than immediate comfort carry a low-grade existential restlessness that no amount of happiness hacking fully resolves. Chapter 7 was about this. If it resonated, go back and spend more time there.

Happy Hack Attack #9: Chronic Stress Without Recovery

Stress is not the enemy. We established that in Chapter 8. Chronic stress without adequate recovery is. The human stress response is designed for acute activation followed by recovery, not for continuous low-grade activation with no genuine off switch. When stress becomes chronic and unrelenting, cortisol stays elevated, the immune system is suppressed, and the capacity for clear thinking, emotional regulation, and genuine connection is significantly reduced. The problem for most people isn't that they experience stress. It's that they never fully recover from it. The recovery practices throughout this book, sleep, movement, connection, meaning, and rest, are not optional extras. They are the biological necessity that makes sustained engagement with a demanding life possible.

Happy Hack Attack #10: Perfectionism

Brenй Brown's research identifies perfectionism not as a healthy pursuit of excellence but as a self-protective belief system built on the conviction that if I look perfect and never make mistakes, I can avoid the pain of judgment and shame. The problem is that it doesn't work. Perfectionism doesn't prevent shame. It amplifies it, because every inevitable imperfection becomes evidence for the belief that you are fundamentally not enough. It also reliably produces procrastination, because the gap between the perfect outcome you're holding out for and the imperfect reality of beginning is too uncomfortable to sit with. The antidote is not lower standards. It's the courage to be seen as imperfect and the willingness to engage fully with life anyway.

One Last Thing

This is the last of 101 practices aimed at one of the most important questions a human life can ask: *How do I live, not just successfully or comfortably, but genuinely, meaningfully, and with as much happiness as this one life will hold?* The answer, woven through every chapter of this book, has always pointed in the same direction: inward to your values and your strengths, outward to the people and the world that need what you have to give, upward to something larger than your own comfort and convenience, and forward, always forward, through whatever hard things arrive between here and the end of the story.

You have already come further than you know. You are already more than you give yourself credit for. And the best chapters, the ones that will ask the most of you and give back more than you can currently imagine, may still be ahead.

Look back long enough to see the ground you've covered.

Then turn forward.

And keep going.

Not because the journey is easy.

Because it is yours.

And because the person you are becoming, through the small daily practices of gratitude and attention, connection and courage, meaning and service and rest and growth, is worth every step it takes to get there.

My sister was right. Pain is inevitable. Misery is optional.

And happiness, it turns out, is not something that happens to lucky people.

It's something that gets built, one small hack and habit at a time, by people exactly like you, in lives that look exactly like yours, starting right now.

Go build something great.

REFERENCES

Algoe, S. B. (2012). Find, remind, and bind: The functions of gratitude in everyday relationships. Social and Personality Psychology Compass, 6(6), 455–469. https://doi.org/10.1111/j.1751-9004.2012.00439.x

Amabile, T., & Kramer, S. (2011). The progress principle: Using small wins to ignite joy, engagement, and creativity at work. Harvard Business Review Press.

Aron, A., Melinat, E., Aron, E. N., Vallone, R. D., & Bator, R. J. (1997). The experimental generation of interpersonal closeness: A procedure and some preliminary findings. Personality and Social Psychology Bulletin, 23(4), 363–377. https://doi.org/10.1177/0146167297234003

Brooks, A. C. (2022). From strength to strength: Finding success, happiness, and deep purpose in the second half of life. Portfolio/Penguin.

Brown, B. (2010). The gifts of imperfection: Let go of who you think you're supposed to be and embrace who you are. Hazelden Publishing.

Brown, B. (2012). Daring greatly: How the courage to be vulnerable transforms the way we live, love, parent, and lead. Gotham Books.

Brown, S. (2009). Play: How it shapes the brain, opens the imagination, and invigorates the soul. Avery.

Bryant, F. B., & Veroff, J. (2007). Savoring: A new model of positive experience. Lawrence Erlbaum Associates.

Burnett, B., & Evans, D. (2016). Designing your life: How to build a well-lived, joyful life. Knopf.

Boyle, P. A., Buchman, A. S., Barnes, L. L., & Bennett, D. A. (2010). Effect of a purpose in life on risk of incident Alzheimer disease and mild cognitive impairment in community-dwelling older persons. Archives of General Psychiatry, 67(3), 304–310. https://doi.org/10.1001/archgenpsychiatry.2009.208

Coan, J. A., Schaefer, H. S., & Davidson, R. J. (2006). Lending a hand: Social regulation of the neural response to threat. *Psychological Science*, 17(12), 1032–1039. https://doi.org/10.1111/j.1467-9280.2006.01832.x

Csikszentmihalyi, M. (1990). Flow: The psychology of optimal experience. Harper & Row.

David, S. (2016). Emotional agility: Get unstuck, embrace change, and thrive in work and life. Avery.

Davis, A. K., Barrett, F. S., May, D. G., Cosimano, M. P., Sepeda, N. D., Johnson, M. W., Finan, P. H., & Griffiths, R. R. (2021). Effects of psilocybin-assisted therapy on major depressive disorder: A randomized clinical trial. *JAMA Psychiatry*, 78(5), 481–489. https://doi.org/10.1001/jamapsychiatry.2020.3285

Duhigg, C. (2012). The power of habit: Why we do what we do in life and business. Random House.

Duckworth, A. (2016). Grit: The power of passion and perseverance. Scribner.

Dunbar, R. (2021). Friends: Understanding the power of our most important relationships. Little, Brown and Company.

Dweck, C. S. (2006). Mindset: The new psychology of success. Random House.

Emmons, R. A., & McCullough, M. E. (2003). Counting blessings versus burdens: An experimental investigation of gratitude and subjective well-being in daily life. Journal of Personality and Social Psychology, 84(2), 377–389. https://doi.org/10.1037/0022-3514.84.2.377

Emmons, R. A. (2007). Thanks!: How the new science of gratitude can make you happier. Houghton Mifflin.

Epley, N., & Schroeder, J. (2014). Mistakenly seeking solitude. Journal of Experimental Psychology: General, 143(5), 1980–1999. https://doi.org/10.1037/a0037323

Feinstein, J. S., Khalsa, S. S., Yeh, H., Wohlrab, C., Simmons, W. K., Stein, M. B., & Paulus, M. P. (2018). Examining the short-term anxiolytic and antidepressant effect of floatation-REST. PLOS ONE, 13(2), Article e0190292. https://doi.org/10.1371/journal.pone.0190292

Festinger, L. (1954). A theory of social comparison processes. Human Relations, 7(2), 117–140. https://doi.org/10.1177/001872675400700202

Field, T. (2010). Touch for socioemotional and physical well-being: A review. Developmental Review, 30(4), 367–383. https://doi.org/10.1016/j.dr.2011.01.001

Flynn, F. J., & Lake, V. K. B. (2008). If you need help, just ask: Underestimating compliance with direct requests for help. Journal of Personality and Social Psychology, 95(1), 128–143. https://doi.org/10.1037/0022-3514.95.1.128

Fogg, B. J. (2019). Tiny habits: The small changes that change everything. Houghton Mifflin Harcourt.

Folkman, S., & Moskowitz, J. T. (2000). Positive affect and the other side of coping. American Psychologist, 55(6), 647–654. https://doi.org/10.1037/0003-066X.55.6.647

Frankl, V. E. (1959). Man's search for meaning. Beacon Press.

Fredrickson, B. L. (2001). The role of positive emotions in positive psychology: The broaden-and-build theory of positive emotions. American Psychologist, 56(3), 218–226. https://doi.org/10.1037/0003-066X.56.3.218

Fredrickson, B. L. (2009). Positivity: Groundbreaking research reveals how to embrace the hidden strength of positive emotions, overcome negativity, and thrive. Crown.

Gilbert, D. (2006). Stumbling on happiness. Knopf.

Gottman, J. M., & Silver, N. (1999). The seven principles for making marriage work. Crown.

Gottman, J. M., & DeClaire, J. (2001). The relationship cure: A 5-step guide to strengthening your marriage, family, and friendships. Crown.

Grewen, K. M., Anderson, B. J., Girdler, S. S., & Light, K. C. (2003). Warm partner contact is related to lower cardiovascular reactivity. Behavioral Medicine, 29(3), 123–130. https://doi.org/10.1080/08964280309596065

Griffiths, R. R., Johnson, M. W., Carducci, M. A., Umbricht, A., Richards, W. A., Richards, B. D., Cosimano, M. P., & Klinedinst, M. A. (2016). Psilocybin produces substantial and sustained decreases in depression and anxiety in patients with life-threatening cancer: A randomized double-blind trial. *Journal of Psychopharmacology, 30*(12), 1181–1197. https://doi.org/10.1177/0269881116675513

Gross, J. J. (2002). Emotion regulation: Affective, cognitive, and social consequences. Psychophysiology, 39(3), 281–291. https://doi.org/10.1017/S0048577201393198

Haidt, J. (2006). The happiness hypothesis: Finding modern truth in ancient wisdom. Basic Books.

Hanson, R. (2013). Hardwiring happiness: The new brain science of contentment, calm, and confidence. Harmony Books.

Hayes, S. C., Strosahl, K. D., & Wilson, K. G. (1999). Acceptance and commitment therapy: An experiential approach to behavior change. Guilford Press.

Hershfield, H. E., Goldstein, D. G., Sharpe, W. F., Fox, J., Yeykelis, L., Carstensen, L. L., & Bailenson, J. N. (2011). Increasing saving behavior through age-progressed renderings of the future self. Journal of Marketing Research, 48(SPL), S23–S37. https://doi.org/10.1509/jmkr.48.SPL.S23

Higgins, E. T. (1987). Self-discrepancy: A theory relating self and affect. Psychological Review, 94(3), 319–340. https://doi.org/10.1037/0033-295X.94.3.319

Holt-Lunstad, J., Smith, T. B., & Layton, J. B. (2010). Social relationships and mortality risk: A meta-analytic review. PLOS Medicine, 7(7), Article e1000316. https://doi.org/10.1371/journal.pmed.1000316

Holt-Lunstad, J., Smith, T. B., Baker, M., Harris, T., & Stephenson, D. (2015). Loneliness and social isolation as risk factors for mortality: A meta-analytic review. Perspectives on Psychological Science, 10(2), 227–237. https://doi.org/10.1177/1745691614568352

Huberman, A. D., Turiault, M., & Bhaskaran, M. D. (2023). Brief structured respiration practices enhance mood and reduce physiological arousal. Cell Reports Medicine, 4(1), Article 100895. https://doi.org/10.1016/j.xcrm.2022.100895

Jamieson, J. P., Nock, M. K., & Mendes, W. B. (2012). Mind over matter: Reappraising arousal improves cardiovascular and cognitive responses to stress. Journal of Experimental Psychology: General, 141(3), 417–422. https://doi.org/10.1037/a0025719

Kaplan, R., & Kaplan, S. (1989). The experience of nature: A psychological perspective. Cambridge University Press.

Kasser, T. (2002). The high price of materialism. MIT Press.

Keltner, D., & Haidt, J. (2003). Approaching awe, a moral, spiritual, and aesthetic emotion. Cognition and Emotion, 17(2), 297–314. https://doi.org/10.1080/02699930302297

Keltner, D. (2023). Awe: The new science of everyday wonder and how it can transform your life. Penguin Press.

Koenig, H. G., King, D. E., & Carson, V. B. (2012). Handbook of religion and health (2nd ed.). Oxford University Press.

Korb, A. (2015). The upward spiral: Using neuroscience to reverse the course of depression, one small change at a time. New Harbinger Publications.

Laukkanen, T., Khan, H., Zaccardi, F., & Laukkanen, J. A. (2015). Association between sauna bathing and fatal cardiovascular and all-cause mortality events. *JAMA Internal Medicine, 175*(4), 542–548. https://doi.org/10.1001/jamainternmed.2014.8187

Laukkanen, T., Kunutsor, S., Kauhanen, J., & Laukkanen, J. A. (2017). Sauna bathing is inversely associated with dementia and Alzheimer's disease in middle-aged

Finnish men. *Age and Ageing, 46*(2), 245–249. https://doi. org/10.1093/ageing/afw212

Li, Q. (2018). Forest bathing: How trees can help you find health and happiness. Viking.

Lindsey, H. M., et al. (2026). Transcranial photobiomodulation promotes neurological resilience in current collegiate American football players exposed to repetitive head acceleration events. *Journal of Neurotrauma.* https://doi. org/10.1177/08977151251403554

Little, B. R. (2014). Me, myself, and us: The science of personality and the art of well-being. PublicAffairs.

Liu, P. J., Rim, S., Min, L., & Min, K. E. (2023). The surprise of reaching out: Appreciated more than we think. Journal of Personality and Social Psychology, 124(4), 754–771. https://doi.org/10.1037/pspi0000402

Lyubomirsky, S., Sheldon, K. M., & Schkade, D. (2005). Pursuing happiness: The architecture of sustainable change. Review of General Psychology, 9(2), 111–131. https://doi.org/10.1037/1089-2680.9.2.111

Lyubomirsky, S. (2008). The how of happiness: A scientific approach to getting the life you want. Penguin Press.

Masten, A. S. (2001). Ordinary magic: Resilience processes in development. American Psychologist, 56(3), 227–238. https://doi.org/10.1037/0003-066X.56.3.227

Masten, A. S. (2014). Ordinary magic: Resilience in development. Guilford Press.

McAdams, D. P. (2001). The psychology of life stories. Review of General Psychology, 5(2), 100–122. https://doi. org/10.1037/1089-2680.5.2.100

McGonigal, K. (2015). The upside of stress: Why stress is good for you, and how to get good at it. Avery.

Neff, K. D. (2011). Self-compassion: The proven power of being kind to yourself. William Morrow.

Nolen-Hoeksema, S., Wisco, B. E., & Lyubomirsky, S. (2008). Rethinking rumination. Perspectives on Psychological Science, 3(5), 400–424. https://doi.org/10.1111/j.1745-6924.2008.00088.x

Pargament, K. I. (1997). The psychology of religion and coping: Theory, research, practice. Guilford Press.

Park, C. L. (2005). Religion as a meaning-making framework in coping with life stress. Journal of Social Issues, 61(4), 707–729. https://doi.org/10.1111/j.1540-4560.2005.00428.x

Pennebaker, J. W., & Smyth, J. M. (2016). Opening up by writing it down: How expressive writing improves health and eases emotional pain (3rd ed.). Guilford Press.

Ratcliffe, C. (2019, October). *The relationship needs circle: A way to understand and improve bad relationship behavior.* BYU I Do. https://www.byuido.org/2019/10/the-relationship-needs-circle-way-to.html

Rogers, C. R. (1961). On becoming a person: A therapist's view of psychotherapy. Houghton Mifflin.

Ross, S., Bossis, A., Guss, J., Agin-Liebes, G., Malone, T., Cohen, B., Mennenga, S. E., Belser, A., Kalliontzi, K., Babb, J., Su, Z., Corby, P., & Schmidt, B. L. (2016). Rapid and sustained symptom reduction following psilocybin treatment for anxiety and depression in patients with life-threatening cancer: A randomized controlled trial. *Journal of Psychopharmacology, 30*(12), 1165–1180. https://doi.org/10.1177/0269881116675512

Schramm, D. G. (n.d.). *New study shows impact of technology on relationships.* Utah State University Extension. https://extension.usu.edu/news_sections/home_family_and_food/new-study-shows-impact-of-technology-on-relationships

Seligman, M. E. P. (2002). Authentic happiness: Using the new positive psychology to realize your potential for lasting fulfillment. Free Press.

Seligman, M. E. P. (2011). Flourish: A visionary new understanding of happiness and well-being. Free Press.

Seligman, M. E. P., Steen, T. A., Park, N., & Peterson, C. (2005). Positive psychology progress: Empirical validation of interventions. American Psychologist, 60(5), 410–421. https://doi.org/10.1037/0003-066X.60.5.410

Sonnentag, S., & Bayer, U. V. (2005). Switching off mentally: Predictors and consequences of psychological detachment from work during off-job time. Journal of Occupational Health Psychology, 10(4), 393–414. https://doi.org/10.1037/1076-8998.10.4.393

Steger, M. F., Frazier, P., Oishi, S., & Kaler, M. (2006). The meaning in life questionnaire: Assessing the presence of and search for meaning in life. Journal of Counseling Psychology, 53(1), 80–93. https://doi.org/10.1037/0022-0167.53.1.80

Turkle, S. (2015). Reclaiming conversation: The power of talk in a digital age. Penguin Press.

van der Kolk, B. A. (2014). The body keeps the score: Brain, mind, and body in the healing of trauma. Viking.

Waldinger, R., & Schulz, M. (2023). The good life: Lessons from the world's longest scientific study of happiness. Simon & Schuster.

Walker, M. (2017). Why we sleep: Unlocking the power of sleep and dreams. Scribner.

Wilson, T. D. (2011). Redirect: The surprising new science of psychological change. Little, Brown and Company.

Wilson, T. D., & Gilbert, D. T. (2005). Affective forecasting: Knowing what to want. Current Directions in Psychological Science, 14(3), 131–134. https://doi. org/10.1111/j.0963-7214.2005.00355.x

Wrosch, C., Scheier, M. F., Miller, G. E., Schulz, R., & Carver, C. S. (2003). Adaptive self-regulation of unattainable goals: Goal disengagement, goal reengagement, and subjective well-being. Personality and Social Psychology Bulletin, 29(12), 1494–1508. https://doi. org/10.1177/0146167203256921

www.ingramcontent.com/pod-product-compliance
Lightning Source LLC
Chambersburg PA
CBHW051304130726
47987CB00004B/1660